Spiritual Trauma Care

Theology and Psychology in Dialogue

Deborah van Deusen Hunsinger

Edited by Preston McDaniel Hill

  CASCADE *Books* • Eugene, Oregon

SPIRITUAL TRAUMA CARE
Theology and Psychology in Dialogue

New Studies in Theology and Trauma

Copyright © 2025 Deborah van Deusen Hunsinger. All rights reserved. Except for brief quotations in critical publications or reviews, no part of this book may be reproduced in any manner without prior written permission from the publisher. Write: Permissions, Wipf and Stock Publishers, 199 W. 8th Ave., Suite 3, Eugene, OR 97401.

Cascade Books
An Imprint of Wipf and Stock Publishers
199 W. 8th Ave., Suite 3
Eugene, OR 97401

www.wipfandstock.com

PAPERBACK ISBN: 978-1-6667-3517-8
HARDCOVER ISBN: 978-1-6667-9198-3
EBOOK ISBN: 978-1-6667-9199-0

Cataloguing-in-Publication data:

Names: Hunsinger, Deborah van Deusen, author. | Hill, Preston, editor.

Title: Spiritual trauma care : theology and psychology in dialogue / Deborah van Deusen Hunsinger ; edited by Preston McDaniel Hill.

Description: Eugene, OR : Cascade Books, 2025 | Series: New Studies in Theology and Trauma | Includes bibliographical references.

Identifiers: ISBN 978-1-6667-3517-8 (paperback) | ISBN 978-1-6667-9198-3 (hardcover) | ISBN 978-1-6667-9199-0 (ebook)

Subjects: LCSH: Pastoral care. | Psychic trauma—Religious aspects. | Pastoral psychology. | Psychology, Religious. | Pastoral theology.

Classification: BV4012 .H83 2025 (paperback) | BV4012 .H83 (ebook)

VERSION NUMBER 05/14/25

"Deborah van Deusen Hunsinger's work is a crucial resource for those providing spiritual care in a world deeply marked by trauma. By bridging theology and psychology, it offers a well-rounded and practical guide for ministers, counsellors, and caregivers. Her sensitive and insightful approach equips readers to navigate the complexities of trauma with compassion, theological depth, and psychological understanding, fostering healing within communities. This book is a must-read for anyone dedicated to trauma-informed Christian care."

— **JOHN SWINTON**, professor in practical theology and pastoral care, King's College, University of Aberdeen

"America's best pastoral theologian, Deborah van Deusen Hunsinger, gives us a remarkable book on uniquely Christian care for the traumatized. Van Deusen Hunsinger thinks in an exuberantly, unapologetically theological way about trauma, as if God matters when it comes to living with and through trauma. Her book is not only our most practical, useful guide for pastors and other Christian caregivers, but also our finest example of astute psychological research and insights on trauma in conversation with the finest Christian theology."

— **WILL WILLIMON**, professor of the practice of Christian ministry, Duke Divinity School

"This book addresses a great need in the world of pastoral counseling and spiritual care. It brings into dialogue the latest insights from trauma theory and research with deep theological reflection and practical guidance."

— **DAVID C. WANG**, Cliff and Joyce Penner Chair for the Formation of Emotionally Healthy Leaders, Fuller Theological Seminary

"This theoretical, clinical, and practical book demonstrates how disciplines can work together, describes how trauma-informed care accesses the all-encompassing love of God, and connects the self-awareness of care-providers to the spiritual care offered. Loving our neighbors as ourselves begins with receiving God's love for oneself. As a chaplain, I hope this book will become a staple for those giving integrated care that is rooted in the expansiveness of God's compassion and I-Thou relationships."

—**Mary Glenn**, assistant professor of the practice of chaplaincy and community development, Fuller Theological Seminary, and chaplain, Los Angeles County District Attorney's Office

"Wise, compassionate and deeply rooted in the gospel of healing and hope, this book is crucial for a time like ours. Never shying away from the lived experience of traumatic loss since it is 'at the heart of the Christian imagination,' Van Deusen Hunsinger roots the work of healing and pastoral care in the gospel and the miraculous grace of the Holy Spirit. There is no saccharine rush past the impact of sorrow and loss, which can be past bearing. At the cross Jesus Christ, the Lord, bears the unbearable, not just alongside us, but for us—taking on himself what cannot be borne by people. The best I have read in this burgeoning field of scholarship."

—**Richard R. Topping**, president and vice-chancellor, professor of studies in the Reformed tradition, Vancouver School of Theology

Spiritual Trauma Care

New Studies in Theology and Trauma

Series Editors:
Joshua Cockayne
Scott Harrower
Preston McDaniel Hill
AND
Chelle Stearns

Formerly Published Books in the Series:
Sarah Travis, *Unspeakable: Preaching and Trauma-Informed Theology*

Joshua Cokayne, *Dawn of Sunday: The Trinity and Trauma-Safe Churches*

Aimee Patterson, *Suffering Well and Suffering With: Reclaiming Marks of Christian Identity*

Contents

Series Preface for New Studies in Theology and Trauma | vii

1. Introduction | 1
2. Bearing the Unbearable: Trauma, Gospel, and Pastoral Care | 10
3. An Interdisciplinary Map for Christian Counselors | 30
4. Pastoral Theology in a Barthian Key | 57
5. A Theology of Koinonia | 79
6. God's Compassion Is over All: Listening with an Open Heart | 104
7. Paying Attention: The Art of Listening | 135
8. Respecting Ourselves as Christian Therapists | 150
9. Vocation: An Inexpressible Gift and Joyous Task | 155
10. A Repentance Unto Life | 181
11. Our Life Together: Called to Compassion | 188
12. Spiritual Trauma Care: Lifelines for a Healing Journey | 199

Bibliography | 213
Index | 221

New Studies in Theology and Trauma

New Studies in Theology and Trauma is a series of entry-level monographs in Christian theology, engaging trauma. The series showcases work at the intersection of trauma and theology from emerging scholars in this new discipline. Each volume will be approximately 60,000–80,000 words long according to the topic at hand. Monographs in the series are aimed at exploring: (i) how trauma studies and trauma theory can inform theological method, (ii) how theology can be used as a frame for understanding trauma, (iii) and how churches and faith communities can facilitate theologically informed, effective trauma care.

Recent neuroscience has confirmed that surviving traumatic violence leaves lifelong scars in the brain and body, and that "the body keeps the score." This persistent reality of trauma poses a unique challenge to Christian communities and churches. Thankfully, many of these communities have begun to recognize that trauma and abuse do not happen "out there" but are horrors that occur within our own ranks, with many Christians calling out for justice for victims who have hidden in the shadows far too long. Christians cannot avoid confronting trauma that is tragically manifesting within our own church communities. When trauma is perpetrated by pastors and Christian leaders, this threatens to undermine a Christian witness to the gospel. As a result, trauma is raising the stakes on theological truth-claims made by Christians. This leaves a door wide open for Christians to explore the intersection of theology and trauma.

Given the emerging state of literature on theology and trauma currently, there is a need to solidify the intuitions shared by scholars in the many disciplines of theology and biblical studies and signal a constructive and generative approach for the future of this growing field. The present series seeks to fill this need by offering a series of monographs grouped around a *double witness*: a witness to the laments and losses involved in surviving trauma and a witness to God's ongoing presence and agency in the aftermath of violence. By promoting a double-witness approach in this series, authors engaging theology and trauma will be provided a coherent and fruitful platform for witnessing both the wounds of trauma and the healing in recovery for communities today.

We have started this series because trauma calls for faithful and generative witness, which is why we have selected the Australian lyrebird as the symbol for our series. The lyrebird is able to listen carefully to sounds of its surroundings, then repeat these back in concert with new voices as part of a broader song. This new song is unique in that it faithfully reflects the original sounds into a new context of richer harmony. Likewise, empathetic listening that faithfully witnesses the wounds of trauma while remaining open to renewed hope within a larger frame is the core idea of the New Studies in Trauma and Theology series.

Series Editors:

Joshua Cockayne, Scott Harrower, Preston McDaniel Hill, and Chelle Stearns

1

Introduction

During the past forty years, the burgeoning literature on trauma theory has grown as trauma comes more and more into common awareness: not only the post-traumatic stress disorder (PTSD) that arises from an overwhelming stressful event in the life of an individual, but also forms of complex trauma that develop in those whose childhood homes were filled with abuse, neglect or violence. There is also a growing awareness of the traumatic impact of larger systems of violence: war; slavery; poverty; racial, gender, and ethnic oppression; as well as the impact of intergenerational trauma. In today's world, with its myriad catastrophes, there are forms of collective trauma that threaten literally every person on the planet.

Christian faith addresses the human plight of sin and suffering. In its own way, it has always known about trauma. Indeed, one might say that "traumatic loss lies at the very heart of the Christian imagination."[1] Our Scriptures do not hide from or deny the harsh realities of human sin and death. They are filled with stories of betrayal, deceit, murder, rape, massacre, slavery, indeed with the downfall and destruction of whole nations. In and with these stories of horror, however, comes an unremitting testimony to a loving and merciful God who delivers all those who call upon the Lord for help. In the book of Psalms, lament and praise are the systole and diastole of the human heart as it cries out to God. Psalm 107 describes one disaster after another, where those who trust in God "cried to the Lord in their trouble, and he delivered them from their distress" (Ps 107:6, 13, 19, 28 RSV). God, so the Scriptures attest, "raises up the needy out of affliction" (Ps 107:41 RSV), "forgives all your iniquity,

---

1. See chapter 1 of this volume.

heals all your diseases, redeems your life from the Pit, crowns you with steadfast love and mercy, and satisfies you with good as long as you live" (Ps 103:3–5). The biblical witnesses to God's mercy toward human failing, disobedience, sin, and suffering, form the bedrock of a faith that is sustained and sometimes even strengthened in times of trouble.

The overriding purpose of this book is to offer theoretical and practical guidance to those who have been called to a ministry of spiritual care for the severely afflicted. Trauma theory can greatly enrich, inform, and deepen this ministry of the church as it seeks to help people grow through times of trial, loss, and suffering. When the impact of trauma on a person's or community's life is understood better, Christian ministers—its pastors, counselors, spiritual directors, chaplains, youth leaders, pastoral caregivers, and caring friends—will better be able to offer the kind of succor that is needed. All ministry is God's ministry, in which we are privileged to participate. Our spiritual care needs to be trauma-informed. The proliferating literature on trauma—in both its theoretical and practical dimensions—needs to be brought explicitly into conversation with our theological understanding and practices of faith. Broadly speaking, two bodies of knowledge—the psychological and the theological—each with their unique conceptualities and purposes, need to be in ongoing conversation with each other because it is the dialogue between them that fosters the kind of understanding needed in order to be of real help. A significant question that therefore arises is: how are these two bodies of knowledge to be related?

Chapters 3 and 4 address this question in some depth. They provide the methodological substance of an approach to interdisciplinary dialogue that seeks to protect the integrity of each field of knowledge while also enabling each to offer its unique gifts to human beings in distress. Christian theology has a distinctive set of conceptualities, with its particular subject matter, aims, methodologies, and linguistic conventions. At the same time, the psychology of trauma has its particular subject matter, aims, methodologies, and linguistic conventions. These two sources of knowledge are very closely related—indeed they have significant areas of overlap whenever we seek to understand a person of faith suffering from trauma—but they are not the same. They cannot be conceptually integrated with each other without doing violence to the distinctive contribution of each field, as well as potentially mislead those we are seeking to help. A psychology of trauma cannot become the overarching framework for understanding the claims of Christian theology. When it seeks to do so, theological knowledge is effectively reduced to a psychological system of thought. They are distinctive conceptualities, each of which can bring its particular wealth of insight and help to a person or community suffering from trauma. They can only do this if each can speak in its own unique voice. Attempts to find a "lowest common denominator" that bring the two together into a conceptually integrated whole inevitably distort the complex interrelated nets of meaning intrinsic to each field.

However, the theoretical and practical resources of both fields can (and should) be integrated into the person of anyone offering care. It is necessary for each helper to work "from the inside out," so to speak, to have traveled along some path of healing and resilience herself, and thereby to have discovered the faithfulness of God firsthand. For, finally, it is trust in God that becomes the lifeline for both the traumatized and their witnesses. Therefore, this book seeks not only clarity about how to use the conceptual resources of trauma theory in relation to the rich theological resources of the Christian tradition, but also how to offer one's presence, faith, and care, along with the concrete skills and practices that will enable that trust to grow. In other words, its purpose is twofold: first, to offer helpers the conceptual clarity they need to use the theoretical resources of both psychology and theology in relation to one another, and second, to offer specific guidance on the dynamic interpersonal processes involved in giving care that leads to healing and resilience.

In a little-known article entitled "Trauma and Spirituality," A. J. van den Blink sets forth a memorable inventory of what Christians need as they seek to heal from trauma.[2] For people of faith, experiences of trauma need to be understood spiritually as well as psychologically. He identifies seven aspects, each of which is of fundamental importance to the whole:

According to van den Blink, Christian spirituality is:

- Shaped by Christian faith and practice;
- Grounded in a theological perspective;
- Accompanied by an awareness of one's experiences of the "numinous" (or as I might put it, accompanied by a deepening sense of communion with God);
- Practiced by participating in a community;
- Motivated by regular spiritual practice;

---

2. Van den Blink, "Trauma and Spirituality," 30–47.

- Manifested as best as one can, in daily life;
- Receptive to help from others, e.g., through spiritual direction or Christian friendship.

As an exercise in spiritual care, this book seeks to include all these determinations. While key findings from the psychology of trauma are integral to the discussion, they do not stand alone. Every chapter seeks to understand these findings spiritually as well as psychologically, by addressing them through a lens of Christian faith and practice. Its explicit theological perspective has been shaped by the theology of the twentieth century Reformed theologian Karl Barth, as it is brought into conversation with trauma theory. Because it assumes that "God is a very present help in trouble," it is oriented toward helping the afflicted to turn toward God for help when overwhelmed by suffering, grief, or loss. Again and again, it emphasizes the essential importance of the community for healing to unfold. We cannot heal from trauma by ourselves. We need the help of others. Regular "spiritual practice" includes the ordinary practices of a "lived faith": individual and corporate prayer, participating in the Lord's Supper, meditating on Scripture as the Word of God, regular Bible study, singing hymns, and common worship in a community of mutual care. These practices support a life of prayer—not only ongoing intercessory prayers but also prayers of lament and thanksgiving, which sustain the community in its vocation to minister to anyone in need. The more we are rooted and grounded in our love for Jesus Christ (the vertical dimension), the further we can reach toward our brothers and sisters in Christ, and indeed beyond them into the wider world (the horizontal dimension). Relationships of mutual care spread throughout the community as we acknowledge our dependence on others to live fully in the promises of the gospel. For finally, it is only by finding a "relational home" in God and in one another, only by knowing in our bones that we belong in community, indeed, that our very lives "are hidden with Christ in God" that we are able to thrive. As our trust in Jesus Christ grows, the community sustained by him also grows in depth and reliability.

Significantly, van den Blink writes, "Spirituality from this perspective requires both a coherent philosophical meta-perspective, a theology in my case, that can be used as a map or lens or point of reference to help discern what is going on in us and around us."[3] This is precisely what is offered in chapters 3 and 4: a map by which to orient ourselves when we

3. Van den Blink, "Trauma and Spirituality," 33.

are faced with the complex phenomena that accompany trauma and as we endeavor to offer psychologically sound and theologically competent help. Chapter 3 was written nearly twenty years before chapter 4, though they explicate the same theoretical territory. They offer an approach to interdisciplinary dialogue that respects the two fields of study—both trauma theory and Christian theology—without confusing or conflating them with each other, on the one hand, nor separating or dividing them into distinct (or divorced) realms, on the other. They also seek to show how our psychological understandings need to be placed within a larger theological framework (rather than the reverse). These chapters form the core methodological substance of the book, on which all the subsequent chapters depend. In other words, all the other chapters of the book presuppose this methodology without drawing attention to it. They are concerned with *using* the method, rather than explicating it.

It goes without saying that fields of study other than the two examined here—psychology and theology—can also contribute to the healing of trauma. I do not wish to be understood as saying that other fields of inquiry are irrelevant. Anything that helps us understand the concrete lived experience of persons and communities can be helpful. History, economics, politics, culture, and neuroscience are all pertinent toward gaining a greater understanding of the intergenerational roots of trauma that pass from one generation to the next. Sociologically oriented understandings of trauma illuminate how oppression, poverty, racism, and sexism all contribute to cultural norms that lend themselves to traumatic affliction. But since the scope of this book is limited to informing the understanding and developing the skills of those persons called to Christian counseling or spiritual care, it draws on the two primary fields of study that offer the most illumination, namely trauma theory and Christian theology. Other fields of study would need to follow the same conceptual ordering. They would need to be brought into dialogue with Christian theology, seeing the overlapping but completely distinctive conceptualities of each field, so that no reductionism takes place, so that each field can offer its particular conceptual gifts and practical skills.

Below, I offer a brief description of each of the chapters:

Chapter 2 seeks to offer an overview of trauma as a lived experience, to outline some of the concrete steps that one can take toward healing, as well as describing the kind of help that is needed from those gifted with compassionate care. It then places all the psychological tools and competencies into an explicitly Christian theological framework, using (though not explaining) the interdisciplinary methodology developed in chapters 3 and 4.

Chapters 3 and 4 are the most difficult of the volume and are best suited to be used in the training of Christian counselors or spiritual caregivers. They presuppose a high level of theological sophistication and a keen curiosity as to how one might best relate the conceptualities of Christian theology to those of trauma theory. These chapters draw on my first and most methodologically substantive book, *Theology and Pastoral Counseling: A New Interdisciplinary Approach*.[4] In that book, one can find a thorough discussion of how a "Chalcedonian" imagination can help one avoid the pitfalls often encountered by practitioners when dealing with these two distinctive conceptualities. Chapter 4 explicitly brings this theological approach into conversation with trauma theory.

Chapter 5 describes how our relationships of compassionate care are nurtured by a life of prayer that depends upon the presence of Christ through the Holy Spirit. It understands our *koinonia* in Christ, our sense of belonging to Jesus Christ and to one another, as the telos of our life together. As we become members of Christ's body, we are knit together with one another in the closest possible communion. As such, we know that we are not isolated in our suffering but learn to reach out to God and to one another with our needs. Since safety and belonging are fundamental to healing and resilience, this chapter shows how the gifts of the gospel offer the *sine qua non* for developing perseverance (*hypomene*) when overcome by trouble.

Chapter 6 shows how our communion in Jesus Christ depends on grounds for hope that utterly transcend this world. Our human capacity for compassionate care can only arise from God's redemptive, compassionate care for the entire world. Our ministry of compassion is therefore a participation in God's ministry. The argument differentiates among three closely related concepts: compassion (from a biblical perspective), sympathy, and empathy (from a psychotherapeutic perspective). It then creates a dialogue between the need to offer ourselves love and self-care, on the one hand, with the New Testament's stark recommendations toward self-denial, on the other. It argues that careful attention to our own needs actually helps us in hearing the needs of others. The chapter ends by offering concrete guidance in transforming negative judgments, first by drawing on the psychological literature, then anchoring it theologically,

---

4. Hunsinger, *Theology and Pastoral Counseling*.

as we learn to place ourselves under the judgment and mercy of the One who truly knows our hearts.

Chapter 7 builds on the previous chapters by shifting our focus to key skills that enable us to welcome the complexity and depth of traumatic suffering. After specifying the extraordinary contribution of empathy, we shift our focus to the richness of "resonance" as a way to welcome both the pain and the beauty of the healing process. As we fully embody our vocation by opening up all our "circuits of emotion and motivation," we may also discover unforeseen spiritual blessings, both in ourselves and in those we serve.

Chapter 8 was originally written as one chapter among twelve, that sought to respond to an essay by Ray Anderson entitled, "Toward a Holistic Psychology: Putting All the Pieces in Their Proper Place."[5] As can be surmised by the title, Professor Anderson had been engaged with many of the same "puzzle pieces" in his long and distinguished career as I have been, namely, psychology, spirituality, Christian faith and practice, and theological reflection. The question I undertake to address in the conversation is an important one for Christian counselors: "How can a Christian psychologist function with integrity when working therapeutically with non-Christians?" I argue that the uniqueness of the gospel is essentially untranslatable, and that we lose the power of its message if we try to translate its terms into other idioms. This chapter shows how an understanding of what I have called a "Chalcedonian" pattern of thought can be helpful in sorting through the "puzzle pieces," so that they can create a helpful coherent picture and not remain in a chaotic, undifferentiated pile.

Chapter 9 is a sermon I delivered some years ago at an academic conference on Barth and Bonhoeffer. It is included in this volume for its emphasis on the importance of repentance in the life of faith. So much attention is given to "forgiveness," in contemporary reflection on the life of faith (forgiving whom, and how, and for what reason). This sermon, by contrast, seeks to discern what true and false repentance looks like. It ponders the difference between what the apostle Paul speaks of as "worldly grief" that produces death with the "godly grief" that engenders a repentance that leads to salvation. Heartfelt repentance leads to joy because it trusts in the merciful judgment of God.

---

5. Anderson, "Toward a Holistic Psychology."

Chapter 10 addresses the question of discerning God's unique call on each of our lives. The purpose of healing trauma is so that we can live out our vocation with joy and commitment. The chapter explores the paradox of our vocation being at once a divine gift and also, mysteriously, a human task. Those whose theological imagination has been shaped by the Chalcedonian pattern will see the underlying logic that organizes the chapter: God's call and our response cannot be separated from one another, but neither should they be confused with one another. It also illustrates the importance of ordering them properly. "The sovereign prevenience of God's gracious call obviously forms the very presupposition and basis of our freedom, our ability to respond in a glad and wholehearted way."[6] This chapter will be of particular interest to those working with young people who are seeking to understand God's call on their lives.

Chapter 11 addresses a real-life event of violation that occurred in my own community, Princeton Theological Seminary, during the summer of 2018. It attempts to speak to the harm a community suffers when it is afflicted with racial tensions and violence. It provides an example of the apostle Paul's testimony that if "one member suffers, all suffer together." The collective trauma that emerges from living in a racist society calls upon all members of the community (both the afflicted and the witnesses) to care for one another in prayer, in listening, and in acts of compassionate service.

Chapter 12 was written during the first four months of the pandemic declared in March 2020. It concerns itself with the complex trauma that arises in individuals and communities when healthy ways of regaining balance and resilience are taken away from us. It speaks of the dangers of isolation and the immense suffering that comes when we cannot be physically in one another's presence, since human beings are created to live in community. This isolation affects us at every level of our being: biologically, sociologically, culturally, and spiritually. It exacerbates the feeling of "alarmed aloneness" that anyone who has suffered trauma already carries within them. Two core human needs—the need for safety and the need to belong (to trust that you matter)—cannot be met when people are cut off from their families and communities. Thus, the final chapter of the book connects substantively with the first chapter but takes the argument further by taking into account the communal and collective nature of trauma. It builds on Daniel Siegel's acronym, C-O-A-L, to

---

6. See chapter 9 of this volume.

demonstrate some of the practical skills involved in learning how to care for yourself when triggered by trauma symptoms: e.g., to develop habits of mind comprised of curiosity, openness, acceptance, and love. Finally, it stresses the importance of developing structures for collective awareness, collective mourning, and collective action, so that we may find our lifeline in the love of God who is our "relational home" and in the mutual care of the Christian community.

Healing from trauma is a mystery. We can describe it, but we cannot prescribe it because faith itself is a gift, and it is the work of grace through faith that "sanctifies our deepest distress." Healing from trauma in the context of Christian faith is more than simple "post-traumatic growth," as wonderful as that is. The gospel understands this healing as the work of God's Holy Spirit. Those who turn to God again and again in their need are given God's miraculous gift of "the fruit of the Spirit" namely, "love, joy, peace, patience, kindness, goodness, gentleness, faithfulness, and self-control" (Gal 5:22 RSV) May it be so as we learn to trust God and to care for one another in mutual love and compassion.

2

Bearing the Unbearable

Trauma, Gospel, and Pastoral Care

Traumatic loss lies at the very heart of the Christian imagination. The souls of those who call themselves Christian are indelibly stamped with the unbearable sorrow of this man, Jesus. After raising the hopes of many, Jesus died a shameful death, indeed an unjust and horrible death. What is more, his friends denied, betrayed, and abandoned him in his hour of need. He was tortured and executed as a common criminal, even though he had done nothing to warrant condemnation. Jesus Christ drank the cup of bitterness all the way to its dregs, and descended into the very depths of hell: how can such a terrible story be borne? Much more than an intellectual puzzle about so-called "theories of atonement" is at stake here. Believers who have survived trauma stake their very lives on the power of the gospel to heal.

Trauma: How can we give it the kind of disciplined attention that it deserves? Holding even a fraction of this suffering steadily in our attention can be challenging. Is it possible to talk about trauma without causing pain to those already bearing trauma in their bodies and souls?[1] Daily through the media, we are bombarded with stories capable of breaking our hearts, yet little attention is given to the impact of such accounts on its hearers. How can we bear these stories with an open heart?[2] Indeed, how do we bear them at all?

Pastoral theology, as I understand it, is first and foremost a theology of God's care for the world in Jesus Christ, in which we are invited to

---

1. Serene Jones asks a similar question: "How can ministers craft sermons that speak to the plight of trauma survivors without re-traumatizing them?" See Jones, *Trauma and Grace*, 85.

2. See Hunsinger, "Keeping an Open Heart."

participate.³ This means that all pastoral care depends upon prayer, leads to worship, and trusts in the promises of God. Such an orientation leads us to confess that though we ourselves, with our enduring failures to love, cannot truly redeem traumatic loss, we cling in hope to the One who can and does. That One drank the cup of bitterness, died a death of anguish, and descends into every darkness that threatens to overwhelm us.

Those who study theology are called to ponder holocausts of every kind, from biblical "texts of terror,"⁴ to grueling historical or theological tracts, to the horrors of the evening news. How can we fortify ourselves, our students, or our children for the kind of world we live in? Whether painted on a vast canvas of national or international significance, or in a miniature of a single family or community, traumatic loss is ubiquitous. When it hits us personally, it changes our lives irrevocably: through the shock of an accident, a criminal assault or tragic death, or through the multiple and complex traumas that arise in relation to immigration, war, imprisonment, torture, domestic violence, or sexual abuse, among others. Unacknowledged and unhealed, trauma often leads to further violence, either against oneself or others, and thus to more trauma. With knowledgeable intervention and wise support, however, trauma can be healed, and may even become "a catalyst for growth and transformation," the turning point of a life, a sign and symbol of God's goodness and care.⁵

As caregivers in the church who seek to help others, how can we be sure that we will, first, do no harm? How can we be a source of spiritual strength and practical support for the communities we serve? Moreover, as witnesses to the trauma of others or as persons afflicted by trauma ourselves, where do we turn for help? In this inaugural chapter, I want to set forth an understanding of the impact of trauma and inquire into the role of the gospel and the church in its healing. I plan to address three basic issues:

- What is trauma and how does it affect us?
- How do we break free from the vicious cycle of trauma's impact?
- How does the gospel with the pastoral care of the church bring healing to the traumatized?

---

3. See Purves, *Reconstructing Pastoral Theology*.
4. Trible, *Texts of Terror*.
5. Cane, *Trauma Healing and Transformation*, 17.

What Is Trauma and How Does It Affect Us?

The twentieth century offered countless opportunities for studying trauma, but it was not until the 1970s that social and political ferment enabled its study to advance decisively.[6] By the mid-1970s, hundreds of "rap" groups had been organized by Vietnam Veterans Against the War where men could speak honestly about the horror of war. At the same time, women gained collective courage as they shared, among other things, their stories of rape, sexual abuse, or domestic violence. No longer willing to allow "denial, secrecy and shame" to render them mute, both men and women were able to transform what had previously been private suffering into powerful public action for social and political change.[7] In the 1970s and 1980s, crisis centers, rape hotlines, and safe shelters were established with painstaking effort in state after state.[8]

At the same time, the Veterans Administration commissioned thorough studies of the war's impact on returning Vietnam vets.[9] Subsequently, a "five-volume study on the legacies of Vietnam . . . demonstrated beyond any reasonable doubt [the] direct relationship [of trauma] to combat exposure."[10] With multiple vectors for social change converging, the American Psychiatric Association included a new diagnosis in their *Diagnostic and Statistical Manual* for 1980 called post-traumatic stress disorder (PTSD). In their first attempt to capture its essence, psychiatrists described traumatic events as lying "outside the range of usual human experience,"[11] a definition that proved untenable since traumatic incidents of one kind or another are quite common.[12] As psychiatrist Judith Herman writes, "Traumatic events are extraordinary, not because they occur rarely, but rather because they overwhelm the ordinary human

---

6. For a fascinating account of the history of the study of psychological trauma, see Judith Herman's classic text, *Trauma and Recovery*, chapter 1.

7. Herman, *Trauma and Recovery*, 29.

8. For a timeline of laws enacted in relation to domestic violence see: "Domestic Violence Timeline." See also Del, *Battered Wives*, 4.

9. Herman, *Trauma and Recovery*, 27.

10. Herman, *Trauma and Recovery*, 27.

11. Herman, *Trauma and Recovery*, 33.

12. "Norris (1992), in a study of 1,000 adults in the southern United States, found that 69% of the sample had experienced a traumatic stressor in their lives, and that this included 21% in the past year alone." Quoted in van der Kolk, McFarlane, and Weisaeth, *Traumatic Stress*, 135.

adaptations to life."[13] In fact, a simple, thumbnail definition of trauma might be: "an inescapably stressful event that overwhelms people's coping mechanisms."[14] When people face "intense fear, helplessness, loss of control, and the threat of annihilation,"[15] and when these feelings persist for more than a month, PTSD becomes the chosen diagnosis.[16] It is important to note, however, that witnesses to horrific events are also vulnerable to trauma. Watching helplessly as a loved one dies, seeing the Twin Towers fall to the earth, or listening in fear as one's mother or sibling gets beaten—such events can also trigger a traumatic reaction.[17]

The subjective experience of feeling overwhelmed uniquely characterizes trauma and differentiates it from those situations that are experienced, perhaps, as exceptionally stressful but not as traumatic. Peter Levine elaborates:

> Traumatized people . . . are unable to overcome the anxiety of their experience. They remain overwhelmed by the event, defeated and terrified. Virtually imprisoned by their fear, they are unable to re-engage in life. Others who experience similar events may have no enduring symptoms at all. . . . No matter how frightening an event may seem, not everyone who experiences it will be traumatized.[18]

The imponderable factor here is that the nature of the triggering event in and of itself does not guarantee a traumatic reaction. One person may experience the event as traumatic while her neighbor, friend, or daughter having the exact same experience may find it stressful but not traumatic.

---

13. Herman, *Trauma and Recovery*, 33.

14. van der Kolk, McFarlane, and Weisaeth, *Traumatic Stress*, 279.

15. Andreasen, "Posttraumatic Stress Disorder," quoted in Herman, *Trauma and Recovery*, 33.

16. Following the criteria for diagnoses can be dizzying since PTSD has so many close cousins, such as acute stress disorder, panic disorder, anxiety disorder, agoraphobia, etc. However, a synopsis of the seven criteria of PTSD are: (1) the traumatic stressor involves death, injury or serious threat (or witnessing or learning about such to another); (2) the response involves intense fear, helplessness, or horror; (3) the person persistently re-experiences the traumatic event; (4) the person persistently avoids stimuli associated with the trauma and tries to numb general responsiveness; (5) symptoms of hyperarousal persist; (6) for a month or more; (7) and the symptoms cause "clinically significant distress or impairment in social, occupational, or other important areas of functioning." See also SAMHSA, "Trauma-Informed Care."

17. See Weingarten, *Common Shock*. See also Weingarten, "Witnessing the Effects," 45–59.

18. Levine, *Waking the Tiger*, 28.

This fact remains completely inexplicable until we realize that *none of us ever actually has the exact same experience* because our minds organize our experiences in a completely idiosyncratic way. Its meaning will be different for each person because our way of making narrative sense of our lives is utterly unique. Thus, feeling overwhelmed or immobilized is a variable that cannot be predicted by either the nature, magnitude, or intensity of the triggering event.[19] "*Consequently,*" writes Carolyn Yoder, "a *traumatic reaction needs to be treated as valid, regardless of how the event that induced it appears to anyone else.*"[20]

I want to underscore this point because I believe it is fundamental to competent pastoral care. Time and again, one hears people minimizing or discounting the anguish of others, essentially encouraging them to "get over it." Wanting those they love to be whole, they try to encourage them by *rationally explaining* why they should not be upset by so small a thing. Yet there is little that so completely obstructs the healing process as having someone offer the free advice to "get over it" or "put it behind" them. While such defense mechanisms—denial and minimization—on the part of friends or caregivers are understandable as human reactions to pain in those they love, they only injure the traumatized further, perhaps to the point of shaming them into silence and truly unbearable isolation.

Yet, why *aren't* they able simply to "get over it?" The various symptoms of post-traumatic stress have been aptly summarized by Judith Herman, as *hyperarousal, intrusion,* and *constriction:* "Hyperarousal reflects the persistent expectation of danger; *intrusion* reflects the indelible imprint of the traumatic moment; *constriction* reflects the numbing response of surrender."[21] While each symptom originates in the triggering event itself, they all have an afterlife in the person's unfolding post-trauma history.

Any kind of physical or emotional shock has the potential to set certain physiological responses in motion. Typical responses include one's heart beating faster, difficulty in breathing, rising blood pressure, and the constriction of one's stomach. One's thoughts may begin to race and the skin may become cold. These responses all stem from the autonomic nervous system putting the body on high alert in response to a perception of threat. The release of hormones mobilizes the body for fight or flight.

---

19. Yoder, *Little Book of Trauma Healing*, 10.
20. Yoder, *Little Book of Trauma Healing*, 11; emphasis in the original.
21. Herman, *Trauma and Recovery*, 35.

When neither fight nor flight seem possible, the physiological response of the body is to freeze.[22]

In the freeze response, "the victim of trauma enters an altered reality. Time slows down and there is no fear or pain. In this state, if harm or death do occur, the pain is not felt as intensely."[23] There is a notable shift in consciousness, in which there is a subjective sense of detachment. Victims of sexual assault, for instance, sometimes speak of "leaving their body" and watching themselves from another point in the room: standing next to the bed or looking down from the ceiling.[24] Metaphorically, it is as if the soul escapes the body to protect the person from the physical pain and the full emotional impact of his or her radical vulnerability.

Like the *fight or flight* response, *freezing* is also heralded by a flood of hormones. In 1844, Dr. David Livingstone described his subjective experience of being seized by a lion:

> Growling horribly close to my ear, he shook me as a terrier dog does a rat. It produced a sort of dreaminess in which there was no sense of pain, nor feeling of terror, though I was quite conscious of all that was happening.... This placidity is probably produced in all animals killed by the carnivore; and if so, is a merciful provision of the Creator for lessening the pain of death.[25]

The capacity of the mind to dissociate like this may reduce the immediate pain and horror of the event, but it does so at a high cost. Studies now demonstrate that "people who enter a dissociative state at the time of the traumatic event are among those most likely to develop long-lasting PTSD."[26]

During a traumatic ordeal, the intense hyperarousal of the emotions often "interfere[s] with proper information processing and the storage of information in narrative (explicit) memory."[27] This means that memory of the trauma is often fragmented; it is not organized in a linear, narrative fashion as normal memories are. Instead, certain features associated with sensory data are vividly remembered such as a particular smell, sound, image, or color. If a dog was barking when the person was assaulted, for instance, the sound of a barking dog might evoke subsequent feelings of

---

22. Rothschild, *Body Remembers*, 8.
23. Rothschild, *Body Remembers*, 10.
24. Herman, *Trauma and Recovery*, 43.
25. See Milbrandt, *Daring Heart*, 15–26.
26. Herman, *Trauma and Recovery*, 239.
27. van der Kolk, McFarlane, and Weisaeth, *Traumatic Stress*, 286.

terror or rage, yet strangely unaccompanied by an explicit memory of the assault. Or, alternatively, the memory of the assault may be explicit, yet strangely dissociated from the accompanying emotions. Bessel van der Kolk comments:

> Although the individual may be unable to produce a coherent narrative of the incident, there may be no interference with implicit memory; the person may "know" the emotional valence of a stimulus and be aware of associated perceptions, without being able to articulate the reasons for feeling or behaving in a particular way. [Pierre] Janet [1859–1947] proposed that traumatic memories are split off (dissociated) from consciousness, and instead are stored as sensory perceptions, obsessional ruminations or behavioral reenactments.[28]

Such intrusive memories can be quite distressing, as aspects of the traumatic event are replayed in the mind over and over again, but without the full picture, without the experience of "normal memory" that enables a coherent sense of self-understanding.

After such an event, the hyperarousal of the nervous system keeps persons on a kind of "permanent alert,"[29] where they may startle easily and sleep poorly. Subject to nightmares and intrusive flashbacks, they may begin to circumscribe their world to avoid anything that might re-trigger the feelings of helplessness, rage, fear, grief, panic, and shame associated with the event. Flashbacks are something like having nightmares while awake. Something triggers the memory of the trauma, perhaps the smell of alcohol, the sound of a particular footfall, a certain tone of voice or characteristic gesture. Indeed, anything can trigger a flashback because of the way the brain organizes data in a vast web of interconnected associations. Neurologists remind us that neurons that "fire together, wire together."[30] Two or more things are forever associated, "wired together," in the brain's neural pathways. Suddenly, one is shaking and sweating in response to an ordinary everyday event.[31] *Yet, knowing that one's response is out of proportion to what triggered it only increases a sense of*

---

28. van der Kolk, McFarlane, and Weisaeth, *Traumatic Stress*, 287.
29. Herman, *Trauma and Recovery*, 35.
30. See Siegel, *Developing Mind*, chapter 4.
31. "Painful life experiences get encoded in our brains and bodies and can be reactivated with great intensity by the right kind of trigger decades later, even if we believe that we have dealt with them or have completely forgotten about them" (van den Blink, "Trauma and Spirituality," 16).

powerlessness, anxiety, and shame. Because such experiences of intrusion are so frightening and because survivors can make little rational sense of them, they often do whatever they can to avoid these states or to deaden the pain by numbing out in some way.

If they do not actively seek help, a whole range of defensive patterns may develop. Rather than facing the pain directly, survivors may turn the intense traumatic energy against themselves. Many addictive behaviors have their source in unresolved trauma that is not consciously faced: substance abuse, workaholism, eating disorders, even rituals of self-mutilation can seem preferable to experiencing the buried pain of trauma.[32] Shame, dread, and helplessness are pervasive, alternating with numbness, depression, or a sense of emptiness. Their sense of agency is damaged; they often feel powerless and alone in a hostile world, wondering whether anyone cares if they live or die.[33] Spiritual questions may become particularly intense with a growing sense of disorientation or even meaninglessness. Living in an unsafe world, survivors of trauma put themselves on constant alert, watching for danger.

While many victims suffer in silence, others will turn the intensity of their suffering outward. Feelings of rage may predominate. Wanting justice, fantasies of revenge may become an obsession. Sometimes narratives are created where the plotline of good versus evil has them perpetually in the role of the "good guy" with "the other" as the "bad guy." The enemy is typically seen as less than fully human. The traumatized begin to tell a predictable tale that seldom varies. Pastoral theologian David Augsburger challenges victims of trauma with a number of pointed questions:

> Can I identify what I get out of rehearsing an offense over and over? Why do I insist on replaying the history of injury? How often have I told and retold the story of the offense to others to gain their support and validation of my role or position as victim?[34]

When such desires for revenge are not consciously wrestled with, attacks on others may seem justified as a way of restoring a sense of dignity,

---

32. Yoder, *Little Book of Trauma Healing*, 33

33. Feeling helpless and alone in a potentially hostile world was Karen Horney's definition of neurosis. See *Neurosis and Human Growth*. Serene Jones speaks repeatedly throughout her book on the damaged sense of agency of the traumatized and their need for experiences of empowerment. See *Trauma and Grace*.

34. Augsburger, *Hate-Work*, 227.

respect, and honor or in the name of justice.[35] In a chilling comment, James Gilligan, director of the Center for the Study of Violence at the Harvard Medical School, comments, "The attempt to achieve and maintain justice, or to undo or prevent injustice, is the one and only universal cause of violence."[36] Pain that is not transformed does not simply disappear. As Ann Ulanov writes:

> Where we repress our grudge-holding, our wish to make someone pay for what has happened to us . . . that repressed shadow does not just go away. It goes unconscious and remains alive with instinctual impulses, emotions, but far out of reach of modification by social or personal reality testing. . . . We put onto others what we do not own in ourselves and identify them with this rejected bit of ourselves. The personal becomes social. But then this live bit of shadow menaces us from the outside.[37]

Instead of the trauma being "acted in" against the self, it is now "acted out" against others. The traumatized feel justified in venting their rage, yet such repeated venting only serves to inscribe the anger and sense of moral outrage more deeply in body and soul. It does nothing to bring healing or peace.

Freud describes "repetition compulsion" as a symbolic reliving of the trauma, as a way the traumatized express their suffering while yet failing to become fully conscious of it. Children who have been sexually abused, for example, may engage in ritual play that gives unconscious voice to the abuse. Those honored for bravery in war may suffer repetitive nightmares[38] or else wreak terrible violence on their families[39] as they struggle with mental pain. The combination of survivor guilt, depression, frozen grief, anguish, and rage act as a kind of seething cauldron beneath the surface, ready to burst forth in a symbolic reenactment of the original horror, often with tragic results.

---

35. Zehr, "Doing Justice, Healing Trauma," 15.
36. Gilligan, *Violence*, 18.
37. Ulanov, *Unshuttered Heart*, 140–41.
38. Wilmer, "Healing Nightmare."
39. See the story told by "Gizelle" in which the unhealed suffering of war leads to sexual assault with tragic effects in Bass and Davis, *Courage to Heal*.

How Do We Break Free from the Vicious Cycle of Trauma's Impact?

Is it possible to forge a path that seeks neither "oblivion" on the one hand nor "revenge" on the other?[40] Is it possible truly to heal? Ann Ulanov describes the predicament of those who have constricted their lives in the aftermath of trauma.

> We swap aliveness for restriction in order to feel safer, avoid pain, survive some blow that seems to us unbearable, that would destroy us. We fear we are empty inside so we cover it up with manufactured control, or made-up excitement, or self-promotion. The emptiness can never change if we refuse to experience it, and in the company of an other. We need an other to depend on when we turn to face our deadness. Whatever we are afraid of, it requires our attention; we must go down into it, look around, not knowing if and how we will come out.[41]

Three key phrases need to be underlined here: First, whatever we are afraid of *requires our attention*. Second, we need to experience it *in the company of an other*. And third, we take these steps *not knowing if and how we will come out*.

Those who seek to reclaim their lives after trauma need to face what has actually happened to them. *It requires their attention.* If their nervous system is in a hyperaroused state, they need to find as much safety as possible. Only true safety will provide the emotional security needed to begin the healing process commonly known as mourning. Giving voice to all that they have experienced—the terror and helplessness, the sense of moral outrage and personal violation, the sorrow, hurt, anger, and grief—becomes the essential first step in piecing together a coherent narrative.

Yet none of this can happen apart from the lively presence of *a caring other*. Who is there that can bear the anguish of such a narrative, without minimizing or denying it, without giving advice or offering strategies to overcome it? Who can listen without offering empty platitudes or switching the focus to a similar story of their own? Who has the wisdom to refrain from asking intrusive questions prompted by their own anxiety, allowing the traumatized space to tell their story in their own way at their

---

40. Van der Kolk dedicates his remarkable anthology, *Traumatic Stress*, to Nelson Mandela and all those who, after having been hurt, "work on transforming the trauma of others, rather than seeking oblivion or revenge."

41. Ulanov, *Unshuttered Heart*, 38.

own pace? Who can offer a compassionate, caring presence, free of pity or sympathy, free of judgment, praise, or blame?[42]

Healing begins as the traumatized manage to piece together a coherent narrative, creating a web of meaning around unspeakable events while remaining fully connected emotionally both to themselves and to their listener. It takes courage even to begin such a conversation. Their feelings can be confusing and difficult to sort out. Often there seem to be no words that adequately describe the horror. Moreover, is it safe to trust the listener? Feelings of shame, fear of judgment, extreme vulnerability are common. Maybe talking about it will make matters worse.

Talking about it can, in actual fact, make matters worse. Any kind of direct processing of the traumatic experience needs to be balanced at all times with a sense of safety and containment. Anchoring oneself in the present, feeling safe with one's listener, processing one small piece at a time, and mourning each of the profound losses involved, all these steps take time, patience, and exquisite self-care. Trauma specialists are trained to pay attention to signs of distress and deliberately slow down the process, remembering the maxim that "the slower you go, the faster you get there."[43] The goal in talking about it is to stay fully connected to the feelings without becoming overwhelmed. Eye contact with the caregiver, slowing down the pace, taking a break from the past, returning to the present with clear focus on one's bodily sensations, all help to put on the brakes.[44] Understanding what is happening and why profoundly assists the healing process as well. This is why a clear conceptual understanding of trauma is important: understanding becomes a part of the holding environment that contains anxiety and increases a sense of empowerment.

Those who have courageously faced trauma give powerful witness to the risks involved. Will they choose life by facing the pain, or will they shrink back once again into numbing defenses?

> When I get into a crisis now, instead of saying, "Oh my God, I'm never going to heal," I see that it's like layers, and the more

---

42. Training in *nonviolent* or *compassionate communication* teaches an exquisite awareness and concrete strategies for the kind of empathic attunement described here. See Rosenberg, *Nonviolent Communication*.

43. Allen, *Coping with Trauma*, 251–53.

44. Babette Rothschild writes: "I never help clients call forth traumatic memories unless I and my clients are confident that the flow of their anxiety, emotion, memories, and body sensations can be contained at will. I never teach a client to hit the accelerator, in other words, before I know that he can find the brake." See Rothschild, "Applying the Brakes."

> I work with it, the more they keep coming around. And even though it's like "But I was feeling good two days ago and now I'm shaking and crying and I can't sleep," I'm beginning to see that I'm not coming back to the same place. I'm coming back at a different level. . . . When I reach the next level where the tears are, where the fear is, where the tiredness is, I have to trust. . . .[45] For me the decision not to identify with the past was a decision, not just a change I went through in the healing process. I had to make a quantum leap that I was no longer going to have the abuse be the cause and my life be the effect. . . . Right now you have to choose what standpoint you are going to live life from. And it's a constant choice.[46]

Trauma survivors need to choose life over death, not once but many times, reaching out with the fragile hope that the trauma can be healed or transformed, that the pain will abate, or that some kind of normalcy will return. Some try to take their lives. Tragically, many succeed, despairing that nothing can stop the eternal recurrence of the trauma. Each person needs the love, support, respect, and understanding of caring others.[47] Those who grow through and beyond trauma do so in part by forging a spiritual framework for what is called post-traumatic growth. Not knowing if or how they will come out, they nevertheless are freed to take steps toward greater and greater freedom. It is to one such framework that I now turn.

How Does the Gospel with the Pastoral Care of the Church Bring Healing to Those Suffering from Traumatic Loss?

When we enter "the strange new world of the Bible," we are confronted with paradox and mystery at every turn. Here we behold a crucified Savior, a God who bears our grief and carries our sorrow, who heals by taking away the sin of the world, both the evil we suffer and the evil we do. It makes no rational sense. Looked at from outside the circle of faith, it is a complete conundrum. "Getting in" on this religion wrenches your

---

45. Bass and Davis, *Courage to Heal*, 457.
46. Bass and Davis, *Courage to Heal*, 438.
47. Sometimes teens and children are overlooked. Where early attachment is threatened or ruptured, children are much more vulnerable to trauma throughout their lives. See the valuable work done by the National Child Traumatic Stress Network for helpful resources, https://www.nctsn.org/.

mind inside out: Is the cross of Christ sheer foolishness or is it the very power of God? (1 Cor 1:18).

At its core, the cross becomes gospel for the traumatized only if they are able to see there a *divine love* willing to bear what is unbearable for mortal, fallen human beings. God bears for us the full weight of both sin and death. If God in Jesus Christ descends into the worst hell imaginable in order to deliver us from the hells we inflict upon one another, then such a God is worthy of our trust. When we stand by helplessly witnessing the suffering and dying of those we love, we have a God to whom we can entrust them in life and in death. For Jesus Christ is not simply a human companion who comforts us by suffering trauma alongside us. As the creeds of the church attest, he is known to us as the risen Lord, the very Wisdom and Power of God, through whom God will fulfill his purpose of redemption. Jesus Christ, the gospel attests, bears what cannot be borne by fragile, fallen human beings. He alone bears the sin of the world, and he alone bears it away.

As the Lamb of God who *takes away* the sin of the world, Christ is known as that One who suffers *for* our sake as well. On our behalf and for our sake, he takes human depravity into his own divine heart in order to transform it, so that it no longer has the power to separate us from God. The powers of sin and death that have such a hold on us—*and that are at the root of all trauma*—are finally nullified. Not only the fear of death, by which human beings are made "subject to lifelong bondage" (Heb 2:15), but also the fear of eternal estrangement from the very Source of Life is proclaimed to be overcome in Christ. Through Christ, we have access to all that we long for: the loving gaze of one who cherishes us, miraculous outpourings of grace, a steady anchor in times of distress, mercy on our weakness, forgiveness of our sins, and most basic of all, the lifeline of basic trust.

If salvation means forgiveness of sin and the promise of eternal life, then all our pastoral arts of healing have *this promise* as its *telos*. Healing, whether physical, emotional, or spiritual, is always set within this larger context of the unimaginable reaches of God's salvation.[48] If our hope is nothing less than the salvation *of the world* in Jesus Christ, it is also a hope held out for the *perpetrators* of trauma as well as for its *victims*. All those human beings from whom we normally seek to separate ourselves

---

48. Hunsinger, *Theology and Pastoral Counseling*. See also Jenson, "Story and Promise," 113–23: "In historical fact and by manifest anthropological necessity, nothing but final hope ever sustains genuine suffering or enables creative historic action."

by every conceivable means, those perpetrators of unspeakable horror—they, too, perhaps more than anyone, need to hear the gospel word of God's judgment and mercy. If One died for all, then he died for those who have brought the terrors of hell, not only upon others, but also upon themselves through their own actions.[49]

Indeed, whenever we affirm that Christ died for sinners, we affirm our solidarity with all who do harm, solidarity in sin as well as in our deliverance from sin. In confessing ourselves as sinners, utterly unable to save ourselves, we recognize that under similar circumstances of deprivation, terror, or colossal historic evils, we, too, would be capable of monstrous crimes toward our fellow human beings. The cross of Jesus Christ is God's response not only to the terror of human trauma but also the anguish of human guilt, bringing succor and healing to the one, and judgment, forgiveness, and the "godly grief" of repentance to the other (2 Cor 7:10). When we affirm the resurrection and ascension of Jesus Christ, we affirm his power to bring every kind of evil to an end.

> Though innocent, Christ suffers as if guilty and ends the logic of evil by taking our suffering onto his body, and not being destroyed by it nor by the death it inflicts. The abyss of love is revealed as stronger than the abyss of death, the power of love as stronger than the power of hate.[50]

This is an interpretive framework that no psychiatrist or therapist has to offer, no twelve-step program or self-help group can claim, but which can be preached and taught week after week in the context of ordinary pastoral care: that in overcoming the world, Jesus Christ saves us from both the guilt and anguish of human sin, as well as the terror and trauma of suffering and death.

These are words of hope to which the traumatized may cling. "Now hope that is seen is not hope" (Rom 8:24). Though our faith holds us fast to this hope, we know that many descend into their graves with nothing but hatred toward those who have harmed them or those they love. Forgiveness, though freely given by God, does not seem to be a human possibility for us in turn. Try as we might, it does not seem subject to

---

49. "More recently there has come an awareness of 'perpetrator-induced trauma' and its role in perpetuating the cycle of victimization and offending; severe offending can itself cause trauma in offenders" (Zehr, "Doing Justice, Healing Trauma," 10). See also, MacNair, *Perpetration-Induced Traumatic Stress*. For a compelling story, see Berry, "Pray Without Ceasing."

50. Ulanov, *Unshuttered Heart*, 150–51.

our human will but comes, when it does, as a miracle of God.[51] While not *subject* to our human will, forgiveness rarely happens apart from an active decision to forgive. One definition of forgiveness, given by pastoral theologian David Augsburger,

> is an act of laying aside one's rational arguments for repayment, my principled arguments for my being truly in the right and you being wholly in the wrong, and at last offering a full and complete pardon to the other, whether or not there are any believable signs of authentic remorse or repentance in the perpetrator. In granting the other person release, one receives one's own.[52]

We have seen this miracle of forgiveness in the testimonies of those who appeared before the South African Truth and Reconciliation Commission. One that has stayed with me is the testimony of Ms. Babalwa Mhlauli. Bishop Tutu writes, "When she had finished telling her story, she said she wanted to know who had killed her father. She spoke quietly and, for someone so young, with much maturity and dignity. You could have heard a pin drop in that hushed city hall when she said, 'We do want to forgive but we don't know whom to forgive.'"[53] We see it in Marietta Jaeger-Lane who has worked tirelessly for both victims *and* perpetrators in the years that followed the kidnapping and murder of her seven-year-old daughter, Susie. Founder of Murdered Victim's Families for Reconciliation, Ms. Jaeger-Lane continues to honor her daughter by offering testimony to end capital punishment for capital crimes.[54] Such stories challenge us to consider those for whom we harbor ill will, those we are unable or unwilling to forgive. Sometimes, we can only lay them at the foot of the cross for God to judge, confessing our inability to fathom either the extent of the evil or its redemption. We can only point away from ourselves to the transcendent hope of the gospel we are called to proclaim.

If maintaining hope is the foundation of all healing, as psychotherapist Jon G. Allen attests, then the Gospel has something fundamental to offer those afflicted by trauma.[55] While ministry cannot replace the work of psychiatry or psychotherapy, it can nevertheless function as an

---

51. Hunsinger, "Forgiving Abusive Parents," 71–98. Augsburger, *Hate-Work*, 232.
52. Tutu, *No Future without Forgiveness*. 149.
53. Tutu, *No Future without Forgiveness*. 149.
54. See Journey of Hope, "Our History," in which the family members of murder victims speak out tirelessly against the death penalty. See also Jaeger, *Lost Child*.
55. Allen, *Coping with Trauma*.

indispensable part of the healing process.[56] When human trust has eluded them, the traumatized desperately need an anchor, a point of reference, something or someone reliable in which to place their trust. Scripture attests again and again that by the power of the Spirit, God comes to those who cry out for help: "I called on Your name, O Lord, from the lowest pit. You have heard my voice: 'Do not hide Your ear from my sighing, from my cry for help.' You drew near on the day I called on You, and said, "Do not fear!" (Lam 3:55–57 NKJV).

We thus facilitate healing when we help the afflicted cry out their sorrow, rage, and tears *to God*. Prayers of lament—crying out to God for deliverance—seem to be faith's only alternative to despair.[57] Instead of protecting themselves against the pain, the afflicted are encouraged to go down into it, clinging to God's promises as they do so. Listen to one such lament, in which the afflicted one directs her anguish toward God.

> There comes a time when both body and soul
> enter into such a vast darkness
> that one loses light and consciousness
> and knows nothing more of God's intimacy.
> At such a time, when the light in the lantern burns out
> the beauty of the lantern can no longer be seen,
> with longing and distress we are reminded of our nothingness.
> At such a time I pray to God:
> "O God, this burden is too heavy for me!"
> And God replies:
> "I will take this burden first and clasp it close to Myself
> and that way you may more easily bear it." . . .
> If God leaves me unanointed, I could never recover.
> Even if all the hills flowed with healing oils,
> and all the waters contained healing powers,
> and all the flowers and all the trees dripped with healing ointments,
> still, I could never recover.
> "God, I will tear the heart of my soul in two
> and you must lie therein.
> You must lay yourself in the wounds of my soul."[58]

---

56. In the United States context, those diagnosed with PTSD will often turn for help to therapists especially trained in trauma. In other contexts around the world, imaginative rituals and collective healing processes have been developed. See, for example, the work of Martha Cabrera, "Living and Surviving," describing her work in Nicaragua.

57. Hunsinger, "Prayers of Lament."

58. Rienstra, *Swallow's Nest*, 230.

These words of Mechthild of Magdeburg, mystic of the thirteenth century, echo down through the centuries, offering a startling image of healing through the palpable presence of Christ's own body. In her fervent prayer, Mechthild offers the wounds of her soul for healing through the intimate presence of Christ's broken body. Here we meet profound mystery. An image of union with Christ rises up from the depths and is given voice in her prayer. Only the full, living presence of a wounded Savior can heal her soul.

Psychologist Robert Stolorow speaks of the fundamental necessity of finding what he calls a "relational home" for traumatic experience. He writes,

> Trauma is constituted in an intersubjective context in which severe emotional pain cannot find a relational home in which it can be held. In such a context, painful affect states become unendurable....[59]

Severe emotional pain cannot be endured if it does not have a relational home, someone to hold what cannot be borne.[60] Ministers of the gospel of Jesus Christ who are rooted and grounded in the love of God provide just such a relational home for all those who groan for the redemption of the world. They offer a steady, sturdy, compassionate, and loving witness to all who have suffered trauma. Insofar as they thus participate in Christ's own compassion, they become witnesses to and mediators of Christ's miraculous grace.

Conclusion

In recent decades, pastoral theology has turned more and more to the public, social, and political dimensions of both affliction and pastoral care. Ministers of the church attend not just to individual members of their congregations but also participate in larger communities of outreach and care. Especially in the light of recent large-scale disasters, pastoral leaders need to respond with sensitivity to the needs of those who do not share the gospel narrative as the overarching context of meaning of

---

59. Stolorow, *Trauma and Human Existence*, 10.

60. See also the example in Hunsinger, "Keeping an Open Heart." The experience described there illustrates the importance of having one's pain "witnessed" as described by Weingarten in *Common Shock*.

their lives. I believe that it is crucial for us also to address questions such as these, even though they lie outside the scope of the present chapter.[61]

As leaders in their own church communities, pastoral leaders need to recognize the power inherent in their position to frame and interpret any traumatic event that has occurred. In so doing, they can either inflame the situation by escalating anxiety (through name-calling, rushing to judgment and blame, using us/them dichotomies, labeling dissenting views, or withholding or misrepresenting the facts)[62] or decrease anxiety and facilitate healing by opening channels of communication among all parties involved.[63] As they offer a secure holding environment to strengthen frayed bonds of trust, and as they call upon God to minister to the community in its pain, they offer space to the hurting to tell their story. In some cases, nearly everyone in the community has been hurt by trauma, but in strangely diverse ways.[64] In this kind of situation, it is essential to refrain from moralizing or blaming but position themselves in such a way that all persons can be heard.[65] The community needs to gather in order to share their common grief, which serves to counteract the fear, shame, isolation, and horror of what has occurred.[66]

The spiritual care of the community finds its final locus in ritual, psalm, and song, in worship and the mystery of the Lord's Supper.

---

61. Jeannette Sutton writes about the wariness that disaster coordinators have toward those providers of spiritual care who volunteer their assistance. "There has been unease about hidden agendas, the appropriateness of religiously oriented interventions, and concern for victims who might feel that contact with some minister-types is intrusive and assaultive" (Sutton, "Convergence of the Faithful," 19). Through ministries of "presence" and "hospitality," spiritual care providers in the public sphere offer comfort and reassurance while helping victims to draw upon their "own religious and/or spiritual resources in order to construct meaning out of chaos." They respect personal boundaries, know how to work in an interfaith manner, and are responsive to training from the disaster assistance professionals such as the American Red Cross.

62. Volkan, *Blind Trust*, as cited in "STAR: Strategies for Trauma."

63. See Zehr, *Little Book of Restorative Justice*, 67–69.

64. It is worth noting that ministers themselves are vulnerable to any trauma afflicting their community. Pastors and church leaders occupy a unique dual role, as those called to give pastoral care, yet at the same time as human beings who are themselves personally affected. Those in caregiving roles need to be exquisitely attuned to their own needs for care, especially when their immediate community is in crisis. Ministers' families are vitally affected and need support as well. Presbyterian Disaster Assistance (PDA) consists of PCUSA pastors, elders, and mental health professionals who are trained in trauma and crisis-response, who offer companionship and support to church leaders in congregations affected by "human-caused disasters."

65. Zehr, *Little Book of Restorative Justice*, 67–69.

66. Zehr, *Little Book of Restorative Justice*, 19–41.

Personal trauma and loss are woven into the losses of the larger community as the liturgy unfolds. That which is most deeply personal becomes part of the communal lament of the people of God through the ages. Walter Brueggemann reminds us that:

> [The] public dimension of grief is deep underneath personal loss, and for the most part, not easily articulated among us. But grief will not be worked well or adequately until attention goes underneath the personal to the public and communal. My expectation is that pastors, liturgically and pastorally, most need to provide opportunity and script for lament and complaint and grief for a long time. No second maneuver after grief shall be permitted to crowd in upon this raw, elemental requirement.[67]

By permitting an unrelieved descent into the raw emotions of grief within the secure boundaries of ritual space, hope and trust may be paradoxically restored.[68]

As the church gathers for worship, we are told of a God who is "the Father of mercies and God of all comfort, who comforts us in all our affliction, so that we may be able to comfort those who are in any affliction, with the comfort with which we ourselves are comforted by God" (2 Cor 1). In worship, we find space both to mourn and to hope, as we wait with painful longing for the redemption of the world. We find comfort in the midst of affliction when we are reminded that the One who descends into every human hell we create, and unwittingly or maliciously perpetuate, is the very One who sits at the right hand of the Father in glory.

The community that responds to trauma in these ways will, by the grace and power of God, find itself stronger, wiser, more compassionate, and more resilient. Its collective story will be one of overcoming adversity together rather than a story of shame, re-victimization, fear, and silencing. By reclaiming the essential practices of our faith—compassionate witnessing, communal lament, and public worship—we "enable people to continue to love God in the face of evil and suffering and in so doing to prevent tragic suffering from becoming evil."[69] As John Swinton writes, "Loving God does not take away the pain that [trauma] inflicts,

---

67. Walter Brueggemann as cited by John Swinton in *Raging With Compassion*, 121.

68. See "Unspeakable Things Spoken," by Johnson, in Greider, Hunsinger, and Kelcourse, *Healing Wisdom*, for a description and analysis of a whole community engaged in a transformative healing process as it confronts horrific historic and ongoing trauma.

69. Swinton, *Raging with Compassion*, 85.

but it *does* transform it."[70] May God work out our salvation by bearing what cannot be borne, by transforming our mourning into longing, our longing into lament, our lament into hope and, through the redemption of this beloved world, our hope into joy.

---

70. Swinton, *Raging with Compassion*, 75.

3

An Interdisciplinary Map for Christian Counselors

Theology and Psychology in Pastoral Counseling

When I worked as a pastoral counselor, I often felt like I was traveling in uncharted territory. Sometimes during a counseling session an image would arise spontaneously in my mind of the counselee and me walking through the woods at night. It seemed as if the light I held in my hand were just barely bright enough for us to see a step or two ahead of us on the path. I hoped it was enough to keep us from stumbling into an unexpected pit. The counselee was on an important journey and had invited me along as companion and guide, but where were we headed? To be sure, I had various maps in hand, some constructed by depth psychologists and others drawn up by various theologians and spiritual guides, but how did they all fit together?

If I followed one map only, we might find a clear path on which to travel, but would our destination be the one we had intended? Were all our efforts straining toward the kingdom of God or toward a more modest goal of healing from psychological trauma? Did the counselee long for the communion of saints or simply for relief from depression and loneliness? Were these different ways of conceiving of our destination compatible with each other, or would they take us in different directions? Where was the particular crossroads where the two sets of maps intersected?

Just where do theology and psychology meet when we are interested in that pastoral art called caring for the soul? This question vexed me for years, and my book *Theology and Pastoral Counseling: A New Interdisciplinary Approach* might be seen as the map I drew after a decade of trying out various paths in the woods.[1] The more I wandered with my counselees, the more urgently I needed an answer to my question. It was confusing to have two sets of maps that charted some of the same territory but in oddly different ways. How could I make sense of them for myself as well as for the people I was trying to help? As I pondered them over time, I became more and more confused and felt more and more hopeless about ever finding a way through the thicket. And yet the question was urgent because it was at the very heart of my sense of vocation: How do we properly conceive of the relationship between these two disciplines, theology and psychology, in the context of pastoral counseling as a ministry of the church? Both theology and psychology were needed to do the work I was called to do, but how were they related to each other?

What were some of the logical possibilities? Perhaps if I removed myself somewhat from the immediate situation with the counselee and approached the question from a more theoretical standpoint, I might be better able to get an overview, a grasp of the whole. If I did that, how might I conceive of the relationship between theology and psychology?

First, I might view the relationship between psychology and theology as a relationship between promise and fulfillment, or between something that is incomplete and something that is complete.[2] Psychology, then, would be conceived as a map that would take a person only part of the way to the destination. Where it leaves off, theology would take over. Psychology, in other words, would be seen as having certain inherent limits; it would need to be extended or supplemented with theological concepts.

Second, I might see that some aspects of psychology conceptualize the same or similar experiences that theology conceptualizes, only using a different vocabulary. Both languages attempt to give shape and meaning to a particular set of human experiences but in different ways. Thus, one would be able to translate back and forth between the two idioms.

Third, I might view theology and psychology as complementary, each having a distinct area of expertise and providing reliable guidance in that area. I would not understand them as contradicting each other because they do not describe the same territory.

Fourth, by contrast perhaps I would view theology and psychology as being directly opposed to each other. They do indeed chart the same

---

1. Hunsinger, *Theology and Pastoral Counseling*.

2. This typology is adapted from George Lindbeck's study of the possible relationships among various religions. Lindbeck also develops an extended cartographic metaphor, in which conceptual theories function as various kinds of maps.

territory, but the paths they map through the woods lead to decidedly different destinations. Those paths might converge for a while but at certain decisive points they would separate, forcing us to make a choice.

Fifth, perhaps I could best understand the relationship between theology and psychology as the relationship between the coherent and the incoherent or between the authentic and inauthentic. Perhaps there are inconsistencies in one map's charting of a particular patch of woods, but the other map presents the way through that part of the woods consistently so that it becomes comprehensible. Maybe people who authentically pursue a psychologically healthy way of life have a similar moral outlook to that of people who authentically practice the disciplines of the Christian faith. If we conceive of the relationship this way, a committed Christian disciple has more in common with someone who is committed to a discipline of intensive psychotherapy than with a nominal Christian. Finally, depending on which aspects of theology and psychology I was investigating, I might attain a proper conception of the relationship through a combination of these possibilities.

A Theological Compass: The Chalcedonian Pattern

Rather than sorting through these logical possibilities, which are intended to be more suggestive than definitive, I would like to propose a different approach. In the midst of such a bewildering and complex set of possibilities, we need a way of orienting ourselves theologically. We need something more basic than a map; we need a compass. I find such a compass in the church's definition of how the divine and human natures of Jesus Christ are to be conceived and related in the teaching of the church. The church fathers who gathered at the Council of Chalcedon in AD 451 confronted many of the conceptual issues that I faced as I pondered the proper way to conceive of the relationship between theology and psychology. The relevant passage from the Chalcedonian definition of the relationship between Christ's two natures reads as follows:

> Therefore . . . we all with one accord teach people to acknowledge one and the same Son, our Lord Jesus Christ, at once complete in Godhead and complete in manhood, truly God and truly human . . . one and the same Christ, Son, Lord, Only-Begotten, recognized in two natures, without confusion, without change, without division, without separation; the distinction of natures in no way annulled by the union, but rather the characteristics

of each nature being preserved and coming together to form one person and subsistence, not as parted or separated into two persons, but one and the same Son and Only begotten God the Word, Lord Jesus Christ.[3]

How did this definition function in its original context? The Council of Chalcedon was called into being after centuries of debate over how to understand the claims of Scripture and the early church that Jesus is Lord, the Son of God. The purpose of the council was not to define the faith of the church in any comprehensive or exhaustive sense, but rather to demarcate clear boundaries for orthodox teaching. The council sought on the one hand to rule out various heretical teachings (such as Arianism and Nestorianism), and on the other hand to hold together the partial truths expressed in various competing understandings of Jesus' simultaneous divinity and humanity (such as those of Christians in Alexandria and Antioch).

The Chalcedonian definition evidences more concern about what it rules out than what it rules in. Its focus is that Christ's two natures are related without separation or division on the one hand and without confusion or change on the other. This was the key move. I came to see that formal nature of these defining or relational terms can be abstracted from the Chalcedonian definition and applied to a wide range of other questions.

The compass that finally provided me with a clear theological orientation was what one scholar has called a "Chalcedonian pattern" of thought.[4] The Chalcedonian definition of how properly to understand the incarnation of the Word of God in Jesus Christ became the basis for my thinking about how properly to conceive of the relationship between the disciplines of theology and psychology in the work of pastoral counseling.

Let me be very clear at this point. I am making a crucial distinction between the Chalcedonian pattern and the Chalcedonian definition. It is the pattern, not the definition, that gives me guidance for thinking about the relationship between theology and psychology. The pattern merely provides form, whereas the definition is substantive. And because the pattern is formal, it can be applied to a variety of different relationships, whereas the substantive definition is specific to Christology. The pattern offers a kind of grammar, whereas the definition sets forth a particular statement in which the grammar is exemplified. There are three formal

---

3. As cited in Loder and Neidhardt, *Knight's Move*, 83.
4. Hunsinger, G., *How to Read Karl Barth*, 185.

features of the Chalcedonian pattern. First, two terms are placed in a relationship in which they exist together without confusion or change so that they remain indissolubly differentiated. Second, those terms are related without separation or division so that they coexist in inseparable unity. Finally, one term is considered to be logically prior to the other; it provides a point of normative orientation, or a framework. In cases in which the two terms generate conceptual conflict, the logically prior term is allowed to prevail. This is what Karl Barth has called indestructible order.[5]

To explicate each of these formal or relational features, I will first ask about their substantive use in the Chalcedonian definition itself. How are Christ's two natures properly understood to be related when we ponder the mystery of the incarnation? Second, in each case I will abstract the formal pattern from the definition by asking what clues it provides regarding the relationship between the discipline of theology and that of psychology.

Indissoluble Differentiation: Without Confusion or Change

What does this relational grammar require when we ponder the mysterious event of the incarnation of God in Jesus Christ? "Indissoluble differentiation" has to do with the importance of maintaining the clear distinction between Christ's divine and human natures. Jesus Christ is said to have not one but two "natures" that are inconceivably united. Their union is said to be inconceivable because nothing could be more radically incommensurable than to be completely divine and completely human at the same time. God alone is eternal; human beings are mortal. God alone is holy; human beings are fallen and sinful. It would be the utmost error to confuse these two natures or to see them as somehow capable of being interchanged.

Kierkegaard captures this characteristic of the incarnation when he speaks of the "infinite qualitative difference" between God and the human being. Following Barth, we might think of this difference as the "ontological divide" that separates divine from human being and which is overcome only when God graciously crosses it in Jesus Christ. Barth asks: "Will not this being of ours be given over to death? Will it not be so questioned that we can be sure only of its not being? And where then

---

5. Barth, *Church Dogmatics* 3/2, 437.

is the comparability between his Creator-being and our creature-being, between his holy being and our sinful being, between his eternal being and our temporal being?"[6] There is no common mode of being that connects the divine nature and the human nature to one another. Although Jesus Christ is both fully God and fully human, the terms of his deity are not to be confused with the terms of his humanity.

When we abstract the formal pattern and apply it to our conception of how theology and psychology are to be related in the work of pastoral counseling, it would seem first of all that we must recognize the clear differentiation between the two fields. Each discipline has relative autonomy; it can delimit its own sphere of inquiry to secure its self-defined integrity. Each discipline proceeds with the investigation of its subject matter according to the methods appropriate to it. A method of investigation based on God's self-revelation would arguably be quite different from the empirical observation of early childhood interpersonal relationships that forms the basis for theories of psychological development.

Even though both theology and psychology may need to deal with basic issues of love and hate, trust and mistrust, they do so within entirely different contexts of meaning. It would be a mistake to consider them to be somehow interchangeable or to determine that they are saying essentially the same thing but in a slightly different vocabulary. We are confused if we think that theological and psychological terms and concepts can simply be translated back and forth so that, for example, we see a client's sins and symptoms as virtually equivalent, or believe that salvation and individuation are two different ways of talking about the same thing. If we are committed to maintaining the clear distinction between theology and psychology, we will be careful not to disregard their irreducible differences. We will be alert to the vastly different subject matters, the different methods employed and the distinctive norms; indeed, we will be alert to the wholly different conceptual universe that we inhabit when we dwell in one or the other thought world.

Inseparable Unity: Without Separation or Division

When we ponder the mystery of the incarnation, we must also ponder the deep paradox that though Jesus Christ was fully God and fully human, he was not two persons, but one. His two natures were inseparably

6. Barth, *Church Dogmatics* 2/1, 83.

united in what is called a *hypostatic* union; he has two natures but one *hypostasis*, a single subsistence or person. We cannot conceive of Jesus Christ properly if we separate his divine nature from his human nature. The whole person, Jesus Christ, human and divine, suffered and died on the cross. Therefore, we can affirm the otherwise incomprehensible mystery that God suffered and died. The whole person, Jesus Christ, divine and human, was raised from the dead. Therefore, we can affirm the otherwise incomprehensible mystery that a human being was raised to eternal life. In all of Jesus Christ's actions and passion he was and is both fully human and fully divine. Thus, though Jesus Christ was without sin because of his divine nature, he took on the sin of the world, becoming what Barth shockingly calls "the one great sinner."[7] Jesus Christ, by virtue of taking on our humanity, suffered and died as a sinner.

How might the formal or relational category of inseparable unity illuminate the relationship between theology and psychology? When we look at human beings in the world and try to understand them in their wholeness, we find that we cannot fully separate or divide theological and psychological perspectives from one another. Though they are clearly distinguishable and need to be distinguished according to their different subject matters, methods, and norms, in the context of pastoral counseling as a ministry of the church, theology and psychology are inseparable. Everything we do and think and speak and suffer we do and think and speak and suffer as psychological beings.

Yet our ordinary human experience in time and space is the very place where God meets us. God comes into our lives in such a decisive way that in the mystery of divine grace, and whether we recognize it or not, we are called to believe, to become persons of faith. At the very core of our humanity is our relationship to God. Through revelation we know ourselves to be created in God's image, to have fallen away from God's intentions for our lives, and to have been redeemed through Christ, and in him promised a new humanity. As seen from the standpoint of faith, these psychic and spiritual realities are, in fact, inseparable. We can no more divide them from one another than we can separate our bodies from our souls. We are a psychospiritual unity even as we are also "embodied souls" or "ensouled bodies."[8] If we want to understand human beings in their essential psychospiritual wholeness, we need to perceive

---

7. Barth, *Church Dogmatics* 4/1, 239.
8. Barth, *Church Dogmatics* 3/2, 327.

them through both sets of lenses, the psychological and the theological. T. F. Torrance captures this kind of complex unity well, and he shows its basis in the incarnation of Jesus Christ:

> Through the incarnation of God's Word and Truth in Jesus Christ, empirical correlates have an ineradicable place both in the mediation of divine revelation to us and in the theological concepts and statements we are bound to employing any faithful interpretation of it. These concepts and statements point indefinitely beyond themselves to the ultimate mystery of the Triune God and must do so if they are to have divine significance and validity, but unless they are correlated with empirical reality in our creaturely world they can have no meaning for us.[9]

Torrance is speaking here not only of the ways in which God uses ordinary human events in time and space to show us his hidden reality, but also of the concepts we need to use to capture those events faithfully. Because Jesus Christ entered fully into human time and space, our strictly theological statements need to find correlations with those statements from other fields that describe ordinary empirical reality; we need to find correlations in history, sociology, political science, anthropology, psychology, and other fields. Though we are focusing here on theology's relationship with psychology, the conceptual relationship between theology and other disciplines would be governed by the same formal pattern.

Indestructible Order: Asymmetrical Relationship

Now we come to the third formal feature of the Chalcedonian definition, the indestructible order of Christ's two natures. According to Karl Barth, Chalcedon's ordering of Jesus Christ's two natures as fully divine and fully human indicates a kind of logical priority or precedence of his divine over his human nature. Barth is not subordinating the Son to the Father but rather is ordering the two natures of Christ, divine and human, in relation to each other.

These two natures, completely distinct and yet united in the one person, Jesus Christ, are not united by virtue of some common element or attribute that they share. Their union, though real, is utterly incomprehensible to the human mind. It is not as if there is some neutral category of being that exists by degrees along a divine-human continuum.

---

9. Torrance, *Christian Doctrine of God*, 82–83.

According to such a mistaken conception, Christ's humanity would somehow be seen as subordinated to his divine being. But such a conception would fail to take note of the radicalness of the distinction between divine and human reality.

There is no common scale by which God and humanity can be measured. Therefore, Christ's two natures cannot be hierarchically related, for hierarchy presupposes a common standard of measure. The word asymmetry more adequately captures the logic of the terms of relationship between Christ's divine and human natures. The preexistent divine Logos, who was with God before the foundation of the world and through whom the world was created, became incarnate as a human being in space and time, as the Jewish rabbi, Jesus of Nazareth, Mary's son. Though Jesus Christ is both fully divine and fully human, the two terms of his person are not equal and reciprocal but are asymmetrically related, with the divine nature having logical priority.

What are the implications of this formal pattern when it is applied to the complex relationship between theology and psychology? When Christian theology is ordered in relationship to psychology, theology is given the place of logical priority. That is, psychological concepts, while retaining their irreducible distinctiveness and autonomy as psychological concepts, are placed properly within a larger overarching context of Christian theology. The implications of the formal pattern of asymmetry are threefold:

1. It is not possible to conceptually integrate theology and psychology because they function on logically different levels.

2. We must not try to translate theological concepts into psychological concepts or vice versa because such translation is possible only with concepts that are symmetrically related.

3. For those who seek to do counseling in the context of Christian ministry, the norms and values internal to faith have logical precedence over all externally derived norms or values, including those of psychology.

I will discuss each of them in turn.

No Conceptual Integration

It is a mistake to try to integrate Christian theology with any type of psychology at the conceptual level. Just as divine being is ontologically other than human being, so theology is logically other than psychology. Theology and psychology may both be languages that speak of the human condition, but they do so with frameworks and assumptions that are logically diverse. They function conceptually at different levels even when they are intertwined in experience.

Michael Polanyi has elucidated the way in which disciplines may function on different levels and how they may relate to each other in what he calls a stratified hierarchy. In his book *The Tacit Dimension* he investigates the nature of human knowledge at various levels of comprehensiveness. By using vivid and apt examples, Polanyi describes exceedingly complex relationships so that they can be apprehended and remembered. One illustration shows clearly what is meant by the difference in logical levels among various bodies of knowledge. "Take the art of making bricks," Polanyi writes,

> It relies on its raw materials placed on a level below it. But above the brickmaker there operates the architect, relying on the brickmaker's work, and the architect in his turn has to serve the town planner. To these four successive levels there correspond four successive levels of rules. The laws of physics and chemistry govern the raw material of bricks; technology prescribes the art of brickmaking; architecture teaches the builders; and the rules of town planning control the town planners.[10]

Each successive level relies on the knowledge of those disciplines lower in the stratified hierarchy. Yet the terms "lower" and "higher" do not denote greater or lesser value. Each discipline is indispensable to the whole. A house that has poorly made bricks because of insufficient knowledge of the laws of physics and chemistry is uninhabitable, even if it is architecturally brilliant. While town planners may have greater power to conceive the total environment of the town, the bricklayers have power over their own sphere, and competence in their task is an irreplaceable contribution toward the desired end. Polanyi's idea of stratified hierarchy is a comment on the logic of the relationships among disciplines. Explaining the contours of this logic, he emphasizes that "the operations

---

10. Polanyi, *Tacit Dimension*, 35.

of a higher level cannot be accounted for by the laws governing its particulars forming the lower level."[11]

Perhaps it will be helpful to look at another vivid example. Polanyi notes that when giving a speech one must have mastery of voice, words, sentences, style, and literary composition. But "you cannot derive a vocabulary from phonetics; you cannot derive a grammar of a language from its vocabulary; a correct use of grammar does not account for good style; and good style does not provide the content of a piece of prose."[12] Each level of mastery relies on the level beneath it, but one cannot logically account for the higher level in the terms of the lower: "Comprehensive entities exist in a peculiar logical combination of consecutive levels of reality.... Each higher principle controls the boundary left indeterminate by the next lower principle. It relies for its operations on the lower principle without interfering with its laws.... The higher principle is logically unaccountable in terms of the lower."[13]

From the standpoint of faith, theology is obviously higher than psychology on the scale of Polanyi's stratified hierarchy. Thus, theology controls the boundary left indeterminate by psychology, but it relies on knowledge gathered by psychology in its own distinct sphere. Theology does not interfere with the free functioning of psychology, but we cannot derive our theology, our ultimate beliefs about God, human beings, and the world, from within the sphere of psychological assumptions. Any attempt to understand the essence of theological affirmations in psychological terms is as fruitless as a brickmaker's attempt to explain architecture by means of his knowledge of the physics and chemistry of brickmaking. Polanyi's case against reductionism is impressive. He regards the effort to account for the higher operations in the terms of the lower as "patent nonsense."[14]

Although Polanyi uses the term stratified hierarchy, he is not presupposing common standards of measurement among the various disciplines. The skills and knowledge necessary for good brickmaking, for example, are incommensurate with the skills and knowledge required by the architect. Remember that it was the issue of incommensurability that led me to reject the term hierarchy and instead to use the concept of asymmetry. Even though we are using terms differently, I believe that

11. Polanyi, *Tacit Dimension*, 36.
12. Polanyi, *Tacit Dimension*, 36.
13. Polanyi, *Tacit Dimension*, 49.
14. Polanyi, *Tacit Dimension*, 37.

Polanyi's description of stratified hierarchy helps elucidate what I mean by asymmetry.

There is a particularity to theology that Polanyi does not discuss. The peculiar logical status of theology, that which makes it radically incommensurable with any other scientific discipline, has to do with the uniqueness of its subject matter. While theology itself is obviously a human enterprise, the event that theology seeks to describe faithfully and to present conceptually is an event that has no parallel or counterpart in human history, namely, God's crossing of the ontological divide by becoming incarnate in Jesus Christ, by living and dying as a human being in history, and by being raised from the dead. All other disciplines seek to ground their knowledge in empirical reality; only theology speaks of an event that is both empirical and transcendent.

Psychology may responsibly speak of a person's conscious concept of God or unconscious image of God. It may examine one's self-understanding in relation to one's understanding of God. It may even speak of how one interprets experiences that one deems religious. But by virtue of its delimited subject matter, psychology cannot speak of God himself in his relationship with human beings. Only a theology that has God's self-revelation as its methodological point of departure can purport to speak of God. Its framework indicates the very different basis on which theological knowledge is based. From a theological perspective, even our knowledge of human beings is derived from God's revelation of true humanity as we come to know it in Jesus Christ. A theological understanding of human beings therefore functions at a different logical level than our knowledge of human beings that is derived from psychology. Theology and psychology cannot be integrated into one comprehensive system of thought without doing violence to the varying logical levels of meaning.

No Translation

Because they function on these differing logical levels, theological and psychological concepts cannot be translated into each other's idioms. As an example, let us think about the concept of shame as it functions within these two different contexts. If we are speaking of the concept of shame from a theological perspective, we cannot assume that a psychological understanding of shame means essentially the same thing. Unlike psychological understandings of shame, biblical understandings of shame are always placed in the context of a person's primary relationship with God. Think of the psalmist's preoccupation with his fear of being put to shame. He repeatedly calls on God to rescue him and to save him from shame for the sake of God's honor. The psalmist sees himself as being graciously delivered from shame in the face of his enemies because he has remained true to God. He believes that because he has taken up God's cause and God's honor, he too will be lifted up above his enemies.

Another primary biblical use of the concept of shame is in regard to the shame of being a sinner before God. Thus, Peter despairs of his sinful heart when he recognizes the holiness of Jesus as Lord: "Depart from me, for I am a sinful man, O Lord" (Luke 5:8 RSV). The publican recognizes his utter sinfulness and stands in shame before God, not daring to lift his eyes. Unlike the foolish Pharisee, he knows how futile human boasting or attempts at self-justification are in the face of God's holiness. While in both of these examples there is a horizontal dimension to the experience of shame (the psalmist is rescued from shame before his enemies, and the publican humbles himself in contrast to the Pharisee, who raises himself up), the primary meaning of the term shame is derived from the vertical dimension, from the reality of being a sinner before God. As sinners we throw ourselves on God's mercy and are thereby delivered from shame. God covers our shame with the cloak of his mercy and righteousness.

By contrast, psychology focuses on shame as an affect that arises in the context of human relationships. Feelings of exposure and inadequacy arise whenever there is a rupture in a relationship with a highly valued other person, or as one writer puts it, when there is a "break in the interpersonal bridge."[15] If a child has such experiences again and again, and if the valued other person does not seek to repair the damage done by the rupture, the child will eventually internalize the shame. Over time such internalized shame will bring about enduring feelings of worthlessness, deficiency, or inadequacy. One's whole sense of identity may become bound up with shame. In such circumstances, there is little that enables a person to build a foundation for positive self-esteem. People who are bound up with shame come to believe that they are in fact inferior, defective, inadequate, or worthless.

But should such feelings of worthlessness be equated with shame over sin in the theological sense? To equate the two would confuse two universes of discourse that function on different levels of meaning. The

---

15. Kaufman, *Shame*, 11.

meaning of the term *shame* changes when we shift from a theological context to a psychological context. Yet there is a vast amount of literature today that glosses over or confuses these important distinctions. In this literature, the language of sin is considered to be harmful to a person's growing self-esteem. New liturgies have even been devised that leave out the confession of sin because it might make people feel badly about themselves. In such cases the creators of liturgy clearly do not understand that the language of sin functions in a radically different context, the context of the gospel as a whole.

In the gospel as I understand it, knowledge of sin and the shame that accompanies it lead to repentance, forgiveness, renewal, vocation, and finally joy (2 Cor 7:9-10). Shame is a single moment along a continuum that leads eventually to the lifting up of the sinner, to the recognition that though one is a sinner, one is a forgiven sinner, indeed, that one is a beloved child of God. Known sin is always forgiven sin because one cannot be aware of what sin is apart from a knowledge of what God has already done in Jesus Christ to overcome and defeat sin. As one who belongs to Jesus Christ in life and in death, one is lifted up with a sense of awe at such an honor. I cannot imagine a more stable foundation for true self-esteem than to know that one's most enduring identity is that of being a beloved child of God.

The Logical Precedence of Theology

If we use faith as a means to an end, as a mere method for improving self-esteem, we will be reversing the asymmetrical order between the disciplines. To make faith a means to an end other than faith itself is to assume that the proposed end is of greater value than faith. In our interdisciplinary field, where psychological norms play an important role in diagnosis and treatment, we sometimes fail to see that in subtle ways what we hold to be normative for the life of faith begins to play a subordinate role to the supposedly greater good of mental health.

This shift has begun to occur, for example, when people understand prayer merely as a resource for healing. Healing is conceived of as the goal toward which all our efforts are straining. If prayer relieves stress and thereby contributes to healing, then it must be used because it is an important resource, the argument goes. Empirical studies have been published, for example, that show a positive correlation between the use of prayer and physical and emotional healing.[16] Some people consider such studies to be a good apologetic for prayer, and some have been convinced enough by the studies to engage in daily prayer for the sake of its practical benefits. But the real focus and purpose of prayer as the means of intimate communion with God has been lost. Everything has been turned upside down. Instead of God being at the center of our lives, our emotional or mental health occupies the center. God thus becomes a helpful adjunct to our self-determined goals. When biblical and theological concepts are put into an overarching psychological framework, this reversal of values takes place. When prayer and confession, Scripture and forgiveness are used as biblical principles and practices to be integrated into psychological counseling, they may subtly begin to serve different ends than those they are meant to serve in the life of faith. They become relativized by their overarching psychological context.

Newton Maloney points out in a recent review of a book that seeks to integrate biblical principles and practices into counseling, "[The author] does not seem to realize that the only legitimate function that any methodology, including spiritual practices, can serve in a counseling situation is to alleviate distress and enhance adaptation to the culture in which a person chooses to live."[17] Maloney's basic assumption is the reverse of my own. He is assuming an asymmetrical relationship between the disciplines, but in the reverse order. He is assuming that the norms and values of psychology set the terms of the overarching context, rather than the reverse. Thus, Scripture and prayer would become the means to the end of alleviating distress and enhancing adaptation. By contrast, I am interested in bringing psychological principles and practices to bear on counseling that is set within a biblical and theological context.

The affirmation of Job, "though he slay me, yet will I trust in him" (Job 13:15 KJV), is incomprehensible to people for whom the norms of psychology have priority. Job could only be masochistic to give voice to such an utterance. But Job is affirming faith in the midst of incomprehensible suffering at the hand of an incomprehensible God who is to be loved and feared above all else. No other value has priority, neither health nor family nor honor nor material goods nor even life itself, but only faith and trust in God, even though Job perceives God as his enemy and slayer. To acknowledge the profundity of Job's faith, even if we cannot remotely

---

16. Duckro and Magaletta, "Effect of Prayer."

17. See Maloney's review of McMinn, "Review of *Psychology, Theology and Spirituality*," 119.

approach it in our own life, is to understand something of what it means to say that the norms and values internal to faith have logical precedence over all externally derived norms and values. Other norms and values are therefore necessarily relativized whenever they come into conflict with faith in God. Faith, or rather God as the object of faith, is to be placed at the very center of our lives. All other values and relationships are ordered around this central relationship.

Before we turn from the topic of the asymmetrical ordering of the two disciplines, I would like to make a few additional comments, lest I be misunderstood. The asymmetrical ordering of the relationship between psychology and theology follows logically, I believe, from the first commandment, that we must have no other gods before God. But that is not to say that the norms and values of psychology are themselves unimportant. Penultimate values may not be ultimate, but they are nonetheless extremely valuable. Who among us would scorn the value of emotional health or good communication skills or nurturing parenting? Who among us would easily cast aside the importance of healthy social adjustment for our children and basic acceptance by their peers?

I am affirming that the gospel makes ultimate claims on us, claims that need to be reflected in our theological concepts, but I do not want to be understood as saying that psychology has little or nothing to offer. On the contrary, I have spent my entire adult life studying psychology. I believe that psychology has much to offer Christians who seek to worship God with all their heart, soul, mind, and strength and to love their neighbor as themselves. I believe that the study of psychology in relation to theology has the potential to enrich and deepen our life of faith, sometimes in unexpected ways. Although I share many of the concerns expressed by those who are worried about what has been called the "triumph of the therapeutic" in the church, I believe that psychology has much to contribute to the pastoral art of caring for the soul. While I do not want to lose theology's distinctive concepts or collapse them into psychological discourse, I do not believe that the solution that will protect our theological inheritance is to ignore the gifts that psychology can bring to ministry.

Before turning to a discussion of three of the gifts that psychology can bring to ministry, let us find a clearing, hold the light directly over our maps, and assess where we have gone thus far. When we started out, we were perplexed in the woods, pondering the various maps we had with us and wondering where they all led. We found our theological compass by extracting the formal pattern of thought from the Chalcedonian definition of the relationship between Christ's two natures. We discussed what it means to affirm that Christ's two natures are related without confusion and change on the one hand and without separation or division on the other. We first asked how these affirmations apply substantively to Jesus Christ in the incarnation and then how the formal Chalcedonian pattern might be applied to the relationship between the disciplines of theology and psychology. Finally, we spent some time on the question of asymmetrical order, trying to draw out the implications of saying that theology has logical precedence over psychology. Now we will focus on the gifts that psychology brings to the pastoral art of the care of souls.

I will focus on only three gifts, though many more could be mentioned. We will consider gifts from the tradition that I know best, the one that arises out of the insights of Freud and Jung, though a different and perhaps equally compelling list of gifts could be drawn up by a cognitive or behavioral psychologist or a family systems theoretician. We will look at three fundamental psychological concepts: first, the theory of the unconscious; second, the therapeutic or pastoral relationship as the context for healing; and third, psychotherapy's attention to process. In each case, I will show how theology can rely on insights from psychology to deepen its own art of pastoral care without reducing pastoral care to psychotherapy. Pastoral care is ministry, and it is appropriately judged by its own intrinsic theological criteria; nevertheless, it can rely on insights from the sister discipline of psychology, which lies directly below it in the stratified hierarchy.

Psychology's First Gift to Theology: The Theory of the Unconscious

Despite a range of questions and criticisms that have been leveled at modern psychoanalytic theory since it began and that persist into the present day, it seems unlikely that the idea of the unconscious will ever lose its illuminating power. To truly love God with all our heart, soul, mind, and strength requires that we know not only something about the object of our love, namely, God, but also something about the subject, namely, the nature of our heart, soul, and mind. The theory of the unconscious assumes that we know very little about who we actually are. It claims that most of what motivates us, most of what we feel, think, desire, and hope for, lies outside of our awareness. The theory of the unconscious provides a way for us to become acquainted with ourselves, with our soul in all its richness, mystery, and complexity.

Both Freud and Jung worked with dreams. Each spent years learning to decipher these strange nocturnal messengers. Anyone who has worked at understanding her dreams over a period of years and has thus mined the depths of her unconscious processes can attest to the inestimable value of learning about aspects of herself that she never imagined were there. My teacher Ann Ulanov used to describe the unconscious as a river of being moving below the surface of consciousness and teeming with life. To fall asleep and to dream is to become present to all of that vitality, to all of those wishes, longings, fears, hopes, sorrows, and joys that lie outside of our awareness much of the time.

The maps of our inner landscape that have been so carefully drawn up by psychologists of the unconscious can also give us insight into the way in which we come to imagine God on the basis of our early life experiences with our parents and other caregivers. We can dismiss such knowledge as a mere projection of our unconscious desires onto the unknown screen of eternity and call it an illusion as Freud did, or we can disregard such knowledge because it tells us nothing about God's actual identity, which can be known only by revelation, as Barth did. But we would be wiser, I believe, to pay attention to those projected images because the stuff of our very psyche is hidden in them. Their value lies not in what they tell us about God (in that I believe that Barth is right), but rather in what they tell us about ourselves. We must not disregard or disparage these creations of our psyches; we need to respect them even when they conflict with the way the Bible depicts God's identity. If we attend to these idiosyncratic images of God, we may learn much about the deeply felt needs and wishes, sorrows and longings of our earliest years. A woman who was abandoned in early childhood, for example, may find herself returning again and again to the contemplation of Christ's moment of utter forsakenness on the cross. A man who was abused as an infant but has repressed all memory of the abuse may find the memory pushing its way into his consciousness by means of his preoccupation with the question of God's trustworthiness. A woman's sense of personal autonomy and agency may have been so undermined because of a traumatic loss at an early stage of her development that she now pictures God as a kind of *deus ex machina*, as the active partner while she remains passive, dependent, and helpless.

These hypothetical examples are not meant to show how God's image can become a veritable Rorschach inkblot test, but rather to suggest that psychology has something to offer Christians as they ponder what they bring into their life with God. Surely, we all distort God's identity, for our human imaginings are so meager and paltry and inadequate. To be sure, our human images are sometimes used by God, in spite of their complete inadequacy, to give us knowledge of who God really is. But we cannot test whether this is the case on the basis of the images themselves. Our images must always be tested in the light of what we learn about God in Jesus Christ. And even when our God representations tell us nothing reliable about God, they always tell us a great deal of value about ourselves. Our representations of God represent the human expectations, desires, and fears that we bring into our relationship with God.

In some cases, a person's conscious understanding of God conflicts with his unconscious image of God. His carefully reasoned theological views may function psychologically as a defense against his very threatening inner image of God. Perhaps you know someone whose theology seems to be a weapon with which to bully those who see things differently. Theological disagreements with him create an emotional atmosphere fraught with tension. I believe that a knowledge of the unconscious might give such a person theoretical and practical tools for self-inquiry. Why is he holding his picture of God so rigidly? Perhaps he is not simply expressing zeal for the Lord. Perhaps he is being threatened from within by an unconscious image of God that contradicts his theologically orthodox, consciously held understanding. He has to defensively uphold his conscious understanding in order to drown out inner voices of self-doubt and fear.

Such a person may consciously love and seek to serve God, but that love might not reach down into his unconscious roots. Hiding underneath the surface might be a powerful image of a sadistic, persecuting God who delights in human misery, or perhaps an abandoning God who doesn't care about human anguish. Whenever people hold theological beliefs defensively, whenever they seem to be greatly threatened by disagreement, we can wonder whether there is a different image of God threatening them from within. Depth psychology offers us tools for investigating such a hypothesis.

Depth psychology and its understanding of the unconscious also give us conceptual tools for understanding events that cannot be understood from within a theological frame of reference but that affect the life of faith dramatically. I recently heard a tragic story of a woman in another culture and country whose pastor and church leaders believed that she was demonically possessed. She was hearing voices, and she believed that she was pregnant with Isaac, the child of the promise. Members of her church prayed for her and with her again and again, but nothing seemed to help. Eventually they held prayer meetings for hours at a time and beat her until she was bruised, trying to rid her soul of the destructive powers that were tormenting her. Her brother learned of these events and did everything he could to intervene. Though he lived literally on the other side of the world from his sister, he persevered until he found a Christian psychologist who could help her.

The psychologist learned that the woman was suffering from depression, rage, and repressed grief over the seven abortions she had undergone at the instigation of her husband's family. In her culture, as in many of the cultures during biblical times, everything depended on having a son. Each time she had been pregnant, this woman had learned with the help of modern diagnostic tests that the child she carried was a daughter. Her husband was the last male descendent of his ancestral line, and he had insisted that his wife wait until she conceived a son before carrying a child to term and giving birth. He and his family had insisted not once or twice but seven times, until her grief and rage could be repressed no longer and issued forth in extreme symptoms.

I do not use this example to suggest that demonic possession is always a case of psychopathology. I do not understand the mystery of demonic possession, but I suspect that such cases may exist. In this instance, however, I believe that the members of the church were in over their heads. They were not good diagnosticians. They did not investigate the woman's history closely. They used the theological and spiritual tools that were available to them without asking whether other tools would be more fitting and appropriate. They disregarded psychological perspectives or collapsed them into a single theological perspective. They understood everything to be a consequence of sin, and they apparently allowed no room for other possible explanations. Their diagnostic framework was too narrowly theological; it was made to do work it was not equipped to do. Because they did not differentiate the psychological side enough, they effectively silenced any independent point of view that it might have offered.

This case is quite dramatic, but there are perhaps dozens of events in any person's life that could bring insight and healing if they were interpreted according to the psychology of the unconscious. "What are the blocks that keep me from forgiving my parents no matter how hard I try?" one young woman asks. Rather than heaping guilt and scorn on herself for not being able to forgive as she has been forgiven, she would do well to investigate whether she has fully uncovered her own unconscious grief and anger. "Why do I keep having sexual fantasies that come into my mind against my will and make me feel degraded?" an older man asks. He could be advised to pray about it, and it would be good for him to do so. But a psychological perspective would begin with the hypothesis that there is an unconscious reason for such fantasies, then would seek their hidden meaning. If the man simply turns in horror from his fantasies and tries harder to repress them, they will return with even more intensity, as repressed contents inevitably do.[18]

In each of these cases, understanding and healing may come not primarily by means of theological investigation and its use of the conceptual category of sin, but rather by means of a search for the unconscious threads that the mind has woven into a pattern of meaning outside of awareness. If we confront these issues solely from a theological perspective, separating them from the underlying psychological dynamics that are at work, we are in danger of misapprehending them. We are unable to give real pastoral help if we insist exclusively on diagnosing sin and offering forgiveness, when instead what is needed is careful attention to how the person has been hurt or traumatized. A knowledge of how the unconscious mind uses various defense mechanisms to cope with trauma can be a priceless treasure for people who desire to learn the pastoral art of caring for the soul.

Psychology's Second Gift: The Pastoral Relationship as the Context for Healing

The church has long known of the healing power of relationship, for we are instructed to place every condition of our lives, whether joyful or sorrowful, in the context of our relationship with God. Our identities as human beings are constituted as persons-in-relationship, and the church as a fellowship of believers is a source of lifelong comfort, strength, accountability, and companionship. We are continually called into fellowship with God in prayer and into fellowship with one another in marriage, in

---

18. See Ulanov, *Functioning Transcendent*, 52–71, for a fascinating case study on this issue.

friendship, in parenting, and especially in the church. What particular gift does psychotherapy bring if the church has known the value of relationship all along?

First, let us consider two closely related ideas: the concept of the therapeutic relationship as a holding environment, and the phenomenon of transference. Child psychotherapist D. W. Winnicott calls the therapeutic relationship a holding environment, comparing it to the primary mother-infant bond. The infant is understood to be threatened by anxiety because she can neither fend for herself in the outer world nor always cope with intense feelings from within. The mother, or mothering person, knows how to help contain this anxiety, first by providing a stable nonanxious presence; second by introducing the world to the child in small, manageable steps; and third by mirroring back the child to herself. The empathetic mother will know how to intervene when anxiety threatens to overwhelm the child.

In an analogous fashion, the empathetic therapist provides a stable environment for a person who is going back and emotionally reliving anxiety-provoking moments from infancy and early childhood. All of the ritual aspects of psychotherapy as a cultural form—a specific time and place, a reliable and empathetic listener, a set fee, a known way of investigating psychic phenomena—are predictable ways of being and interacting that help to provide a secure and safe structure for the relationship, which functions as a kind of container for the person's anxiety.

In the life of faith innumerable issues may raise our anxiety, and there are few places where those issues can be explored safely. In many churches, any exploration of sexuality provokes intense anxiety. Furthermore, a congregant's questions about what he believes deep down about God, or his fears about whether his beliefs are orthodox or about whether he is saved may be sources of nagging, ongoing concern. Sometimes people experience shame or anguish over their sins or wrongdoings and fear judgment by their fellow believers. In all of these instances, a relationship with a pastoral counselor who is pledged not to exploit counselees' vulnerability and who will explore the consequences of their sin without playing God by standing in judgment may be a container strong enough and safe enough to provide the kind of stability that is needed.

The second, closely related, idea is psychotherapy's concept of transference. "Defined most simply, transference is a phenomenon when one person becomes the carrier for an unconscious content activated in another person. That content carries into the present moment conflicting and unassimilated feelings about figures in the past that distort the perception of the present person or situation."[19] Transference is similar to projection except that it is not so much a matter of a single trait being projected as it is matter of a whole complex of issues that belong to a relationship in the past being transferred to a relationship in the present. Transference occurs unconsciously; one consciously thinks that one is accurately perceiving the other in the present.

How might a knowledge of transference phenomena be helpful to those who seek to care for the soul? The skillful pastoral counselor who understands transference phenomena will know how to work with a counselee's intense feelings. First, she will understand that many of the feelings that the counselee has toward her do not belong personally to her but are instead clues to understanding the counselee's past relationships, particularly those of early childhood. For painful, unresolved issues from the past become present in the transference. The present relationship thus provides access to issues that would otherwise remain inaccessible. In a very real sense, the past is never really past, for it lives on within the unconscious mind. Whatever has not been healed pushes for recognition and attention in the present relationship.

One simple example is so common that it is the subject of rueful humor among therapists: the client's reaction to the therapist's annual vacation. From a conscious standpoint, the fears of abandonment that begin to arise in the counselee when the therapist prepares to go on vacation may seem unreasonable and out of proportion, even to the counselee. Intense, irrational, and vivid, these fears in all their fullness are not to be denied. What is going on here? Now that the counselee is in a relationship that provides enough safety, that functions as a protective container for his repressed anxiety, he can afford to experience the terrors that he felt as a child but that he had to repress at the time. The transference relationship therefore offers him an opportunity to regain lost parts of himself. Those feelings of fear and anger long hidden can now surface and be integrated into his adult ego. Once these feelings become fully conscious, they will lose their determining power over his choices. Whenever feelings that were unconscious are made conscious, the ego is strengthened.

When Freud generalized about the nature of transference, he emphasized two issues of overriding importance, namely, unresolved feelings of a sexual or aggressive nature. Conflicts about need and dependency,

---

19. Ulanov, *Functioning Transcendent*, 123.

about sexual desire and longing, and about power and authority were the issues that he found to be most problematic. Untrained counselors who do not understand the nature of these phenomena can easily fall into destructive power struggles, on the one hand, or destructive sexual acting out, on the other. Theology does not have the conceptual resources for working directly with these kinds of unconscious dynamics. Simply labeling aggressive or sexual wishes as sinful and then struggling against them consciously, trying to keep them repressed, actually increases their power because repressed wishes continue to push for expression. By contrast, allowing those wishes into awareness by means of the transference, and suffering them consciously, reduces their power.

Psychology's Third Gift: Attention to Process

The third gift that psychotherapy brings to people who are learning the pastoral art of caring for the soul is its detailed attention to process. There are numerous questions of primary importance in the work of counseling that have to do not essentially with content, but rather with process. How do you develop emotional rapport with another human being? How do you ask questions that deepen emotional contact but are not invasive? How do you accurately read the meaning of a person's body language, eye contact, or tone of voice? How do you confront someone in a way that maximizes your chances of being heard instead of being dismissed defensively? How do you show a counselee that you have heard her accurately, and how do you communicate your respect for her? How do you tune into your own feelings as a way to help you understand the possible feelings of the person you are counseling? How do you address transference and countertransference issues in a way that minimizes possible embarrassment and maximizes potential insight? When is it appropriate to use a story from your own life to show a counselee that you have understood him? How do you develop a sense of timing, learning to make interpretations in the right way and at the right time? In all of these ways and many more, psychotherapy has much to teach people who are engaged in the practice of the pastoral arts.

These kinds of issues are addressed by every pastoral-counselor-in-training, every beginning chaplain, and every student of clinical pastoral education. Some of us take these issues so much for granted that we lose sight of just how much there is to learn, and how much we have already learned from the field of psychotherapy. But curiously we have not yet fully integrated these insights into our pastoral functioning. Pastors and pastoral counselors seem quite able to function in these ways when they are operating out of a psychological frame of reference, but when they move into their strictly pastoral role, they seem less capable of continuing to pay attention to issues of process. One prominent pastoral theologian writes:

> Prayer and theological reflection are crucial resources to be used in some form within the counseling process. However, much of my praying and theological thinking takes place outside the actual counseling hour and counseling relationship. I offer prayers of intercession for my counselees in the privacy of my own devotional life. The counseling relationship also generates many insights of a spiritual and theological nature, but I do not share them with the counselees because I am reluctant to turn the counseling session into a classroom, fearing that prayer and the sharing of theological insights would disrupt the therapeutic process.[20]

Why should prayer necessarily disrupt the therapeutic process? Why should the sharing of theological insight necessarily turn a counseling session into a classroom? Could the counselor not share a theological insight with the same kind of careful attention to timing, body language, and overall process that she would have if she were sharing a psychological insight?

I believe that process skills are best learned through apprenticeship: by undergoing counseling oneself, by observing and imitating one's mentors and teachers, by undergoing supervision of one's counseling work, and by participating in a process group. Pastoral counseling is a process that involves us as whole persons; it is not simply a skill that can be mastered. Counseling is not a matter of an expert telling a beginner "how to do it." Sometimes all the counselor can do is provide general guidelines. When offering a prayer, the pastoral counselor must not only be true to the scriptural witness, but also address the particularities of the situation before her. The prayer must be sensitively attuned to all the issues of context, both the wider context and the more immediate interpersonal context. Similarly, the counselor should introduce interpretations using theological concepts in the same manner in which she would introduce interpretations using strictly psychological concepts. She should give the

---

20. Wimberly, *Prayer in Pastoral Counseling*, 15.

same kind of exquisite attention to the particular situation, need, and language of the counselee. In no sense should the counselor turn the counseling room into a classroom. The counselor should always consider the process dynamics of intervention.

In pastoral counseling, every level of the counselor's person is engaged—his thinking, his feeling, and his willing. Therefore, though I am very much against the conceptual integration of theoretical categories of interpretation, I am very much for personal integration—intellectually, emotionally, and spiritually. The more fluently the counselor speaks the language of faith and understand the concepts of theology from the inside, the better. The more the counselor can integrate skills such as active listening and asking noninvasive questions into his normal way of functioning, the better. The more the counselor becomes a person of prayer and feels at home in taking everything before God, the better. Pastoral counseling is not just a role that one puts on like a lab coat when one goes to work; rather, it needs to be wholly integrated into one's personal way of functioning.

Conclusion

By emphasizing the asymmetrical ordering of theology and psychology, I have sought to illustrate what it might mean to "seek first God's kingdom" (Matt 6:33 NASB) in the context of pastoral counseling as a ministry of the church. But as we seek that kingdom together, let us not neglect the conceptual and practical tools that psychology and psychotherapy have given to the church.

When we considered the disciplines of theology and psychology in relation to each other, we affirmed six basic theses:

1. When theology and psychology are used as interpretive frameworks in the context of pastoral counseling (or spiritual care), each has autonomy in terms of its distinctive methods, aims, norms, and linguistic conventions.

2. When we seek to understand persons in their psychological and spiritual wholeness, it is important not to separate these two conceptual frameworks from each other. Though they are to be clearly distinguished, they are not to be separated from one another.

3. The counselor must conceive of these conceptual frameworks as suitable languages that function on different logical levels; it would be a mistake to try to integrate them with each other at the conceptual level.

4. The counselor must place psychological discourse into the larger theological framework of meaning, rather than the reverse.

5. People who seek to learn the pastoral art of caring for the soul can study psychology and apply some of its concepts and skills to pastoral counseling, in particular psychology's theory of the unconscious, its understanding of the therapeutic relationship as the context of healing, and its attention to questions of process.

6. Although it is a mistake to strive for systematic or conceptual integration of the theological and psychological modes of discourse, it is crucially important to integrate them in practice at the level of personal integration—intellectually, emotionally, and spiritually—so that the skill of using these ways of thinking and speaking becomes a part of the counselor's ordinary way of functioning.

To do the work of pastoral counseling is one way among others that the church has for seeking to love God with all our heart, soul, mind, and strength, and our neighbors as ourselves.

4

Pastoral Theology in a Barthian Key

Pastoral theology is by definition interdisciplinary. At least as it is undertaken in the United States today, it engages in a substantive way with a number of other disciplines, most especially the psychological disciplines. Karl Barth's theology, on the contrary, is often characterized as being completely resistant to interdisciplinary dialogue. Barth's unequivocal rejection of apologetics, his insistence on God's "wholly otherness," his critique of religion's captivity to culture, and his emphatic *"Nein!"* to Emil Brunner's natural theology, have led many to believe that Barth simply was not open to dialogue with thinkers from other disciplines. Yet this conclusion is belied by the actually existing dialogue—substantive engagement with contemporary and historical thinkers—that Barth carried on throughout his life.

This chapter seeks to understand what is at stake when one does pastoral theology with strong dogmatic commitments as developed by Karl Barth in his *Church Dogmatics*. It delineates Barth's normative criteria for an adequate theological anthropology and argues that recent work in pastoral theology (with particular attention to the field of trauma studies) can be understood to fulfill these criteria. By developing a "Chalcedonian imagination," pastoral theologians can mine various secular disciplines and offer them to theological, spiritual, and pastoral workers as "parables of the truth." These living parables seek to offer human wisdom within an overarching context of prayer as an obedient response to God's promise and command.[1]

Although there is scant reference to psychology in Barth's opus, he did engage with numerous other disciplines throughout the course of his

---

1. Lin, "All This is from God," 16, see especially n142.

theological career, open to truth wherever he found it, while objecting to claims that would compromise, dilute, or distort the gospel. Whether it was engaging with socialist politics in his early years as the "red pastor" in Safenwil, Switzerland, articulating his assessment of a variety of philosophies and theologies, entering into dialogue with contemporary science, or opposing Hitler's regime, Barth was assiduous in discerning what was and what was not compatible with his understanding of the gospel of Jesus Christ.

Because the subject matter of theology is the living Lord, Jesus Christ, who is the same yesterday, today, and forever and yet new every morning, theology can never be made into a system. A person is not a system, nor is a relationship. The relationship between God and human beings can be described in a narrative with a history-like character, but it cannot be captured with a set of principles or abstract thought organized into a system. It is important to note that Barth did not consider himself to be a "systematic" theologian, but rather a "dogmatic" one. His task was to elucidate Christian dogma. The opening sentence of the first volume of his magisterial *Church Dogmatics* announces this with clarity: "As a theological discipline, dogmatics is the scientific self-examination of the Christian Church with respect to the content of its distinctive talk about God."[2]

Six Normative Criteria for an Adequate Theological Anthropology

At the very center of this distinctive talk is God's relationship with humanity in and through Jesus Christ. Barth developed six normative criteria as to what constitutes an adequate understanding of this relationship based on God's self-revelation in Jesus Christ as depicted in Holy Scripture.[3]

1. God is *present* to human beings, not as an idea, principle, or symbol, but as a living person, Jesus Christ, who is both fully God and fully human. Jesus is not only present to us but is also the one through whom we are made present to God. In and through Jesus Christ, we belong to God.[4]

---

2. Barth, *Church Dogmatics* 1/1, 3.
3. Hunsinger, G., *Evangelical, Catholic and Reformed*, 246–49.
4. Barth, *Church Dogmatics* 3/2, 68, 73.

2. The *history* of our fellowship with God is a history of deliverance. In Jesus Christ, God comes to us again and again as Savior.

3. Our human life is not an end in itself. In and through Jesus Christ, we live for the *glory* of God.

4. God's *lordship* and sovereign power is revealed in Jesus' death and resurrection. Through God's love and freedom, we are delivered from the bondage to sin and death.

5. Because of Jesus' *freedom* to obey God, human beings are free to respond to God's grace by aligning our lives and our wills to God's own purpose of redemption. Human freedom consists in loving and deciding for God. "Freedom in the substantive sense does not include the possibility of rejecting grace because when grace is rejected, freedom contradicts itself and is lost. It enters into the bondage of sin and death."[5]

6. Just as Jesus' life was one of *service,* so our human lives are lived for the sake of serving God. We serve God when we bear witness to God's presence, history of deliverance, glory, lordship, freedom, and service as it has come to us in Jesus Christ. When our lives are shaped by a corresponding service to God and others, we fulfill our life's vocation.

In setting forth these criteria based on the biblical witness, Barth establishes the unqualified uniqueness of dogmatic thought. Describing the singular history of God with us, as revealed in Jesus Christ and attested in Scripture, is the work of Christian dogmatics. No other discipline engages this *unique and unrepeatable history.* "Jesus Christ as the one Word of God" became Barth's way of giving voice to what lay at the center of his entire opus: Holy Scripture finds it unifying and controlling center in the person of Jesus Christ.

No other discipline that strives to give an account of human life and its purposes is guided by this singular narrative of God with us. Neither philosophy nor psychology, neither sociology nor history, nor indeed any of the sciences or humanities. No discipline or theoretical system has *this particular concrete content* as its subject matter. Barth writes:

> What other word speaks of the covenant between God and the human race? What other of its character as the work of God,

---

5. Hunsinger, G., *Evangelical, Catholic and Reformed*, 248.

and indeed of the effective and omnipotent grace of God on the basis of eternal love and election? What other of the fulfillment of this covenant in the humiliation of God and the exaltation of the human race? What other of a comprehensive justification of the human race by God and sanctification for it? What other of the fact that this reconciliation of God with the human race and the human race with God is no mere idea but a once and for all event? . . . What other is directed so concretely to each and every human being?[6]

A theological anthropology based on the scriptural witness to this particular account of human life has a very different character and mode of investigation from any of the "nontheological anthropologies." According to Barth, these are of two types: what he calls a "speculative theory of man," and the "exact sciences of man."

Speculative Theories versus Exact Sciences

"Speculative theories" of human beings set forth a philosophy or worldview by articulating their "axiomatic principles" apart from the Word of God. When they claim to define human reality apart from its relationship with God, they cannot help but conflict with a theological anthropology based on the Word of God. They attempt too much. They proceed as if they are developing a "system of truth exhaustive of reality as a whole."[7] Barth considered such approaches to knowledge of human beings to be an "enemy" of Christian faith, that must be opposed.[8] He writes,

> We are not able to see the essence and nature of [human beings] apart from the Word of God. We cannot enter that sterile corner, nor can we argue from it. And there can be no question of theological anthropology being constrained or even able to enter the framework of an anthropology that has such a different basis.[9]

Here we can recognize Barth's unequivocal "*Nein!*"

By contrast, the "exact sciences," which are more hypothetical and tentative in their findings, acknowledge the relativity of their conclusions and accept their partial character. They study human life from a

---

6. Barth, *Church Dogmatics* 4/3, 107–8 rev.
7. Barth, *Church Dogmatics* 3/2, 22.
8. Barth, *Church Dogmatics* 3/2, 23.
9. Barth, *Church Dogmatics* 3/2, 23.

particular standpoint as phenomena to be understood according to current research, that might grow as deeper understandings of the phenomena grow. Barth acknowledges the possible contributions the exact sciences can make toward "the wider investigation of the nature of [the human being] and the development of a technique for dealing with these questions."[10] Because of their hypothetical character, they are open to the Christian witness and do not conflict with it.

The problem with speculative theories, according to Barth, lies precisely in their presupposition that it is possible to know human reality apart from the Word of God. Since Barth considered our relationship to God in Jesus Christ to be the very center of human life, he thought it imperative to guard the "frontier" against all such speculative theories. At the same time, however, he was open to the possible contributions of the "phenomena of the human" described by the "exact sciences." The difference between these two sorts of knowledge (their presuppositions and their claims) explains why in one conversation Barth could intone an unambiguous *"Nein!"* whereas in another, he would show remarkable openness.

Barth appreciated Calvin's openness to thinkers outside of Christian faith because he agreed essentially with Calvin's conviction that Jesus Christ is the "only fountain of truth." Calvin wrote:

> Whenever we meet with heathen writers, let us learn from the light of truth which is admirably displayed in their works, that the human mind, fallen as it is, and corrupted from its integrity, is yet invested and adorned by God with excellent talents. If we believe that the Spirit of God is the only fountain of truth, we shall neither reject nor despise the truth itself, wherever it shall appear, unless we wish to insult the Spirit of God.[11]

While Barth preferred to speak of the Word of God, rather than the Spirit of God, as the only source of truth, he, like Calvin, also believed that truth can be found even among those ignorant of the gospel. If Jesus Christ is Lord of all creation, and not just Lord of the church, we can trust that he is at work in myriad ways throughout the world. God's speech and action—indeed God's living presence—is not limited to the church, nor to its worship, but can be discerned in "an infinitely bewildering variety of ways."[12]

---

10. Barth, *Church Dogmatics* 3/2, 25.
11. Calvin, *Institutes of the Christian Religion*, book 2, 15.
12. Barth, *Church Dogmatics* 2/1, 319.

> Words of great seriousness, profound comfort, and supreme wisdom are found not only in the church but also in the world. . . . How can it be otherwise if Jesus Christ is really sovereign over the whole world of creation and history?[13]

Barth went so far as to say, "God may speak to us through Russian Communism, a flute concerto, a blossoming shrub, or a dead dog. We do well to listen to him if he really does."[14]

The question, then, is not whether or where the truth might appear, but rather, how would we recognize the truth when we see it. How do we test the truth of nontheological disciplines that strive to teach us about human beings? This becomes the quintessential question for interdisciplinary dialogue.

There obviously needs to be a certain kind of fit between the nontheological discipline and the gospel as given in Holy Scripture. Not every insight from a hypothetical science could be brought into a fruitful relationship with dogmatic theology that has Jesus Christ as its unifying center. But there are clearly some disciplines that, though they approach their subject matter differently (phenomenologically or empirically rather than proceeding from faith in the scriptural witness) offer deep insight into something essential about human life. Their truth is determined by the "faithfulness, genuineness and reliability of what they impart."[15] When found to be faithful, genuine, and reliable, they would have for Barth the status of "secular parables of the truth" or "parables of the Kingdom."[16]

Secular Parables of the Truth: Four Criteria

Such parables will be recognizable to those with eyes to see and ears to hear. In order to assess their adequacy *as* parables from the standpoint of the gospel, the phenomena would be subject to four criteria:

1. *The phenomena need to be in agreement with the witness of Holy Scripture.* No secular word will be adequate if it contradicts or usurps the "general line" of the biblical message. The Bible needs to be "understood in the light of its center." Therefore, the definitive test is that the secular word "will harmonize at some point with the

---

13. Barth, *Church Dogmatics* 4/3, 97.
14. Barth, *Church Dogmatics* 1/1, 60.
15. Barth, *Church Dogmatics* 4/3, 110.
16. Hunsinger, G., *How to Read Karl Barth*, 234–80.

whole context of the biblical message as centrally determined and characterized by Jesus Christ."[17]

2. *They need to be in agreement with the historic dogmas and confessions of the church.* Barth considered the confessions of the church to be authoritative guideposts—e.g., the Apostles' Creed, the Nicene-Constantinopolitan Creed, and the Chalcedonian Definition—in helping the church to understand and interpret Scripture faithfully,[18] as well as to learn "new things" about God, as new knowledge is tested in relation to the historic confessions and affirmations.[19]

3. *They may be tested by the fruit which is borne.* Barth considered this to be the preeminent practical test. Is this the fruit given by the Holy Spirit? "Now the fruit of the Spirit is love, joy, peace, patience, kindness, goodness, faithfulness, gentleness, and self-control" (Gal 5:22–23 RSV). "In what direction do they [the phenomena being studied] lead human beings?" Barth asks. "What spirits do they seem to evoke? ... Have they led to ... greater freedom or ... greater bondage? Is the phenomenon one which is uplifting to the human spirit or does it cast one down into the mire?"[20]

4. *The phenomena may be significant for the life of the community.* "If it is a true secular parable, it will help the church to reflect on the truth which is attested, bringing it to a place of repentance on those issues where it has strayed from its own path. Yet it will also offer a voice of comfort, a voice which lifts up and edifies the church."[21] Because God's grace is more powerful than human sin, parables of the Kingdom will have this two-sided aspect: a word that acknowledges the reality of human disorder and evil, while remaining open to possibilities for good to arise.

Barth would test the insights and arguments from other disciplines with these criteria, using them to assess whether they are compatible with the gospel. Obviously, nontheological anthropologies base their study of human beings in methods foreign to a theology based on biblical revelation. They base them on empirical observation, statistical data,

---

17. Barth, *Church Dogmatics* 4/3, 125.
18. Barth, *Church Dogmatics* 4/3, 125.
19. Barth, *Church Dogmatics* 4/3, 268.
20. Barth, *Church Dogmatics* 4/3, 268.
21. Barth, *Church Dogmatics* 4/3, 268.

or phenomenological description. Theology alone relies on revelation as its determinative source of knowledge. These two disparate sources of knowledge have different aims, subject matters, methods of investigation, and linguistic conventions. Nevertheless, the secular sciences can genuinely be of service to the theological imagination and to the work of the church.

A Chalcedonian Imagination

Barth's particular way of relating the normative claims of theology and faith to the truths of other disciplines can be more clearly understood if we study the underlying patterns that govern his thought. One such pattern has been identified as a "Chalcedonian" pattern of thought, which governed Barth's thinking whenever he sought to relate contemporary political, social, or cultural issues to theology.[22]

"Chalcedonian" refers, first of all, to the church's understanding of the mystery of the Incarnation of Jesus Christ. How is this person, who is proclaimed as God among us, to be understood? The historic church council held in Chalcedon in AD 451 was called so that the church fathers could find a way to speak clearly and truthfully about an incomprehensible mystery, namely that Jesus Christ is at once both fully God and fully human. They did not seek to define the faith of the church in a comprehensive or exhaustive sense, but rather to demarcate clear boundaries for orthodox teaching. The Chalcedonian Definition of Christ's identity as one person with two natures stated that Jesus Christ is

> perfect in Godhead and also perfect in manhood, truly God, truly [human] . . . one and the same Christ, Son, Lord, only-begotten, recognized in two natures, *inconfusedly, unchangeably, indivisibly, inseparably*; the distinction of natures being by no means taken away by the union, but rather the property of each nature being preserved, and concurring in one Person and one Subsistence, not parted or divided into two persons, but one and the same Son, and only begotten, God the Word, the Lord Jesus Christ.[23]

The Chalcedonian Definition of Christ's person is intended to affirm an inconceivable mystery, namely that this person is both completely

---

22. Hunsinger, G., *How to Read Karl Barth*, 85.
23. Schaff, *Creeds of Christendom*, 63.

God and completely human. The two terms of his identity are not to be confused with or changed into one another, nor are they to be separated or divided from one another. Barth thought that the logic of the relationship between the two natures also demands that conceptual or logical priority be given to Jesus' divine nature. The eternal Son of the Father, who was with the Father from before the foundation of the world, joined with the particular Jewish human being, Jesus of Nazareth, Mary's son, at a particular place and time in history. The two natures, divine and human, are utterly incommensurable, yet inscrutably united in one person.

The formal features of this Chalcedonian Pattern of thought, according to Barth, are thus "indissoluble differentiation" (without confusion or change), "inseparable unity," (without separation or division), and "indestructible order" (with conceptual priority assigned to the divine over the human). The pattern is first seen in the Chalcedonian Definition, but its formal features can be discerned in Barth's thinking about a wide variety of matters. When Barth writes about the relationship between heaven and earth in the totality of creation, for example, or about how to understand the relationship between the doctrines of justification and sanctification, or between the claims of the gospel and those of the law in the Word of God, or between faith and works in our human response to God, or the relationship between church and state, in each case (and others), this overall pattern of thought can be seen to govern the discussion.[24] George Hunsinger aptly states, "It is probably safe to say that no one in the history of theology ever possessed a more deeply imbued Chalcedonian imagination."[25]

The Chalcedonian Definition is substantive, whereas the pattern is merely formal. Because the pattern is formal it can be applied to a variety of different relationships, whereas the definition is specific to Christology. The pattern offers a kind of "grammar" while the definition sets forth the christological prototype of the grammar. The pattern, being merely formal, can be abstracted from the definition and applied to relationships between Barth's dogmatics and other disciplines.[26]

"Indissoluble differentiation" between a theology based on revelation and secular disciplines that contribute to our knowledge of human beings means that each discipline has its own relative autonomy. Each can delimit its own sphere of inquiry to secure its self-defined integrity.

24. Barth, *Church Dogmatics* 3/2, 343.
25. Hunsinger, G., *How to Read Karl Barth*, 85.
26. Hunsinger, "Chalcedonian Pattern," 27–28.

Each discipline proceeds with the investigation of its subject matter according to the methods appropriate to it. Even though there may be overlapping themes (such as various approaches to love, for example, which are rightly examined by a variety of disciplines—by philosophy, theology, psychology, ethics, poetry, sociology, etc.), they each do so within their own unique context of meaning. It would be a mistake to consider their discipline's use of the word to be interchangeable with another discipline's use of it, or to think that they are saying essentially the same thing but with a different vocabulary. No, the particular linguistic and disciplinary context of the word means that it cannot be translated back and forth among disciplines without distorting the uniqueness of its meaning in its own context.

"Inseparable unity" would mean that a theology of revelation cannot be divorced from perspectives that describe human beings phenomenologically. Just as Jesus Christ is both fully God and fully human, so our human lives have at once a hidden spiritual dimension known only to the eyes of faith and an empirical dimension that can be perceived and described phenomenologically. Sin and grace, for example, cannot be seen; they can be perceived only through the lens of faith. Human wickedness can be seen by looking at how abominably human beings have treated one another through the ages, but one needs the scriptural witness to interpret this evil as sin. Sin, like grace, cannot be understood apart from God's revelation. Nevertheless, understandings of human wickedness (e.g., the horror of the Holocaust, the terror and trauma of war, the wickedness of human slavery, the tenacious evils of racism and sexual abuse, the economic violence of capitalism) have helped the church through the ages to work and pray toward ending these evil practices and to offer concrete help and solace to those who suffer oppression and victimization. When our inhumanity against others is acknowledged as sin (because of faith's perception of God's work in the world), the whole conversation is reconfigured to include not only God's judgment and wrath toward such evils but also God's grace, mercy, and forgiveness, which makes possible human repentance and amendment of life.

"Indestructible order" means that concepts from the "exact sciences," while retaining the irreducible distinctiveness and the autonomy of their particular sphere of study, are understood to be placed properly within a larger overarching context of Christian theology that has Jesus Christ as its center. Ordering theology in relation to other disciplines in this fashion follows logically from the first commandment, to put no other gods before God. In this way, the norms and values of other disciplines are placed within an ultimate context of our relationship with God. Thus, Job's affirmation, "Though he slay me, yet will I trust in him" (Job 13:15 KJV) gives witness to this ultimate value. Psychological norms would likely question such an affirmation and characterize it with a completely different set of conceptual understandings. One can imagine that a psychologist might interpret such a statement as a sign of deep depression or even masochism, rather than a statement of ardent faith. Yet, from a theological perspective, Job is affirming faith in the midst of unfathomable suffering at the hands of an incomprehensible God who is to be loved and feared above all else. No other value has priority, not his mental or physical health, nor family, nor honor, nor material goods, nor even life itself, but only faith and trust in God. Although Job calls God his enemy, he never gives up on God. He will not "curse God and die," nor will he relinquish his importunate insistence on hearing directly from God. To acknowledge the profundity of Job's faith is to understand something of what it means to say that the norms and values internal to faith have logical precedence over any possible externally derived norms or values. Other norms and values are inevitably relativized whenever they threaten to displace the centrality of our relationship with God. Faith, or rather God as the object of faith, is to be placed at the very center of human life. All other values and relationships are to be ordered in relation to this central relationship.[27]

Of course, from a psychological point of view, Job might aptly be diagnosed as someone who is profoundly depressed. Such a diagnosis could be true and accurate, but it would function on a different logical level from the theological affirmation based on faith. It would be a mistake to try to integrate them with each other at the conceptual level. Theology and other disciplines are "logically diverse even when they are existentially connected, that is to say, even when they reside in the same breast. In that case, one could not systematically co-ordinate the two."[28] The psychological understanding needs to be placed into the larger theological framework of meaning if we are to understand it rightly.

Barth was clear that the one Word of God "cannot be combined with any other, nor can he be enclosed with other words in a system prior to both him and them."[29] And most significantly for interdisciplinary

27. Hunsinger, "Chalcedonian Pattern," 36.
28. Frei, "Afterword," 103.
29. Barth, *Church Dogmatics* 4/3, 101.

dialogue, there can be no "systematic coordination" with truths governed by other norms. "As the one Word of God he wholly escapes every conceivable synthesis envisaged in them."[30] It is important to state this explicitly because it differentiates Barth's way of engaging other disciplines from "correlational" or "revised correlational methods" that are often assumed in contemporary pastoral theology.[31] It also guards against misunderstanding the Chalcedonian Pattern as just another systematic or comprehensive method, as a cookie-cutter approach to interdisciplinary dialogue. Any such dialogue needs to proceed on an *ad hoc* basis, not a systematic one. In each case, the conversation needs to be shaped by the particulars being investigated, and in no case can one simply appeal to the "Chalcedonian Pattern" as if it provided some kind of magical key to unlock all methodological doors. (In a private letter to a contemporary colleague, New Testament scholar, Markus Barth, in fact speaks of his father's characteristic use of this pattern of thought as a "master key." He writes that "the references to the 'Chalcedonensian' Creed [*sic*], . . . its formulations on the interrelation of Christ's two natures, [are] the only or supreme *passe-partout* for depicting and applying to contemporary issues the Christology of my father."[32]

While Barth acknowledged the pervasiveness of this formal pattern of thought in his work and remarked on its potential fruitfulness, he was aware of the hazards that would accompany any attempt at conceptual integration or systematic coordination between the unique Word of God and other approaches to understanding human life. He writes:

> We are certainly not required either to systematize this formal connection or to discern it everywhere. There are important points of Christian knowledge where we cannot speak of such analogy and where only a combination of lack of taste and direct error would try to discover it. . . . In each case, we must consider whether and how far the points concerned may be brought into mutual relationship, in cross connections. At this point no certain conclusions result from logical possibilities alone. For theological truths and relationships of truth have in their own place and way their own worth and fullness, the light of which can be increased but may also be easily diminished when they are set in relation to others.[33]

30. Barth, *Church Dogmatics* 4/3, 101.
31. Miller-McLemore, "Cognitive Neuroscience."
32. Hunsinger, "Master Key," 22.
33. Barth, *Church Dogmatics* 3/2, 343.

The Chalcedonian Pattern must be adapted to the particular subject matter being studied. In no case should the subject be squeezed into a fixed and predetermined form. No conceptual synthesis or essential equivalence can be developed between Barth's theology and other disciplines because the intertwined factors represent fundamentally different levels of interpretation. There is simply "no totality" by which divine being and creaturely being can be systematically united. Any actual connections that occur are contingent and *ad hoc*, being strictly grounded in God's initiative and divine freedom.[34] Nothing can obscure more completely the sovereign freedom of God to act, nor indeed the free human response to God's grace, than trying to encapsulate them both in some kind of overarching systematic scheme.

Our life narratives, whether focused at the personal, communal, or national levels, need to be placed within the larger narrative that we find in Scripture. It follows that we are not to attempt translating the scriptural idiom into contemporary thought forms (as is common in various contemporary "liberal" theologies), but rather the reverse. We are to place our little life narratives into the larger narrative that has Jesus Christ at its center. According to the logical ordering of the Chalcedonian Pattern, it is important to emphasize that they are asymmetrically, not hierarchically, related. Divine and human being are *incommensurable*; they share no common standard of measure.[35] Therefore, they cannot be ordered hierarchically. Ordering them asymmetrically in this way with logical priority given to theology, does *not* mean that theology somehow has divine standing or that it cannot err. It is obviously a fully human enterprise, and just as subject to sin and error as any other human undertaking. It simply means that nontheological claims about humanity need to be tested by *theological* criteria to assess their truthfulness, reliability, and fruitfulness for human life.

Psychological norms, for example, cannot function as ultimate norms for human life, into which theology must place itself. On the contrary, psychological norms need to be placed into a theological framework of meaning, not the reverse. An example of "reverse asymmetry" would be one in which theological norms are put into an overarching psychological framework. When prayer and confession, Scripture and forgiveness are used as biblical principles and practices to be integrated into a framework of psychological counseling, for instance, they serve

---

34. Hunsinger, *Theology and Pastoral Counseling*, 235–36.
35. Hunsinger, G., *How to Read Karl Barth*, 286–87.

different ends than those they are meant to serve in the life of faith. When placed into such a psychological framework, their intended meaning is subject to distortion. Newton Maloney once asserted, for example, that "the only legitimate function that any methodology, including spiritual practices, can serve in a counseling situation is to alleviate distress and enhance adaptation to the culture in which a person chooses to live."[36] When prayer is thus understood as a resource for healing instead of as a means of intimate communion with the living God, God becomes little more than an instrumental adjunct to achieve our self-determined goals. While prayer may indeed help us to alleviate distress or to adapt to a culture, this way of ordering the norms of the two disciplines puts our emotional or mental health at the center of our lives instead of God. It makes a big difference whether we conceive the task to be one of integrating biblical principles and practices into psychological counseling or to be one of bringing psychological principles and practices to bear upon counseling set within a biblical and theological context. Only the latter way of understanding the relationship between disciplines honors the "indestructible order" of a Chalcedonian Pattern of thought.[37]

A Case Study: Human Trauma

In the final decades of the twentieth century, thinkers from a variety of disciplines began to investigate the profound effects of psychological trauma on human beings. Sadly, the twentieth century offered countless opportunities to do so—with two world wars and the Holocaust bringing unimaginable horror and intergenerational trauma in its wake.[38] The war in Vietnam that raged for more than a decade sowed seeds of awareness that traumatic symptoms were normal responses to violence and terror and had nothing to do with cowardice in the face of death. At the same time as veterans were becoming aware of the necessity to offer one another mutual support by starting "rap" groups where their traumatic symptoms could be openly discussed, women began to speak out about the multiple traumas of rape, sexual abuse, and domestic violence.[39]

36. Maloney "Review," 119.
37. Hunsinger, "Chalcedonian Pattern," 35–36.
38. Weingarten, "Witnessing the Effects," 45–59.
39. Herman, *Trauma and Recovery*, 20–32.

Neuroscientists subsequently deepened our understanding of trauma by studying Adverse Childhood Experiences (ACE), demonstrating how early experiences of neglect and abuse in childhood actually change the neural pathways in the brain such that people become prone not only to trauma but also to other dysfunction and disease for the rest of their lives. Children who had been emotionally, physically, or sexually abused as children have been found to be at much higher risk for adult ill-health as much as a half century later. Those with high ACE scores were more likely not only to have "increased health risks for alcoholism, drug abuse, depression, and suicide attempts, smoking, sexually transmitted disease, physical inactivity and severe obesity" but also for "heart disease, cancer, chronic lung disease, skeletal fractures and liver disease."[40]

This growing body of research, undertaken for more than thirty-five years, has made great strides toward contributing to "the wider investigation of the nature of human beings and the development of a technique for dealing with these questions."[41] Indeed, multiple avenues for healing trauma have been developed, from medication to meditation, from talk therapy to group therapy, from dream analysis to mindfulness, from deep breathing and relaxation to yoga and movement.[42] The analyses of trauma and the methods developed for its amelioration or healing have drawn upon a wide variety of resources. Yet the psychological researchers without exception consider two things to be of fundamental importance for healing and growth to occur: first, the primary importance of interpersonal connection, and second, the necessity of creating a personal narrative that makes some kind of sense of traumatic suffering. If we were to boil down the essential presuppositions at work, we might state them in this way:

- Emotional healing and growth occur in the context of an emotionally significant relationship.
- And they occur in a context of developing a meaningful personal narrative.

---

40. Felitti et al., "Relationship of Childhood Abuse," 246.
41. Barth, *Church Dogmatics* 3/2, 25.
42. Herman, *Trauma and Recovery,* 158–60; Wilmer, "Healing Nightmare," 47–62; Allen, *Coping with Trauma,* 249–78; van der Kolk, *Body Keeps the Score,* 265–78.

Dialogue Between Trauma Studies and Barth's Theological Anthropology

Let us examine these presuppositions in the light of Barth's criteria for fruitful interdisciplinary dialogue.

1. *The phenomena need to be in agreement with the witness of Holy Scripture.* Since Barth sees our relationship with God to be central to human life, the focus on the quality of our relationships does seem to correspond to the "general line" of the biblical message. Since God comes to us as our deliverer and Savior, our interpersonal relationship with God could in fact serve as a constant wellspring of hope in the midst of incessant temptations to despair. Persons afflicted by trauma can place their lives in God's hands, offering prayers for healing, not for themselves alone but for all persons who suffer from terror or victimization. Barth assumes that our relationship with God is clearly the most emotionally significant relationship we have. At the same time, since Jesus Christ is not to be understood apart from his people, his followers also have emotionally significant relationships with one another, who care for each other and hold one another in prayer. Even though "secular" approaches to trauma do not take their bearings from Holy Scripture, their presupposition about relationship being at the center of healing and hope makes it possible in turn to set their findings into a biblical framework. There is thus a kind of fit between the empirical findings of the secular parable and the larger framework of the gospel narrative.

   In order to develop a meaningful personal narrative of the traumatic event, the survivor learns how to speak aloud to another human being what she considers unspeakable. Feelings of outrage, grief, bewilderment, and shame need to be felt and acknowledged. Those who are successful in recovering from trauma through this process are able to "reconstruct a coherent system of meaning and belief that encompasses the story of the trauma."[43] Clearly, both the norms and limits of the therapeutic relationship require that the therapist make no assumptions about the specific meaning the traumatic event has for the person,[44] nor does she attempt any substantive contribution of her own toward the person's unfolding

---

43. Herman, *Trauma and Recovery*, 213.
44. Herman, *Trauma and Recovery*, 179.

narrative. Instead, her role is "not to provide ready-made answers, which would be impossible in any case, but rather to affirm a position of moral solidarity with the survivor."[45] In delimiting her role to one of moral solidarity, Judith Herman conveys respect for the person's faith (or lack of it). She also demonstrates respect for the modest, but indispensable role of her psychological work. She makes no claim to any absolute truth for all times and places, but pays exquisite attention to the particularities of the situation the person finds herself in. Psychological counseling helps the person to create a personal narrative, while spiritual and theological guidance helps the person to place that narrative into the larger narrative of God with us. By giving the person opportunities to lament the evil done to her as well as confess the evil she has done, the gospel offers a path toward new life in the midst of catastrophic loss.[46]

2. *They need to be in agreement with the historic dogmas and confessions of the church.* Dogmatic affirmations about humanity as being made in God's image would mean at a minimum that the dignity of human life would be upheld by the secular investigator. At the same time, some acknowledgment of the human capacity for evil would honestly need to be made. Although secular authorities cannot speak of sin (for the category of sin is by definition unique to biblical revelation), they can—and do—speak honestly of the terrifying reality of humanity's seemingly endless capacity for evil. For example, Judith Herman comments on the enormity of difficulty of creating a narrative that makes sense of the traumatic event: "She [the survivor of trauma] stands mute before the emptiness of evil, feeling the insufficiency of any known system of explanation."[47]

3. *They may be tested by the fruit which is borne.* This criterion, which Barth considers the "pre-eminent practical test," is where the field of trauma studies potentially shines. As persons engage in healing relationships, they are led toward greater freedom as well as toward deepened capacities for love and trust. When put into the larger narrative of their life in Christ, trauma victims may create a new narrative in light of their faith. Jesus' loving compassion toward those who come to him for help may become a dependable source

---

45. Herman, *Trauma and Recovery*, 179.
46. Hunsinger, *Bearing the Unbearable*, 1–21, 83–100.
47. Herman, *Trauma and Recovery*, 178.

of ongoing hope. While there may not be any "system of explanation" that adequately accounts for the evil they have suffered, victims of trauma are nevertheless given comfort by the living presence of God. Their healing becomes a "sign" pointing toward their ultimate "salvation" in Christ.[48]

The Chalcedonian Pattern of thought, discussed above, would stipulate the importance of (a) *keeping clear conceptual distinctions* between trauma and sin, on the one hand, and between healing and salvation, on the other. Trauma may occur because of human sinfulness but these two concepts cannot simply be equated with each other. Trauma comes about not only because of sin, but also because of tragedy or overwhelming suffering or any number of natural evils. The concept of sin functions in a completely different context from that of trauma, and they need to be kept distinct. Only those who have faith in God understand the analogies that might be drawn between trauma and sin. They see trauma as pointing analogically toward the realm of sin and death from which Jesus Christ delivers us. Similarly, psychological healing is not the same thing as forgiveness or salvation. They function on different conceptual levels. (b) It is also important to *recognize the unity* of the psychological concepts with those of theology when the person afflicted with trauma places her personal narrative into the larger narrative of faith. Human beings are at once fully biological, psychological, social, *and spiritual* beings. When we seek to understand ourselves in our wholeness, we cannot separate or divide ourselves into component parts. We are instructed to understand our lives not only as an empirical reality, but at its center as an unfolding dynamic of faith. (c) Finally, we need *to give priority to God's narrative* as given in the scriptural witness over empirical observations that construct our life narratives. The gospel promise of our ultimate deliverance from sin and death is unimaginably greater than anyone's little life story. Personal healing in the context of therapeutic work points *beyond itself* analogically to the salvation won for us in Jesus Christ. Reading Scripture with its realistic depictions of overwhelming horror (war, rape, dismemberment, murder, disease, betrayal, the downfall of whole civilizations) not only displaces our own little lives from the center of our preoccupation, but also puts us in spiritual communion with

---

48. Hunsinger, *Theology and Pastoral Counseling*, 65–74.

those who have suffered throughout the ages. When the gift of faith is given, the scriptural narrative becomes a life-giving wellspring of hope for deliverance.[49]

4. *The phenomena may be significant for the life of the community.* "If it is a true secular parable, it will help the church to reflect on the truth which is attested, bringing it to a place of repentance on those issues where it has strayed from its own path. Yet it will also offer a voice of comfort, a voice which lifts up and edifies the church."[50] Three brief examples may suffice to indicate the significance of trauma studies as a "secular parable" for the life of the church:

- *Sexual abuse by clergy*: When people of faith listen with compassion to those who have suffered sexual abuse by their priests and ministers, they can see the long-lasting—sometimes lifelong—nature of such traumatic suffering. Not only is there a loss of trust in these church leaders, but often a catastrophic loss of faith in God. Trauma studies help the church to imagine the scope of the devastation of people's lives, and call the church to repent, make amends, and offer restitution to the victims and their families. When such repentance is genuine, relationships of trust can, by the grace of God, sometimes be restored, and faith deepened.

- *Violence toward women and children*: The traumatic harm that has been done for years (perhaps for centuries) by the church when those in authority encourage easy forgiveness or the "dutiful submission" of wives toward their abusive husbands is well documented.[51] Such easy forgiveness is nothing but "cheap grace."[52] Similarly, when children are taught to "honor [their] father and mother" when abusive parents are unworthy of being so honored, children become alienated from the church community and rightly consider it an unsafe place.[53] When this trauma is acknowledged and understood, abusers can be

---

49. Hunsinger, *Theology and Pastoral Counseling*, 90–94; Hunsinger, *Bearing the Unbearable*, 13–18.
50. Barth, *Church Dogmatics* 4/3, 128.
51. Fortune, *Keeping the Faith*, 275–88.
52. Bonhoeffer, *Cost of Discipleship*, 43–56.
53. Hunsinger, *Bearing the Unbearable*, 42–69.

held accountable and called to repentance. For the survivors of violence, the gospel can once again be clung to as a source of comfort and hope.

- *War:* The traumatic impact of war cannot be overestimated. The horror of what is witnessed, the moral injury inflicted by being required to act against one's own conscience, the terrifying nightmares, hallucinations, and tenacious sense of overwhelming evil—both the evil one has suffered and the evil one has perpetrated—all these features of war mean that the church needs to wake up to its responsibility to become witnesses and agents for peace. Trauma studies bring to life the stories of veterans who may languish for decades trying to numb their pain with alcohol and drugs, sometimes living an entire life at the edge of rage, desperation, and despair. By bringing empathic understanding to this traumatic suffering, the church can offer genuine comfort and hope to soldiers and their families and rededicate itself to become a church committed to peace.[54]

Trauma studies acknowledge that under certain favorable conditions, recovery from trauma is possible. One author writes: "When I have been traumatized, my only hope for being deeply understood is to form a connection with a brother or sister who knows the same darkness."[55] On the interpersonal plane of psychological or philosophical study, this is as large a claim as one can make. Yet, how much incomparably deeper and wider is the darkness known by God in Jesus Christ, who bears in his body the magnitude of the world's sin in order to bear it away.

When confronted with its complicity in afflicting human beings with trauma, the church will recognize that "godly grief that produces a repentance that leads to salvation" as the narrow gate that leads to new life (2 Cor 7:10 RSV). When the church is brutally honest about the extent of its participation in incalculable webs of sin, it will find God's comfort and mercy as it turns in grief and penitence toward making amends.

---

54. Tietje, "*Contra* Rambo's," 22–38
55. Stolorow, *Trauma and Human Existence*, 49.

Conclusion

While Karl Barth does not have a systematic methodology for determining how to engage in interdisciplinary dialogue with nontheological anthropologies, he does have a characteristic way of going about it. It is of paramount importance to Barth that God's sovereignty, initiative, and freedom as a living, acting God not be compromised or imprisoned by any system of thought, and certainly not by a system that effectively denies the centrality of Jesus Christ. Speculative theories that make (sometimes implicit) theological claims about what it means to be human are rejected while Barth remains open to learning from what he calls the exact sciences.

Those who appreciate Barth's understanding of the incommensurability between a theology based on revelation and a science based on empirical research or phenomenological description will be unlikely to conflate or confuse concepts from one field with those of another. One cannot "translate" a psychological concept into a theological one the way that one can translate English into French or vice versa. It is not a matter of saying the same thing in a different idiom. No, the disciplines do not function at the same logical level. The logic (and the scope) of the claims they make about the nature of human reality is not equivalent from one discipline to the next. Spiritual reality is not only more comprehensive than biological, emotional, interpersonal, social, or cultural realities, it also requires the kind of spiritual perception that comes with the gift of faith. At the same time, this perception cannot be separated from empirical contextual knowledge. It learns from these other disciplines and needs them in order to address human life in its particularities.

Such a "Barthian" approach to pastoral theology will eschew reducing theology and other disciplines to a supposed "lowest common denominator." Instead, where analogical comparisons among the various disciplines might prove fruitful, promising concepts from the sciences can be understood as "parables" of the kingdom of God. If we by faith believe that the Gospel itself is the source of what is ultimately and finally true in the world, that the witness to Jesus Christ as given in Scripture is what orients us toward reality, then we can expect to see parables of this truth in other forms of thought. Thus, psychotherapeutic approaches to healing, while certainly not offering salvation, can be seen as possible eschatological signs when placed into a theological framework of meaning.[56] It is important to notice that in saying this, we are starting within a hermeneutical circle that already has Jesus Christ at its center. We are not beginning with some kind of supposed "neutral ground" of common human experience.

While no conceptual synthesis is possible between an "exact science" based on empirical observation and a theology such as Barth's, a Chalcedonian approach to the dialogue among disciplines offers clear guidelines that allow theology to retain its distinctiveness and its logical priority. Each discipline brought into conversation with theology retains its integrity as a discipline and has the freedom to develop methods appropriate to its own sphere of investigation. Theology can say nothing about the methods they choose as long as they remain hypothetical in character and do not make sweeping claims that conflict with the overall character of what is claimed by the gospel.

A theological anthropology that is faithful to the scriptural witness affirms God's presence as a living being in the person of the resurrected Jesus Christ. At all times, God's lordship and sovereign power, divine freedom, and initiative are acknowledged. This divine freedom becomes the condition for the possibility for human beings to respond to God freely and gladly in obedience.

When Barth's dogmatic theological anthropology provides the overarching framework for our psychological, ethical, and social approaches to human problems and their amelioration, we can see exactly how valuable the "exact sciences" can be. Trauma studies, as one form of pastoral theological inquiry, when placed within a framework of the living gospel with its living, active Lord, offers human beings concrete practices that can help persons move toward renewed interpersonal relationships based on trust. A new narrative can be created that recognizes Jesus Christ at its core as Deliverer and Savior. The person can even flourish through what is known as "posttraumatic growth."[57]

---

56. Martyn, "Child and Adam," 285.
57. Tedeschi, "Violence Transformed."

5

A Theology of Koinonia

Spiritual care cannot be Christian unless conducted in a spirit of reverence. The work of prayer is integral to every step. If we believe that it is finally God who provides what is needed, then prayer is not optional. God bids us to pray in times of trial—"Call upon me in the day of trouble" (Ps 50:15)—and promises his help: "Ask, and it will be given you; seek and you will find; knock and it will be opened to you" (Matt 7:7). Prayer is, as John Calvin recognized, the "chief exercise of faith."[1] Through it, faith is nourished, hope is renewed, and our love for God is strengthened. Spiritual care arises from prayer and leads back to it.

Prayer in the context of spiritual care is prayer on behalf of another. It is our response to another's need offered up to God. When we intercede for another, God draws us into communion with himself, providing the strength to face the situation at hand. We sense our complete dependence upon God, and yet see that God uses the human community to effect his purposes. Through common prayer our spirits are knit together, giving us a foretaste of the communion of saints. By these living spiritual connections courage is renewed, faith is deepened, and Christian fellowship is revitalized. *Koinonia* is the *telos,* as well as the indispensable means, of all true spiritual care.

Frank Lake, founder of the Clinical Theology Movement in Great Britain, states that true dialogue is "initiated by the pastor's willingness to listen" to the parishioner and is "concluded when both of them are listening to Jesus Christ." As the transaction of listening moves from the one plane to another, "we have an epitome of that for which the world exists."[2]

---

1. Calvin, *Institutes of the Christian Religion* III.20.1, 850.
2. Lake, *Clinical Theology*, 15.

Though Lake focuses on the relationship between pastor and parishioner, his claim would apply to anyone who cares for another in Christ's name. When persons gather in this name, listen to each other in the light of faith, and express their needs in prayer, they fulfill God's purpose of *koinonia* or spiritual fellowship. This communion is the "epitome" of which Lake speaks.

The Greek noun *koinonia* (and related words with the same root meaning) occurs 119 times in the Bible.[3] It is variously translated into English as communion, community, or fellowship. But these single nouns do not quite capture its richness or range of meaning. Biblical passages that speak of our participation *in Christ* or of our having a share in Christ point to what is meant by *koinonia*. For example, in the eucharistic passages in 1 Corinthians, Paul speaks of the cup of blessing as a participation (*koinonia*) in the blood of Christ, and the bread which we break as a participation (*koinonia*) in the body of Christ. As we partake of the consecrated elements, we become members of Christ's body. We participate in Christ's life even as we take Christ's body into our own bodies. We are *in Christ* and Christ is *in us*.

Koinonia draws together the vertical dimension (our relationship with God) with the horizontal dimension (our relationship with each other) by means of our common life in Christ. In 1 John 1:3, the author uses the concept of *koinonia* (usually translated as fellowship) to draw these dimensions into relationship with each other:

> The life was made manifest, and we saw it, and testify to it, and proclaim to you the eternal life that was with the Father and was made manifest to us—that which we have seen and heard we proclaim also to you, so that you may have fellowship with us; and our fellowship is with the Father and with his Son Jesus Christ. And we are writing this that our joy may be complete. (1 John 1:3 RSV)

Fellowship in the church *means* fellowship with the Father and the Son. The communion which the church shares is its communion with God in and through Jesus Christ. Our spiritual fellowship with one another connotes our common participation in Christ's suffering and comfort (2 Cor 1:7) as well as our partnership in the Gospel (Phil 1:5).

Further, *koinonia* points to the church's living hope that it will *participate in* or *partake of* the divine nature.

---

3. See Reumann, "Koinonia," 134–36.

His divine power has granted to us all things that pertain to life and godliness, through the knowledge of him who called us to his own glory and excellence, by which he has granted to us his precious and very great promises, that through these you may . . . become *partakers* (*koinonia*) of the divine nature. (2 Peter 1:4 RSV)

Koinonia is the word used in what may be the most familiar of all benedictions: "The grace of the Lord Jesus Christ, and the love of God, and the fellowship (*koinonia*) of the Holy Spirit be with you all" (1 Cor 13:14). The *koinonia* of the Holy Spirit is the perfect fellowship the church enjoys when it is one in the Spirit, living out its unity in Christ. *Koinonia* is thus an eschatological concept, pointing toward a fulfillment not fully realized here on earth, of a true communion of saints that finds its identity and hope in Christ. This spiritual fellowship in Christ is strengthened whenever members of Christ's body gather together for prayer.

Koinonia is the fellowship that makes spiritual care possible. When *koinonia* flourishes, so does spiritual care. In this chapter, I proceed as follows: First I trace the theological ground and reality of *koinonia* in the perfect fellowship of the Holy Trinity itself. The love and freedom between the Father and the Son in the Spirit become a template for understanding our relationships with each other. Jesus Christ is mediator of the fellowship not only between God and ourselves, but also in our relationships with each other. The central role of Christ in mediating *koinonia* is then delineated. Turning more specifically to spiritual care, I argue that *koinonia* is an end in itself, not merely a means to some other end. Prayer in the context of spiritual care draws persons into intimate fellowship with God and one another. It is God's gift to the church. We learn to pray in community, and we depend upon the community to uphold us in prayer. Since spiritual care is the work of the whole community, not simply the ordained staff, the chapter ends by arguing for the priesthood of all believers. All the saints need to be equipped for the work of ministry. All need to participate in ministries of intercessory prayer and spiritual care to build up the body of Christ.

Koinonia Relationships

The Christian understanding of the Trinity arose out of the church's intuition of God's perfect *koinonia*. As depicted in Scripture and affirmed in the creeds, God is not solitary but uniquely relational. The Father loves the Son, and the Son loves the Father through the Holy Spirit to all eternity. The trinitarian fellowship they enjoy is one of mutual indwelling. Even in their irreducible differences, they remain an indivisible unity, one God. Their fellowship does not diminish but rather enhances the personal integrity of each. The Father remains the Father in all eternity, loving the Son through the Holy Spirit. The Son alone becomes incarnate, suffers, dies, and is raised from the dead. He is mediator and advocate between the Father and all humanity. The Holy Spirit is the living presence that flows eternally between the Father and the Son, not only as the bond of love between them, but also as the active agent of their love in the world. As he binds the Father and the Son in eternity, so he also binds us to the Father through the Son here on earth. Each member of the Trinity retains his particular identity, yet they are completely one in purpose, action, and essence. As the trinitarian persons of the Godhead relate to each other in mutual love and freedom, so we are called to become fully human through loving relationships with others and with God.

The mutual indwelling that characterizes the Holy Trinity becomes a template for understanding our relationship to Jesus Christ. Christ so dwells in us that we are made members of his body, the church. We are *in Christ,* and he is *in us* through the Holy Spirit. When we come to God in prayer and join one another in the Spirit through the Son, we do not lose our individual identity but find it. In our relationship with God, we are granted the freedom to be our true selves. God does not overwhelm us with his presence but liberates and sustains our particularity by it. Our uniqueness is discovered in relation to God and others, not apart from them.

Our fellowship with Christ is similar in intimacy to the eternal communion of the Trinity, but different in the following respect. In ourselves and apart from Christ, we remain sinners who are unable to enter God's holy presence. But in and through Christ, we are made righteous before God and given access to the Father as adopted children. Our union with Christ becomes the ground for the grace to address the Creator of all things as *our* Father. As members of Christ's body, we are enabled to approach God with familiarity and trust. Our being *in Christ (koinonia)* allows us to claim God as our Father.

The eternal flow of love and freedom between the Father and the Son, and between Christ and the church, is also meant to characterize our relationships with one another. Human beings were created for community. "The eye cannot say to the hand, 'I have no need of you,' nor again the head to the feet, 'I have no need of you'" (1 Cor 12:21). Paul's understanding of the church as the body of Christ (Rom 12; 1 Cor 12) sees it as a differentiated unity in which each part plays an indispensable role for the good of the whole. In the creation story (Gen 2:18–25), human beings made in God's image as male and female recognize one another as true counterparts who need each other. Although irreducibly different, they are made for fellowship. Their differences are not effaced, nor are the boundaries between them blurred, yet only *together* do they form the *imago Dei*. "So, God created man in his own image, in the image of God he created him; male and female he created them" (Gen 1:27). The humanity made in God's image is thus not the male creature alone as the tradition has sometimes implied, but only male and female together. Though all persons reflect the image of God, they cannot be fully human as isolated beings. The image of God, as Barth suggests, is not an intrinsic quality in humankind, such as our rational or intellectual capacity, but rather our being created in relationship with God and one another.[4] Only as relational beings do we find our true identity as God's image.

Barth speaks of *mitmenschlichkeit* (translated as co-humanity) to convey the interrelatedness (literally "*with*-ness") in which we are not human without the other. We become God's covenant partners together in community. Only the whole church knit together in love can become what it is: the true marriage partner of Christ (Eph 5). Human beings need one another in order to be human. Isolation is a sign of human misery. To deny our need for others is a defense against the pain of isolation. Human flourishing requires human community—people bonded together in mutual giving and receiving.

As Barth describes it, we are not fully human apart from: 1) mutual seeing and being seen; 2) reciprocal speaking and listening; 3) granting one another mutual assistance; and 4) doing these all with gladness. First, as we allow others to see us as we truly are, neither hiding nor withholding ourselves, we affirm our common humanity. Second, as we speak and listen to one another, we seek to know the other in her uniqueness and to be known in ours. "Each fellow-human being is a whole world, and the

---

4. Barth, *Church Dogmatics* 3/2, 324. The main point being made here is an analogy between God's differentiated unity (Father, Son, and Holy Spirit) and humanity's differentiated unity (human beings as male and female). This is not to say that one has to be married in order to reflect God's image, only that to be human means to be in relationship.

request which he makes of me is not merely that I should know this or that about him, but the person himself, and therefore this whole world."[5] The purpose of speech is to reveal our true self to the other and to help the other to see the world through our eyes. It is an act of self-revelation and self-interpretation that seeks to create a bridge of mutual understanding. Third, we grant one another mutual assistance, thus acknowledging my need of the other and the other's need of me. None of us is self-sufficient, for "my humanity depends upon the fact that I am always aware, and my action is determined by the awareness, that I need the assistance of others as a fish needs water."[6] At the same time, I maintain a constant awareness of the other's need of my assistance. I recognize that I am called to assist others in order to retain my own humanity. Finally, we do all this with gladness. We are gladly open with the other, letting ourselves see and be seen. We gladly speak and listen. We gladly receive and offer assistance. Barth calls this gladness "the secret of the whole." Each receives the other as a gift. "Human nature is the human being himself. But a person is what he is freely and from the heart. And freely and from the heart he is what he is in the secret of the encounter with his fellow-human being in which the latter is welcome, and he is with him gladly."[7] As we give and receive one another gladly as incomparable gifts, we find our true humanity.

If the *imago Dei* is our being with and for one another in co-humanity, then the paradigmatic form of prayer in spiritual care will join us together in our common life in Christ. Prayer finds its basic context "wherever two or three are gathered" in the name of Christ. Spiritual care flourishes as the community prays together. Not only do we learn to pray in community, but the community is called to pray with and for each individual member of the body. Prayer as a communal activity builds up the body of Christ even as it cares for each individual member. Moreover, the prayers of each are determined by the prayers of all. They are in principle the prayers of the whole community, even as the prayers of the community are applied in practice by each believer.

---

5. Barth, *Church Dogmatics* 3/2, 258.
6. Barth, *Church Dogmatics* 3/2, 263.
7. Barth, *Church Dogmatics* 3/2, 264.

Jesus Christ as the One Mediator

These relationships of love—between the Father and the Son, between Christ and the church, and among the members of the church, all in and through the Holy Spirit—are discernible in Christ's high priestly prayer. As depicted in the Gospel of John, in taking leave of his disciples, Jesus prays:

> I am praying for them. . . . For they are thine; all mine are thine, and thine are mine and I am glorified in them. . . . I do not pray for these only, but also for those who believe in me through their word, that they may all be one; even as thou, Father, art in me, and I in thee, that they also may be in us, so that the world may believe that thou hast sent me. The glory which thou hast given me I have given to them, that they may be one even as we are one, I in them and thou in me, that they may become perfectly one, so that the world may know that thou hast sent me and hast loved them even as thou hast loved me. (John 17: 9–10, 20–23)

This passage establishes the central place of prayer in our life of faith. Jesus Christ prays to the Father for the church, for its unity throughout the ages. Though he prays first for his disciples, he also prays for every generation that follows, for those who depend upon their apostolic witness. The same Spirit who unites the Father and the Son in mutual indwelling also incorporates the church into the intimacy of the divine life. When the church finds its identity in God, it gives a credible witness to the world. The glory which the Father gives the incarnate Son is shared with the disciples so that they might become one. As the Father dwells in Christ through the Spirit, so Christ dwells in the church. The church receives the glory of God as it participates in Christ's own life and finds its identity in him. As we are "in Christ" we receive and find our unity. Everyone who comes to him dwells in him and is knit together into his body. When the church speaks with one voice about who Christ is, the world receives its witness. The world recognizes God's love when it is awakened to what God has done in Christ for the sake of the world.

Jesus Christ is the key to this whole series of interconnections. As attested by Scripture, he is our only Mediator and Advocate. Through him, the love and knowledge of God are communicated to us. He is the self-revelation *of God* because he is himself fully divine, at one with the Father. He is the actual presence of God's love *to us* because he is fully human as well, sharing our human nature. As he mediates God to us, he also mediates us to God. He not only reveals God's love and makes it present to us, he also mediates our love and gratitude back to God. When we offer prayer to God in Christ's name, we acknowledge this mediation in both directions.

> We can only pray "in the name of Christ" because Christ has already, in our name, offered up our desires to God and continues to offer them. In our name, he lived a life agreeable to the will of God, in our name vicariously confessed our sins and submitted to the verdict of guilty for us, and in our name, gave thanks to God. We pray "in the name of Christ," because of what Christ has done and is doing today in our name, on our behalf.[8]

Our love for one another likewise occurs through the mediation of Christ. Through him we have God and God has us, and through him we have one another. "We have one another only through Christ," writes Bonhoeffer, "but through Christ we really do *have* one another. We have one another completely and for all eternity."[9] Thus Christ is the hidden center of all our relationships. Present through the Spirit in every encounter, he enables our words to bear fruit. The mediations, in which Christ is at the center, thus exist in three modes:

- God's love for human beings descending from heaven to earth, mediated by Christ and communicated in the power of the Holy Spirit. (The vertical relationship downward of God's grace and love for humanity through Christ.)

- Human love for God ascending to heaven, mediated by Christ and communicated in the power of the Holy Spirit. (The vertical relationship upward of the human response of love and gratitude toward God through Christ.)

- Mutual love among human beings as mediated by Christ in the power of the Holy Spirit. (Horizontal relationships of love and freedom between human beings, as mediated by Christ.)

God's love within the Trinity itself—the Father for the Son and the Son for the Father through the Holy Spirit, in God's own eternal and transcendent being—is the eternal ground of Christ's mediation in all its modes.

These spiritual relationships undergird the vocation of the community. All our prayers participate in Christ and in his high priestly prayer to the Father. He is the One who mediates our prayers to God. His high

---

8. Torrance, *Worship, Community and the Triune God*, 35.
9. Bonhoeffer, *Life Together*, 34.

priestly prayer incorporates every prayer we offer in his name. When we pray the Lord's Prayer, he adopts us as brothers and sisters into his relationship as Son to the Father. He makes his Father to be ours as well, so that we can utter the first word of the Lord's Prayer. If he were not the Son of the Father, on the one hand, nor fully human like us, on the other, we could not participate in the mystery of adoption. And if we were not God's adopted children, we could not claim God as the One to whom we belong in life and in death. As Barth writes:

> It is he—Jesus Christ through the Spirit, the Spirit as the Spirit of Jesus Christ—who makes good that which we of ourselves cannot make good, who brings our prayer before God and therefore makes it possible as prayer, and who in so doing makes it necessary for us. For Jesus Christ is in us through his Spirit, so that for his sake, praying after him as the one who leads us in prayer, we for our part may and must pray, calling upon God as our Father.[10]

The mediation of Christ is both vertical and horizontal. It is Christ who makes it possible for us to pray at all, and also to be present to each other in his name. When he stands between us and the persons we seek to serve, the relationship is reconfigured. His presence affects every aspect of the conversation. He is the lens through which we see another, or the light by which we glimpse another's heart. An ancient prayer of St. Patrick's that speaks of Christ's mediating presence in all our interpersonal relationships conveys this idea well.

The Eye of God

The eye of God betwixt me and each eye,
The purpose of God 'twixt me and each purpose,
The hand of God betwixt me and each hand,
The desire of God betwixt me and each desire.

I sing as I arise today
God be in every breath,
As the mist scatters on the crest of the hill,
May each ill haze clear from my soul today.

The dearness of Christ 'twixt me and each dearness,
The wish of Christ 'twixt me and each wish,

---

10. Barth, *Church Dogmatics* 3/4, 94.

> The pain of Christ 'twixt me and each pain,
> The kindness of Christ 'twixt me and each kindness.
>
> I sing as I arise today
> God be in every breath.
> As I clothe my body with wool
> Cover my soul with thy love, O God.
>
> The eye of God 'twixt me and each eye,
> The purpose of God 'twixt be and each purpose
> The hand of God 'twixt me and each hand,
> The desire of God 'twixt me and each desire.[11]

When God's eye comes between my eye and that of another, then our mutual seeing is sanctified. When God's hand mediates our common action, then our shared work is made holy. The sanctifying presence of Christ purges our natural human desires of anything base or unworthy. Yet it must also be said that even our most noble aims need to be judged and transformed by the purposes of God. Christ's mediation reconfigures even our loftiest aspirations.

This transfiguration of desire is illustrated in John Baillie's *A Diary of Private Prayer*. Though the language is archaic, Baillie portrays the shift from high moral striving to those aims as reconfigured by Christ:

> O omnipresent One, beneath whose all-seeing eye our mortal lives are passed, grant that in all my deeds and purposes today I may behave with true courtesy and honor. Let me be just and true in all my dealings. Let no mean or low thought have a moment's place in my mind. Let my motives be transparent to all. Let my word be my bond. Let me take no unchivalrous advantage of anybody . . . Yet, O Lord God, let me not rest content with such an ideal of manhood as men have known apart from Christ. Rather let such a mind be in me as was in Him. Let me not rest till I come to the stature of His own fullness . . . Let me love as He loved. Let my obedience be unto death. In leaning upon His Cross, let me not refuse my own; yet in bearing mine, let me bear it by the strength of His.[12]

The prayer calls upon God to grant a mode of conduct that has true human dignity, as it recognizes the value and dignity of others. It desires all that is gracious and honorable by the culture's highest standard. Yet, the

---

11. Eddy and Eddy, *Cry of the Wild Goose*, 36–39, altered.
12. Baillie, *Diary of Private Prayer*, 49.

second half of the prayer deepens the request of the first. While the first part of the prayer holds up an ideal of true humanity, it becomes clear that even such noble ideals are utterly transcended by Christ. Christ's mind and stature, his love and obedience far surpass even our noblest aspirations. Even our highest values are judged and transfigured by the cross. The prayer thus stretches the imagination beyond human knowing, trusting that God's grace will be sufficient during trial or testing. It asks for something that outstrips human capability, believing that Christ will grant strength where human strength fails. It is a prayer that trusts finally in Christ's mediation.

Prayer also changes our relationship to *ourselves*. St. Patrick's prayer invokes Christ's intercession in human pain. Whenever Christ stands between us and our own suffering, then all that would otherwise be meaningless or unbearable can be borne in and through him. When our suffering is offered to Christ, it is wholly encompassed in his. It is taken up into his cross, which by the power of God's mercy redeems us. His presence gives suffering a dimension of depth that can enable us to endure.

> No one suffers the mental pain of persecutory emptiness without [Christ's] participation. Since this is true, and God has, in Christ, reconciled the world of the persecuted to Himself through His Cross, it is of the utmost importance that we should learn how to make this fact meaningful to those who suffer like Him.[13]

The cross of Jesus Christ borne for our sakes imparts the gift of perseverance. Our communion with Christ thus reconfigures not only our desires and our actions, but also our suffering. It entrusts all our relationships—with God, with one another and with ourselves—to Christ, having faith in his intercession. With each new petition, St. Patrick's prayer offers a glimpse into the unexpected richness of his presence.

Koinonia as an End in Itself

Koinonia itself is the central purpose of our life together. The loving communion of persons, both human and divine, is its *telos*. Being fully present to others, listening with care, and praying for their needs are ends in themselves. They are not a means to some other end. Because psychotherapy has come to dominate the practice of pastoral care, many pastors assume that providing pastoral care means becoming a positive "agent for change."

13. Lake, *Clinical Theology*, 194.

Pastoral care becomes a strategy, sometimes even a "treatment plan." Programs in pastoral care equip students with practical tools to help people in their marriages, their parenting, and other relationships. Interpersonal communication and developmental psychology are studied, and psychosocial systems are analyzed. Concrete skills and conceptual maps are developed. Action plans are created, delineating steps to be taken in various pastoral encounters: how to set up short-term counseling contracts, how to make a psychodynamic assessment, how to analyze pertinent social and cultural factors, how to refer people to other professionals.

When *koinonia* is seen as the purpose of pastoral care, this whole orientation is transformed. While it is not discarded, it is necessarily reconfigured. Practical strategies for change are subordinated to more basic *spiritual* aims. Consider a young minister in her first pastorate. After she had preached a sermon on the presence of God in the midst of trial, a man thirty years her senior approached her with a problem in his marriage. It was a complex situation, and clearly one that she, as a woman in her twenties, had never before encountered. As she cast about wondering how to help him, she panicked, telling herself that she had nothing to offer. Anxiety overtook her as she assumed that it was her job to bring about effective change in his life. Not only did she underestimate the power of her care as it pointed toward God's own compassion, she also forgot that God was already at work in the midst of the crisis. The man's "problem" was not hers to solve. His whole life story was known to God and God was at work in him, "both to will and to work for his good pleasure" (Phil 2:13). As Bonhoeffer has written:

> Because Christ stands between me and another, I must not long for unmediated community with that person.... Because Christ has long since acted decisively for other Christians, before I could begin to act, I must allow them their freedom to be Christ's. They should encounter me only as the persons that they already are for Christ. This is the meaning of the claim that we can encounter others only through the mediation of Christ.[14]

The young pastor had taken too much responsibility for her parishioner, forgetting God's work both through her and apart from her.

John Patton makes a similar point when he defines "the presenting problem" as the *context* rather than the *focus* of pastoral care. He writes,

---

14. Bonhoeffer, *Life Together*, 44.

> If the people of God are called to care for one another through their hearing and remembering... then the central act of pastoral caring is not problem solving. *It is the hearing and remembering in relationship, and the human problems are the contextual background for the more important task of care.*[15]

Koinonia does not negate the value of other frameworks that reflect on the human condition. It includes them for such knowledge is often useful in the fulfilling of God's purposes. The point here is that though pastoral care is informed by other disciplines, it uses their insights in the service of spiritual aims. The minister took her presence and caring for granted, without perceiving their centrality to the pastoral care task. By seeing "the problem" as the *context* rather than the *focus* of her time with her parishioner, the pastor would be able to see her task differently. She would see his psychological issues *in theological perspective*. Matters of compassionate understanding and spiritual discernment would be more prominent than psychological diagnosis or cure. How might she best hear the substance of his needs at that time? Had his faith been strengthened or undermined by the trials he faced? What had enabled him to reach out to her for help? What did he need and how did he understand where God was leading him? Their conversation would be shaped more by the common faith they shared, as informed by God's word, than by any assumed cultural, psychological, or sociological commonality.

We Learn to Pray in the Church Community

All Christian prayer is first the prayer of Jesus Christ, then the prayer of the community, and last of all our own individual prayer. As we have seen, even our most personal prayers belong to the community before we give them voice. We never pray as isolated individuals, but always as members of the body of Christ. Christ sanctifies our prayers by incorporating them into his own. He accepts, elevates, and corrects them. Through the Spirit, he discerns the core longings of our hearts and mediates them to the Father. In a similar way, our individual prayers are shaped and sanctified as they are incorporated into the historic prayers of the church.

In our common life of worship, we gather together with a church that prays without ceasing. As we "join our voices with angels and archangels and with all the company of heaven" in the great prayer of

---

15. Patton, *Pastoral Care in Context*, 40; emphasis added.

thanksgiving, we are connected to the saints throughout the ages. Our theological imaginations are shaped by theirs. The great hymns, liturgies, and prayers of the church deepen our understanding of the God to whom we pray. Prayer is thus never an individualistic act, even though it is undertaken by individuals. Karl Barth writes:

> But as he prays in community, he does so in anticipation with and for all other human beings. He does as an individual what they all can and should do. Hence, he does not merely represent himself, or the community in the world, but humankind and the world as a whole before God. His asking as an individual thus acquires a genuinely universal character.[16]

In prayer, we cannot separate ourselves from the members to whom we are joined. The "we" who pray to "our" Father pray for and on behalf of the whole world, which also belongs to Jesus Christ, even when the world does not know it.

Pastoral Care as the Work of the Whole Community

Like prayer, pastoral care is the work of the entire community. It is not something that only pastors do. All Christians are called to care for one another, just as they intercede for others, both inside and outside the church. This vocation is conferred not by ordination but by baptism. In baptism, every Christian is called to live out the priesthood that belongs to the whole church.

The "priesthood of all believers," so important to the Reformation, has been lost in large segments of the contemporary church. The clericalism of the Middle Ages that Luther deplored has been replaced by "professionalism." Only "professional" Christians, those set apart by education, training, and ordination, are now the "real" Christians. Ordinary believers lack the mystique of such a caste. Only professionals can interpret the Bible or pray in a given situation. The dignity of the faithful is thus lost.

If we were to retrieve the dignity of every Christian's calling, what would that entail? In his book, *The Church*, Hans Küng comments that this doctrine only makes sense "if every member of the community really does exercise priestly rights and functions."[17] In pastoral care, every

---

16. Barth, *Church Dogmatics* 3/4, 103.
17. Küng, *Church*, 372.

"priestly" function has significant concrete content. Küng lists these functions as:

- Direct access to God
- Spiritual sacrifices
- The preaching of the Word
- Baptism, the Lord's Supper, and the forgiveness of sins
- Mediating functions

Because they are all rich with implications for pastoral care, it is important to consider each in turn.

First, all Christians have direct access to God. Jesus Christ as the one mediator gives access to all who call upon him in faith. In the Old Testament, a special cadre of priests alone could enter the holy of holies. The coming of Christ brought such priestly mediation to an end because his unique sacrifice was a perfect offering that needed no repetition or renewal. It sufficed to make human fellowship with God possible, reconciling us to God in spite of our sin and uncleanness. The Letter to the Hebrews contrasts the sacrifices of the high priests of Judaism with the Christ's perfect and unrepeatable sacrifice.

> And by that will we have been sanctified through the offering of the body of Jesus Christ once for all. And every high priest stands daily at his service, offering repeatedly the same sacrifices, which can never take away sins. But when Christ had offered for all time a single sacrifice for sins, he sat down at the right hand of God ... or by a single offering he has perfected for all time those who are sanctified. (Hebrews 10:10–14)

Unlike the priests of the Old Testament, Jesus Christ offers himself once for all. His perfect sacrifice accomplishes what nothing else could ever accomplish: the forgiveness of sins. In faith, through baptism and by the power of the Holy Spirit, all who participate in Christ's self-offering are given access to the Father. There is no longer a barrier that separates us from God, but rather a fellowship that joins us with God through Christ. Küng writes:

> Every believer, as a member of the community ... has an ultimately direct relationship with God, which no human being ... can take away from him.... It is in this most intimate personal sphere that ultimate decisions between an individual and God

> are taken, as also between an individual and his fellow human beings. This is where God's grace makes direct contact with us, God's Spirit guides us. This is where we find our ultimate freedom and our ultimate responsibility. No one can judge, control or command the decisions which are made in this sphere of direct contact between God and God's people.[18]

The inviolable sphere in which each person stands before God with her own responsibility needs to be respected. Each person is accountable for her own choices; here no one can take responsibility for another, neither spouse, nor parents, nor pastor. Each person finally answers directly to God for the choices she has made. Each is called into the obedience of a specific calling and is answerable to God in a unique relationship of love and trust. As we recognize each person's unique relationship to God, we are able to focus more on our own responsibility and less on that of others. An attitude that respects this sacred sphere respects God's mysterious work in every individual life. Christian counselors and spiritual caregivers will acknowledge that primary relationship with God in all that they do and say.

Second, all Christians are called to make spiritual sacrifices as "priests" of God. Because Christ's sacrifice is sufficient, we are not required to atone for our sins, nor could we possibly do so. As people who discover our forgiveness in Christ, the sacrifices we offer are those of praise and thanksgiving. When we offer ourselves as a living sacrifice to God, we do so with praise to God for the gift of salvation received in faith. As Paul writes in his Letter to the Romans, "I appeal to you therefore, brethren, by the mercies of God, to present your bodies as a living sacrifice, holy and acceptable to God, which is your spiritual worship" (Rom 12:1). Our prayers and praise to God, as well as our service of love toward others, are our spiritual sacrifices to God through Jesus Christ.

Some of the most consequential choices of our lives are efforts to balance out the moral ledgers of the past as we seek to atone for our own sins or perhaps those of our forebears. However, these misguided efforts cannot succeed. We act as if Christ had not come when we try, of ourselves, to redeem the past. Children who attempt to atone for the choices of their parents, for example, can become entangled in a history for which they are not responsible. Bert Hellinger provides an example of such spiritual entanglement.

---

18. Küng, *Church*, 373.

> A doctor once told a group that his father had been a doctor for the SS and had supervised many human experiments in the concentration camps.... The son's question was, "What shall I do about my father?" I said to him, "In the moment your father impregnated your mother, he wasn't acting as an SS officer. The two things are different, and you can and must keep them separate." Like this doctor, it's possible for a child to acknowledge his or her father *as a father* without assuming responsibility for the father's actions. Children in such situations must not minimize or excuse their father's actions, but they can say, "What you did is your responsibility. Still you are my father. Whatever you have done, we're related. I'm glad that you gave me life. Even when what you did was horrible, I'm your son, not your judge."[19]

It requires discernment to know one's true responsibility and to allow others their own. In addition, it requires courage to take responsibility for one's own misdeeds, and faith to accept the atonement of the Gospel. The work of atonement—the overcoming and undoing of our guilty past—belongs to Christ alone. Christ won an actual atonement that our futile efforts attempt, but by definition cannot achieve, since none of us is Savior or Judge. Yet each of us can offer praise and thanksgiving for the reconciliation accomplished in him. Thanks and praise are integral to the work of prayer, particularly in situations of remorse and repentance (see chapter 9).

Third, all Christians are called to bear witness to the Word of God. "You are a royal priesthood ... that you may declare the wonderful deeds of him who called you out of darkness into his marvelous light" (1 Peter 2:9). "Preaching the message of salvation" is the "primary command which Jesus gives to his disciples," which is why there are so many different terms (about thirty) to describe this activity.[20] The Word is entrusted to all believers, not simply to an educated elite. The whole community, and each person within it, serves the world by bearing witness to Christ and to the salvation of the world effected through him. This means that each person is called to give his or her unique witness. While in some quarters of the church, there is a regular forum for such witness, other churches lack an institutional means for personal testimony. In some churches, there is a reluctance to give one's own witness. Could it be that

---

19. Hellinger, *Love's Hidden Symmetry*, 99.
20. Küng, *Church*, 375.

the ability to interpret one's life through the lens of faith is disappearing from sectors of the church?

A major factor in the explosive impact of the Reformation was the translation of the Bible into the language of the people. This gave previously unheard-of access to the Gospel. Eventually, millions of Christians were able to read Scripture themselves. But with the advent of the historical-critical study of the Bible, many came to believe that interpreting their lives in light of the biblical witness was a specialized skill that only experts could tackle. As something essentially beyond their ken, the Bible was no longer perceived as a book through which God's Spirit spoke to ordinary people. Habits of reading and study developed over generations began to decline and biblical illiteracy became widespread in a relatively short span of time. As a result, many persons ceased to do the ongoing work of interpretation essential to the life of faith. Scripture became little more than a collection of odd historical data, rather than a sacred text giving shape to history, personal identity, and destiny. As George Lindbeck writes, "The use of Scripture is not part of people's lives, and thus reading and hearing it (when they do read and hear it) has little impact."[21]

In the priesthood of all believers, every person is to offer her own witness to the grace of God. While not all are called to preach on Sunday morning, all *are* called to give their personal testimony. No one can speak for another in such an act. The varied richness of the entire community's witness is edifying to the church and has power to speak to the world. "When you come together, each one has a hymn, a lesson, a revelation, a tongue, an interpretation. Let all things be done for edification" (1 Cor 14:26). Every member of the community is called "to give an account of the hope" that is in her (1 Peter 3:15), to preach, persuade, or testify according to the faith she holds.

Fourth, the community is called to baptize, to forgive sin, and to celebrate the Lord's Supper. When Jesus' disciples are instructed "to make disciples of all nations, baptizing them in the name of the Father and of the Son and of the Holy Spirit" (Matt 28:19), they are doing so as representatives of the whole church and not as a specialized class.[22] Similarly, Jesus' words about loosing and binding sin (Matt 18:18) are addressed to the church as a whole, not to a clerical elite. Jesus' command to the disciples to drink the cup and break the bread in remembrance of him is also

---

21. Lindbeck, "Scripture, Consensus and Community," 75.
22. See Küng, *Church*, 379–80.

to be enacted by the whole church for the sake of all. While certain individuals are set apart by ordination to perform these functions, they do so on behalf of the community and not as private individuals. Pastoral care not only enacts the sacramental significance of baptism as it reaches out to people in need, but it also extends the forgiveness of God in the Lord's Supper. Moreover, the work of compassionate care is itself sacramental. By virtue of their baptism, caregivers take on a representative role, interceding for others and offering Christ's forgiveness in return. Eucharistic celebrations at the end of life, as family and friends gather round hospital beds, are especially rich in meaning, giving spiritual depth to mutual forgiveness. Though churches set apart ordained ministers to consecrate the elements, all Christians are called to partake.

Fifth, all Christians are called to pray for others, thus mediating in a secondary way between God and the world. While there is only one Mediator, Jesus Christ, every Christian is called to mediate between God and the world insofar as he or she intercedes on behalf of others.

> All Christians have their own circle of those who have requested them to intercede on their behalf, or people for whom for various reasons they know they have been called upon to pray. First of all, this circle will include those with whom they must live every day.... A Christian community either lives by the intercessory prayers of its members for one another, or the community will be destroyed.[23]

In prayer, we know the dignity of a calling to stand with those who suffer, to bear their burdens with them, to support them in times of trial, and to comfort them with the comfort of God, with which we ourselves have been comforted (2 Cor 1:4). As those redeemed by Christ, we are to live not for ourselves but for the sake of all for whom Christ died.

God wills to include every person in the working out of his purposes. Our sense of identity as well as our deepest joy arise from an understanding of this vocation. Barth writes: "God tells each one of us that he needs us in a definite and concrete respect, that he has a use for us. Not one of us is to pass our short span of life in vain."[24] To be given an essential part in God's purposes is the source of our human dignity, honor, and worth. Since it is an honor that God confers upon us, we cannot disown it, whatever our personal struggles. By calling human beings as

---

23. Bonhoeffer, *Life Together*, 90.
24. Barth, *Church Dogmatics* 3/4, 657.

his witnesses and to do works of service in the world, God confers upon us the greatest possible significance.

> We each have our honor before God and from God. No circumstances and no human being can increase or diminish it, can give it to us or take it from us. Even we ourselves cannot do this. God alone is competent to decide our dignity and worth.[25]

Equipping the Saints for Ministry

How are we to be equipped for this vocation? Where do we find the confidence to carry out these ministries? If our common priesthood has been neglected by the church, how can we reclaim it? The task is daunting only if we forget that God has already given us the gifts we need. Just as the saints of the church refer to all those sanctified by Christ, so the gifts of the Holy Spirit are lavished upon the whole church and not upon a single elite. They are neither "exceptional, miraculous [n]or sensational."[26] Nor are they intrinsically connected with ordination. Though such misconceptions are widespread, the gifts of God are completely ordinary. Seldom are they characterized by extraordinary signs and wonders. St. Paul labors to refute the view that the unusual gift of ecstatic speech is the only gift to be esteemed. On the contrary, he insists that interpretation is even more desirable than tongues, for whatever is edifying to the congregation is of the greatest value. Küng states:

> [Paul] emphatically reduces in importance this sensational gift, by insisting that it is nothing compared with the charism of interpretation; it is not of itself edifying for the community, nor does it clarify the understanding of the [one] who prays.[27]

The criterion by which we are to judge the value of any gift is its power to build up the community. Yet such gifts are everyday phenomena in the life of the church, both in the early church and today. Küng lists several examples with their scriptural reference: exhortation, acts of mercy, service, teaching, utterances of wisdom and knowledge, faith, discernment, helping, administration, and the most common gift of all, love, which is above all the others.

---

25. Barth, *Church Dogmatics* 3/4, 678.
26. Küng, *Church*, 181.
27. Küng, *Church*, 181.

Such gifts obviously are not given only to ordained leaders. On the contrary, they are bestowed on all members of the church to meet the needs not only of the community but also the world around it. Thus, any natural talent may be a potential charism. When brought into the service of Christ, our gifts are transformed by the Holy Spirit to be used for the good of all. In a point that is especially pertinent to those who serve the afflicted and traumatized, Küng notes that even our suffering might be a charism to strengthen the faith of others, citing Paul's words in Colossians 1:24: "Now I rejoice in my sufferings for your sake, and in my flesh, I complete what is lacking in Christ's afflictions for the sake of his body, that is, the church." If even our capacity for suffering could be edifying for the church, then whatever befalls us can be used by God. Our afflictions, borne in patience and hope and given over into Christ's keeping, would thereby serve a worthy end. Such an insight points toward the essentially mutual nature of all Christian ministry. For even those who are homebound, even the utterly incapacitated, would have a gift to offer the community. Suffering borne in faith can function as a powerful witness to the sufficiency of God's grace and build up the body of Christ.

All Christians, therefore, not just those with spectacular gifts, enable the church to fulfill its call. Ordinary but indispensable gifts are spread throughout the community and are not by any means limited to those in ordained leadership. Nor are they limited to just a small group. St. Paul asks, "Are all apostles? Are all prophets? Are all teachers? Do all work miracles? Do all possess gifts of healing?" (1 Cor 12:29–30). The varied gifts of God spread among the people cannot function in isolation from each other. On the contrary, each of us needs the others in order to function properly as a whole. Here again, *koinonia*, our mutual partnership in Christ, is the mysterious gift of the Spirit that enables the church to carry out its work. As St. Paul develops the idea of the church as the body of Christ, he shows the indispensability of each part for the sake of the whole.

> For the body does not consist of one member but of many. . . .
> If the ear should say, "Because I am not an eye, I do not belong to the body," that would not make it any less a part of the body. If the whole body were an eye, where would be the hearing? If the whole body were an ear, where would be the sense of smell? (1 Cor 12:14, 21)

Each member of the body has at least a small but essential part to play for the good of the whole. None can say that she does not belong simply because she is unable to do something that another member can do with ease. None of us is to judge or to undervalue the particular gift that we have been given. Rather, we are to develop and use it to the greatest extent possible. Those who are tempted in this way would do well to meditate on the parable of the talents (Luke 19). For we will not be judged by the standard set for our neighbor, who may have been given many talents and used them well, but rather for what we have done with the single talent given us.

Given the wealth of the community's gifts, how are they to be developed? James C. Fenhagen has argued that "it is more important for the ordained ministers in a congregation to enable others to identify and carry out their ministries than to do it themselves."[28] While clergy need to know how to offer prayer for their congregations, it is also crucial for them to nurture gifts of prayer in their people. As they develop their capacity for discerning their congregation's gifts, they also need to offer encouragement so that those gifts can be claimed and cultivated. Equipping the saints for ministry entails a scope of preaching and teaching that cannot be overemphasized. The whole congregation needs to be called forth week after week with continual opportunities for service, witness, and prayer.

All persons need help in discovering their gifts. All need help in developing them for the mission of the church. The church loses something of its distinctive identity when it sees its task merely to be one of finding the right "volunteers" for various committees. Instead, constant discernment is required to identify and call forth the entire range of gifts that lie nascent within the community. Even this is not the exclusive work of the clergy, but rather that of the whole body. While the ordained pastor might model such a process, all members need to observe and encourage the gifts of others. This is part of what it means to live in the mutual relationships that characterize our partnership (*koinonia*) in Christ.

The ordained pastor's role is to hold up a vision that not only values the gifts of all but requires the congregation's participation in discerning and eliciting those gifts. Such a task is clearly the work of many individuals over time. The Holy Spirit uses the wisdom of others to call specific individuals in particular ways. A person discovers the uniqueness of her

---

28. Fenhagen, *Mutual Ministry*, 105.

A THEOLOGY OF KOINONIA

vocation by hearing what others see in her, especially when that seeing has been subjected to prayer. One man confided his "rule of thumb" in spiritual discernment: if three persons unknown to each other called his attention to something in particular, he seriously pondered it as a matter of utmost importance. He subjected the matter to prayer, believing in the power of the Holy Spirit to communicate through these ordinary means (see chapter 10 in this volume).

In a time of personal crisis, the care of the community makes the grace of God palpable. Few would single out the ordained minister, no matter how essential her role, as the only one through whom God's grace operates. Rather, it is the ongoing care of the whole people of God that makes one feel loved by God. The cards, letters, casseroles, flowers, phone calls, and offers of help that pour in from the community during a time of illness or loss speak far more eloquently of God's compassion than any single official pastoral visit could. Don Browning states the obvious but frequently overlooked point, "The minister's pastoral care is only a small part of the total care of a congregation."[29] After studying a number of congregations in terms of their actual patterns of care, Browning and his colleagues came to the conclusion that the corporate acts of caring done by the congregation as a whole, as well as various important subgroups in it, were far more meaningful to its members than anything that the ordained pastor did alone. Browning goes on to say that this finding does not devalue the importance of an official pastoral visit, especially during a life crisis or major life transition, but rather places such visits in perspective. Ordained ministers, he argues, should consider their task to be more nearly one of facilitating "natural patterns of care" that already exist than of seeing themselves as providing all the pastoral care needed. Especially since loneliness was the greatest single problem cited, whatever skills pastors might have in making bridges between people would be much more valuable than trying to be "all things to all people" themselves.

If the work of prayer is truly to be the work of the whole congregation, then equipping the saints for ministry happens as every member takes responsibility to call forth others as members of Christ's body. Churches need to understand that mutual caring is not the "job" of the pastor, but rather of the entire community. As Browning suggests, failing to understand our vocation as "agents," and not just "recipients" of care, we are in danger of perceiving the pastor as a hired "professional"

---

29. Browning, "Pastoral Care," 117.

Christian, doing the work of the community rather than facilitating and enabling the work that all are called to do.

Churches who do such equipping provide guidance in listening to others with compassion, in interpreting Scripture as the Word of God, in praying with those in need, in hearing another's confession and offering Christ's forgiveness, in blessing God in every circumstance of life. These are not esoteric matters about which only the professionally initiated need to know. Rather, they are common everyday matters in what it means simply to be a Christian.

Conclusion

Whether one's church is in a more rooted, rural culture or in a more mobile, urban culture, few churches are immune to the societal patterns that make loneliness such a primary source of suffering in the United States today. With institutions and cultural patterns that schedule every hour into some kind of programmed activity, allowing scant time for ordinary interaction, people find themselves cut off from each other. The impact of replacing communal forms of recreation and entertainment with television and electronic media should not be underestimated.[30] With so many persons, both in and outside the church, feeling emotionally and spiritually isolated, the rich vision of God's fellowship where all can share their heart's longing, and where each has a needed gift to offer, can be both healing and renewing. It is precisely into a world such as this that relationships of trust, mutual sharing, and prayer are most needed.

The New Testament assumed churches that were small, interdependent units, where each person was needed for the community to thrive or sometimes even survive. Though the intense economic interdependence of the New Testament church (cf. Acts), is rarely feasible today outside

---

30. Rodenburg, *Need for Words*, 38. Rodenburg describes the losses incurred with the advent of television: "I remember witnessing the introduction of TV into a small village in Portugal in the late 1970s. The first set appeared in a workers' café, a local gathering place where gossip was exchanged and stories told. It was an exciting place to visit because it was so alive with talk, especially in the summer when words would drift far into the night. It was also a place where every level of society and age mixed. Children would listen to elders and become part of an ongoing story which was that village and those people. Then the television set arrived. Gradually the place fell silent. Watching replaced talking. Then mainly watching. Rather than remaining a tightly knit group of speakers, speaking for themselves, the people in the village surrendered to the patterned speakers beamed in from Lisbon."

of particular sect groups, with clear intentionality and accountability, church communities can, by God's grace, achieve a proximate form of interdependence that will enable genuine spiritual growth in the Christian life. Indeed, it is difficult to imagine how even basic spiritual sustenance can take place apart from intentional small groups designed to nurture spiritual vitality. For there is no growth in faith apart from the mutual edification of those in community. The kind of upbuilding described in the New Testament is a matter of the heart, the emotional, intellectual, and spiritual core of the human being; and to share from the heart is to give of ourselves, with the whole of who we are.

The spiritual fellowship to which we are called invites us into intimate communion with God and one another. Life in the church is meant to mirror the mutual indwelling of the Holy Trinity. Since we are fallen creatures, such mutual love and freedom is merely glimpsed and not fully grasped. Nevertheless, a vision of mutuality has been given to us as part of the Gospel's treasure. Our unity in Christ, our dependence upon Christ, and our willingness to offer and receive help from one another are all part of this rich vision. Real interdependence becomes a reality when we reach out to one another in love. Only as we consent to open up our inner lives to each other will we grow in trust. Only as we take steps to pray together will we find the unity we are called to realize. Each of us is called to listen and intercede for others on the basis of their true need. Each of us is called to give our witness of the One who sustains and renews our lives. Each of us is responsible for exercising the gifts we have been given for the good of all.

6

God's Compassion Is over All

Listening with an Open Heart

> *The LORD is good to all, and his compassion is over all that he has made. —Psalm 145:9*

God's love is the wellspring from which we draw when we need compassion for ourselves or another. It is noteworthy that throughout the gospels the word "compassion" is used only to describe Jesus or the God-figure in Jesus' parables.[1] The New Testament witness thus affirms God alone as the source of all compassion. Jesus Christ as the only Son of the Father reveals both the depth and breadth of divine compassion. His life-story shapes our understanding of its very meaning. We remember his compassion toward each human soul who cries out to him for help: the blind, the deaf, the lame, those stricken by disease or burdened with grief. We remember his lament over the city of Jerusalem as he perceives the blindness and wretchedness of its inhabitants. We recall his compassion for the thousands who are hungry not only for bread but for the smallest morsel of hope. When we contemplate his compassion toward those who crucify him, we ask, who *is* this one praying for his tormentors? What immeasurable compassion resides in this human breast?

"Compassion," writes Andrew Purves, "reveals the inner nature of God."[2] Christ's compassion becomes "a window of access into the nature of . . . God's vulnerability and willingness to suffer with us."[3] The Lord who has compassion over all that he has made does not leave us to suffer the anguish of our mortal condition, nor the consequences of our sin, alone, but actively wills to share it.

---

1. Purves, *Search for Compassion*.
2. Purves, *Search for Compassion*, 12.
3. Purves, *Search for Compassion*, 16.

> The mercy of God lies in his readiness to share in sympathy the distress of another, a readiness which springs from his inmost nature and stamps all his being and doing. It lies, therefore, in his will, springing from the depths of his nature and characterizing it, to take the initiative himself for the removal of this distress. . . . The personal God has a heart. He can feel and be affected. . . . God is moved and stirred . . . in his innermost being . . . open, ready, inclined . . . to compassion with another's suffering and therefore to assistance.[4]

Though we cannot fathom the depth of such love, nor comprehend the mystery of Christ's atoning sacrifice, his life-story enables us to envision a transcendent ground for hope, which is a vision nothing short of the redemption of the entire world, for the kingdom of God to come on earth as it is in heaven.

The church is both called and enabled to "participate in God's continuing compassion for the world."[5] When our compassion is grounded in God's own love, we connect to a transcendent source, which enables us to keep our hearts open in trying situations, rather than close ourselves off in self-protection. Though compassion cannot be sustained over the long haul by means of our own meager resources, it can be renewed daily by means of our connection to the core of God's love. While nonviolent communication[6] emphasizes the importance of our listening to others with compassion, Bonhoeffer grounds it as a spiritual practice of the church by showing its foundation in God's listening to us. Just as God shows his love for us by listening to our prayers, so we are to demonstrate our love for others by listening to them.

> The first service that one owes to others in the community involves listening to them. Just as our love for God begins with listening to God's Word, the beginning of love for other Christians is learning to listen to them. God's love for us is shown by the fact that God not only gives us God's Word but also lends us God's ear. We do God's work for our brothers and sisters when we learn to listen to them.[7]

---

4. Barth, *Church Dogmatics* 2/1, 369–70.

5. Purves, *Search for Compassion*, 12.

6. Marshall Rosenberg's book, *Nonviolent Communication: A Language of Life* is discussed in some detail in this chapter, since it provides so many helpful tools to spiritual caregivers.

7. Bonhoeffer, *Life Together*, 97. See also Hunsinger, *Pray Without Ceasing*, 51–78.

Listening to our brothers and sisters in Christ is one way that we are invited and enabled to participate in Christ's work. Learning to hear the cry of another's heart is not only a gift to be cherished, it is also a skill to be honed.

Compassion, Sympathy, and Empathy

Let us make some distinctions among several closely related concepts: compassion, sympathy, and empathy. Compassion, as I understand it, is first of all an attribute of God. Indeed, it is descriptive of a central aspect of God's character, the steadfast love that is merciful toward all that God has made.

> Bless the Lord, O my soul, and all that is within me, bless his holy name. Bless the Lord, O my soul, and do not forget all his benefits, who forgives all your iniquity, who heals all your diseases, who redeems your life from the Pit, who crowns you with steadfast love and mercy, who satisfies you with good as long as you live so that your youth is renewed like the eagle's. . . . As a father has compassion for his children so the Lord has compassion for those who fear him. For he knows how we were made; he remembers that we are dust. (Psalm 103:1–5, 13, 14 NRSV)

The psalm speaks of multiple aspects of God's compassionate nature: it is forgiving, healing, and redemptive in character. God's mercy crowns our lives; his goodness renews it. The compassion of God reaches out toward those who are poor and needy; here it is compared to the love of a father for his children. Throughout both the Old and New Testaments, God's compassion toward the widow, the orphan, the slave, and the oppressed, indeed anyone especially in need, is repeatedly attested. The scriptural terms, *rahamim* in Hebrew (related to "womb") and *splagchna* in Greek (related to "bowels"), "carry the thought of yearning over another with great feeling."[8] As Christians, we believe that insofar as someone has true compassion for others, it is ultimately derived from this transcendent source.

In his Letter to the Romans, the apostle Paul speaks of the special gifts of the saints, each one of which is needed for the body of Christ to function properly. After naming prophecy, ministry, teaching, exhortation, giving, and leading, he speaks of the gift of compassion. "We have

---

8. Harrison, "Compassion," 132.

gifts that differ according to the grace given to us: prophecy, in proportion to faith; ministry, in ministering; the teacher, in teaching; the exhorter, in exhortation; the giver, in generosity; the leader, in diligence; the compassionate, in cheerfulness" (Rom 12:6–8). When compassion is a gift of the Spirit, it shines forth with special luminosity. Certain saints of the church come to mind. We think of someone like Marietta Jaeger-Lane, a woman whose seven-year-old daughter was abducted and murdered. Jaeger-Lane not only became a founding member of Murder Victims' Families for Reconciliation (MVFR), but also has spent her entire life since the tragedy working for the abolition of the death penalty. We think also of Bishop Desmond Tutu, Martin Luther King Jr., and Nelson Mandela, who have inspired generations of those working for reconciliation among people of different races. In *No Future Without Forgiveness*, Tutu speaks of the costliness of bringing healing to a traumatized nation. It is a cost that he and thousands of others have borne; to do so with an affirmation of their common humanity with those who have harmed them is a compelling witness to the God who has sustained them.[9]

The second closely related word is sympathy. By sympathy, we mean the feelings that are evoked in us when we listen to or observe the feelings of another. In sympathy, we find ourselves spontaneously sharing another's feelings. If she expresses sadness and despondency, we may sympathetically notice similar feelings arising in us. Alternatively, we might begin to feel joyful as we hear about the joyful, expansive feelings of another. If he is in acute pain, we might become aware of an analogous pain in ourselves, sometimes to the point of feeling it viscerally. Judith Jordan recounts an especially vivid moment witnessing such sympathetic feeling in a child only eighteen months old:

> A mother inadvertently jammed her hand in the door of the playroom and was in obvious pain. Her 18-month-old daughter immediately picked up a soft, cuddly toy with which she had been comforting herself earlier and took it to the mother, standing close to her, looking worried and rubbing it against her mother's cheek. When the mother smiled and said she was all right, the child's face lit up.[10]

From what Jordan observes, we imagine that the child experienced some sort of anguish analogous to her mother's and moved swiftly to alleviate

---

9. Tutu, *No Future without Forgiveness*.
10. Jordan, "Meaning of Mutuality," 87–88.

her mother's pain. She could not be at peace until she knew that her mother was comforted.

Because the brain is "hard-wired" for relationship, such sympathetic feelings can arise quite early in life. Daniel Siegel states: "Within the brain are clusters of cells that are designed to fire in response to eye contact and facial expressions. . . . For example, seeking proximity to a caregiver and attaining face-to-face communication with eye gaze contact is hard-wired into the brain from birth. It is not learned."[11] The child observed by Jordan had the capacity to "feel with" her mother and express it (though without words) at a year and a half. That she was able to share her mother's feelings in this way indicates a prior history of a secure attachment.

> Attachment at its core is based on parental sensitivity and responsivity to the child's signals, which allow for collaborative parent-child communication. Contingent communication gives rise to secure attachment and is characterized by a collaborative give-and-take of signals between the members of the pair. Contingent communication relies on the alignment of internal experiences, or states of mind, between child and caregiver. This mutually sharing, mutually influencing set of interactions—this emotional attunement or mental state resonance—is the essence of healthy secure attachment.[12]

Though a capacity for sympathy may be innate, it flourishes in an environment characterized by a secure attachment with a caring parent.

Sympathy often arises in the context of sharing a common loss. Although each person's grief is uniquely her own (and thus needs to be understood in its particularity), shared feelings of sadness often bring consolation. At funerals, we sometimes find comfort in hearing the qualities of our loved one praised by another; even to have his foibles described can bring unexpected delight. At the same time, a sense of isolation can arise if the particularity of our own loss is not acknowledged. When someone says *sympathetically*, "I know *just* how you feel," we want to protest that she simply does not, indeed cannot, know how we feel, for our pain is unique.[13]

---

11. Siegel, *Developing Mind*, 138.
12. Siegel, *Developing Mind*, 117.
13. "Death is the great leveler, so our writers have always told us. Of course, they are right. But they have neglected to mention the uniqueness of each death—and the solitude of suffering which accompanies that uniqueness. We say, 'I know how you are feeling.' But we don't" (Wolterstorff, *Lament for a Son*, 25).

Sharing similar feelings may be healing, but empathy provides a depth of understanding that sympathy typically cannot reach. Empathy recognizes and acknowledges difference in the midst of similarity. Paradoxically, we have a greater sense of companionship when the uniqueness of each person's grief is acknowledged. Empathy is a disciplined undertaking in which one momentarily sets aside one's own unique feelings and needs in order to connect with the other's unique feelings and needs. The focus in empathy is on fully connecting with the other person, whereas in sympathy we are often more connected with our own feelings than we are with the other's. The boundary or distinction between your feelings and mine is blurred.

Psychotherapists have endeavored for years to capture the distinctive character of empathy. Heinz Kohut considers it the "single most essential quality that enable[s] emotional well-being."[14] The human being, he said, "can no more survive in a psychological milieu that does not respond empathically to him than he can survive physically in an atmosphere that contains no oxygen."[15] Carl Rogers, one of Marshall Rosenberg's mentors, describes empathy in this way:

> To sense the client's private world as if it were your own, but without ever losing the "as if" quality—this is empathy, and this seems essential to therapy. To sense the client's anger, fear, or confusion as if it were your own, yet without your own anger, fear, or confusion getting bound up with it, is the condition we are endeavoring to describe.[16]

With this definition, note that Rogers also distinguishes between empathy and sympathy. If one's own anger, fear, or confusion get bound up with the anger, fear, or confusion of the speaker, one is responding sympathetically rather than empathetically.

When there is a sturdy empathic connection between persons, the listener is able to sense the other's feelings and needs even if they are not explicitly stated. When we observe parents who are receptive to the needs of their newborn, for instance, we see how they seek to understand the child from within, sensitively attuning themselves to a range of nonverbal signals. They attend to the quality of the child's cries, to its facial expressions, tone of voice, and bodily movements as they attempt to discern the

---

14. Hunsinger, *Pray Without Ceasing*, 55–56.
15. Kohut, *Restoration of the Self*, 253.
16. Rogers, "Necessary and Sufficient Conditions," 98.

child's needs. This kind of exquisite attention to the other also underlies effective psychotherapy, which is frequently described as a kind of re-parenting process.

> Responding to the patient's nonverbal signals, including tone of voice, facial expressions, eye gaze, and bodily motion, can reveal the otherwise hidden shifts in states of mind. Resonating with these expressions of primary emotions requires that the therapist feel the feelings, not merely understand them conceptually. Resonance involves the alignment of psychobiological states between patient and therapist.[17]

This kind of resonance enables a person to "feel felt" which may well be "an essential ingredient in attachment relationships . . . [and] vital to close relationships of all sorts throughout the lifespan."[18]

Resonating with another "requires that the therapist feel the feelings, not merely understand them conceptually."[19] How does this statement square with Rogers's insistence that the therapist's own feelings are not bound up with those of the client's? What actually happens when the listener seeks to empathize with another? Is she feeling what the other feels? Or is she simply seeking to understand her conceptually? Theorists at the Jean Baker Miller Training Institute (formerly the Stone Center) of Wellesley College insist that both cognitive and affective components are actively engaged in effective empathy. On a feeling level, there is a profound sense of connection between two people that has a physiological basis. This quality is akin to the sympathetic sharing of a feeling that we described above. "In part, they [genuine empathic moments] have a physiological quality in which our posture, our teary eyes, our tense muscles unconsciously reflect the state of the patient, thereby transmitting to us a kind of visceral experience of the patient's emotional state."[20] In these instances, we are not feeling grief or anxiety related to our own life experiences (as in sympathy) as much as we are experiencing the effect of being attuned to the experience of the person sitting before us. In other words, as we resonate with another's feelings, we find ourselves mirroring them, usually unconsciously. As we physically mirror the other, our own body imparts information about what the other might be feeling. Siegel

---

17. Siegel, *Developing Mind*, 290.
18. Siegel, *Developing Mind*, 272.
19. Siegel, *Developing Mind*, 290.
20. Kaplan, "Empathic Communication," 46.

explains: "The signals from the body also directly shape our emotions. Our awareness of bodily state changes—such as tension in our muscles, shifts in our facial expressions, or signals from our heart or intestines—lets us know how we feel, though bodily feedback occurs even without awareness."[21] We thus get a sense of the other's feelings by raising into awareness the feedback our own body is giving us.

Another dimension of the affective component of empathy has to do with the personal associations that enable the listener to guess at the other's feelings and needs. Alexandra Kaplan calls it "associative empathy."[22] The listener associates something comparable from her own experience as she listens. These associations come effortlessly to mind, like the "free-floating attentiveness" recommended by Freud.[23] The ability of the listener to notice these associations and then to detect their emotional impact assists her in guessing the other's feelings and needs. She uses these memories as a reference point for connecting with what the other might be feeling and needing in the present. But the central focus of her attention is not on her own experiences; it is on the experience of the other. She notes her own feelings and needs, not in order to explore them or to share them, but as possible clues about what the other might be experiencing.

Simultaneous with these essentially affective dimensions of empathy are cognitive components that go in a different direction. While one may feel an intense sense of connection with the other, there is at the same time clarity about one's own distinct identity. As Kaplan explains, "The cognitive component of empathy follows a different, essentially contradictory, course from that of the affective. Specifically, while there may be an interpenetration of affect, identity remains differentiated. The therapist, throughout, never loses sight of herself as a distinct being; at the same time, she is emotionally joined with another."[24] Clarity about her own differentiated identity enables her simultaneously to connect with others emotionally, understand their feelings and needs as if from the inside, while holding a completely different point of view. For this reason, accurate empathy does not imply agreement. One can understand another and yet have quite different feelings and needs in relation

---

21. Siegel, *Developing Mind*, 143.
22. Kaplan, "Empathic Communication," 46.
23. Hunsinger, *Pray Without Ceasing*, 67.
24. Kaplan, "Empathic Communication," 47.

to the matter at hand. One is "affectively connected and cognitively differentiated at the same time."[25]

While a vast amount of literature on empathy has originated either in infant studies or in assessing therapeutic effectiveness, empathy is a vital quality in all our relationships throughout life if we are to thrive. Indeed, any relationship characterized by empathic attunement inherently fosters emotional growth. It provides an environment in which persons feel fully alive, connected to themselves and others, with a felt sense of belonging. Jean Baker Miller and her colleagues identify five features that arise out of such relationships: zest, action, knowledge, self-worth, and connection.[26] The feeling of zest is the energetic, expansive feeling that comes in the wake of "feeling felt." A surge of vitality accompanies the sense of emotional connectedness. When one has little sense of emotional connection, by contrast, this feeling of zest is noticeably absent. As one experiences oneself being fully heard and gains a greater sense of self-connection, one is also empowered to act. One feels less stuck and has more of an internal sense of freedom to take action in any situation.

Empathy also expands one's knowledge. As one is given the freedom to explore many facets of one's life situation, one becomes aware of components that previously had remained hidden from view. A more comprehensive picture emerges. Previously unconscious feelings rise to the surface and one is able to articulate needs that were heretofore unacknowledged. At the same time, one grows in feelings of self-worth. A caring attitude on the part of the listener conveys to the speaker that she is worthy of another's time and attention, which increases the sense that she matters. Inevitably, the experience of connection fosters a desire for even more connection. Enduring emotional bonds are forged over time in relationships that have empathy at their core.

In conclusion, compassion, as we are using the term, is a spiritual gift, sympathy arises naturally in secure relationships, and empathy is a finely honed skill. When the apostle Paul exhorts the Christians in Rome to "rejoice with those who rejoice and to weep with those who weep" (Rom 12:15), he sees them as joined together as one body in their love for Jesus Christ. That love is the source of their compassion for one another. Whenever we share a common feeling or strongly identify with another's feelings, we give voice to feelings of sympathy. And finally, when we seek

25. Kaplan, "Empathic Communication," 47.

26. Miller and Stiver, *Healing Connection*, 30. See also Hunsinger, *Pray Without Ceasing*, 57.

in a disciplined way to understand the particularity of each person's feelings and needs, we are practicing the skill of empathy.

The Art of Self Empathy

You shall love your neighbor as yourself. —Matthew 22:39

In the Gospel according to Matthew, Jesus says that "the great and first commandment" is: "You shall love the Lord your God with all your heart, and with all your soul, and with all your mind" (Matt 22:37). He then goes on to say that a second is like it: "You shall love your neighbor as yourself" (Matt 22:39). "On these two commandments," says Jesus, "depend all the law and the prophets" (Matt 22:40). It is an astonishing summary for its clarity and economy. We are to love God with everything that we are, single-mindedly and wholeheartedly, with all-out passion from the depths of our being. And we are to love our neighbors as we love ourselves, to care about their welfare and take their longings to heart in the same way that we care about our own wellbeing. In saying this, Jesus assumes a love of oneself as the basis for illuminating what he means by loving one's neighbor. As we love and care for our own bodies and souls, so we are to love and care for our neighbors.' We are to regard our neighbors' needs as having the same importance as our own.

Yet how are we to understand what it means to love ourselves in light of other New Testament injunctions to deny ourselves? Is self-love less honorable than love of neighbor or even worse, intrinsically sinful? Numerous biblical passages can be brought to bear on such an interpretation: that we ought to "deny ourselves" (Matt 16:24), "hate even life itself" (Luke 14:26), and "put to death the deeds of the body" (Rom 8:13). Similarly, we must "do nothing from selfishness or conceit, but in humility count others better than [ourselves]" (Phil 2:3).[27]

A theologically adequate understanding of self-love becomes even more difficult when we consider the Bible's denunciations of human sin. Old and New Testaments alike speak of the pervasiveness of sin. "Indeed, I was born guilty, a sinner when my mother conceived me" (Psalm 51:5). "All have sinned and fall short of God's glory" (Rom 3:23). "For I know that nothing good dwells within me, that is, in my flesh" (Rom 7:18). Entire theological traditions, specifically those stemming from John Calvin's

---

27. This partial list of biblical passages is found in Ray Anderson's book, *Self Care*, 105.

thought, affirm the "total depravity" of human nature. Some have claimed that the self is inherently evil. They have argued that God calls us solely to a life of self-abnegation. Anything less is selfish and sinful. So, we are left wondering, does Scripture teach us to hold ourselves in contempt?

Perhaps surprisingly, Calvin's own theology can help us answer these questions. In the *Institutes of the Christian Religion*, Calvin defines "the sum of the Christian life" as "self-denial." By this, he means the setting aside of "the yearning to possess, the desire for power," as well as "arrogance, ostentation . . . [and] avarice."[28] Self-denial resists the tendency to exaggerate the faults of others, enabling us to relate to others with "true gentleness"[29] and "to look upon the image of God in all men, to which we owe all honor and love."[30] In other words, juxtaposed with this emphasis on human sin is the affirmation of the goodness of humanity, which is made in the image of God. Scripture teaches us to value our life, body, and soul, as a precious gift from God. It teaches us to honor our bodies as temples of the Holy Spirit and to know that we are beloved children of our maker. Passages that emphasize self-denial, humility, and even "hatred" toward our own lives are meant to counteract the human tendency to think only of ourselves. As in the injunction to "love our neighbor as ourselves," self-love is the assumed point of reference. It is taken for granted that we will cherish our lives and the needs of our bodies and souls. What we need to hear is that our neighbors' lives deserve the same kind of tender solicitude as our own.

The tradition of interpretation that portrays human beings in a completely negative light wants to emphasize that there is no aspect of human nature untouched by sin. However, the Calvinistic affirmation of "total depravity" does not mean that there is nothing lovable or worthy about human beings, but rather that human beings are incapable of acting or even willing the good apart from God's grace. Such a confession does not negate the affirmation of our having been created in God's own image. Though sin corrupts or distorts the image of God, it does not destroy it. Scripture states that after God created the world and all its creatures, including human beings, "God saw everything that he had made, and behold, it was very good" (Gen 1:31). Indeed, God creates human beings in God's own image and honors us by calling us to a life of love, witness, and service. Though we sin, God continues to extend

---

28. Calvin, *Institutes of the Christian Religion* 2, 3.7.2, 691.
29. Calvin, *Institutes of the Christian Religion* 2, 3.7.2, 694.
30. Calvin, *Institutes of the Christian Religion* 2, 3.7.2, 696.

steadfast love toward human beings. In an effort to see our true situation before God, especially the gravity and pervasiveness of sin, we are not to lose sight of the fact that God loves and cherishes us as beloved children. If we are the object of the Lord's compassionate care in spite of our sin, then we also ought to have compassion for ourselves. We are to care for ourselves in correspondence to the tenderness that God extends toward us. Remembering this is particularly important for those who have suffered the trauma of emotional abuse as children. They have been taught to disregard their own needs and focus solely on the needs of others. They have been taught that it is "selfish" to have compassion for themselves and to trust that they matter to God and to others.

It is paradoxically the case that we cannot love either God or others if we do not love ourselves. Love of self is intrinsically tied to love of neighbor. Even the so-called "golden rule" makes no sense without a proper regard for the self. We must respect ourselves and cherish our own lives if we are to respect and cherish others. As Ray Anderson observes, "Love of self and neighbor, as grounded in God's love of both, is not two separate commands to love, nor two kinds of love. Rather, this command to love includes three aspects: God, the neighbor, and the self. One cannot despise oneself and truly love God or the neighbor."[31] When Paul admonishes husbands to love their wives, his reasoning also proceeds from the basic assumption of a proper love of self.[32] "In the same way, husbands should love their wives as they do their own bodies. He who loves his wife loves himself. For no one ever hates his own body, but he nourishes and tenderly cares for it, just as Christ does for the church, because we are members of his body" (Eph 5:28–30). Because we are equally members of Christ's body, so Paul seems to say, we are to cherish every member equally. All have worth and value, including ourselves. Love of self and neighbor is one love that flows in both directions. Everything depends upon the mutual and reciprocal care between our neighbor and ourselves.

We come to esteem ourselves only as we are cherished by others, by our parents or early caregivers and by friends and family thereafter. We

---

31. Anderson, *Self Care*, 106.

32. I recognize that this passage of Scripture has been interpreted throughout church history in ways antithetical to the vision for mutual love that I am setting forth in this chapter. Specifically, it has been used to subjugate women and deny their full humanity. I am suggesting that contrary to these interpretations, Ephesians 5, when interpreted in light of the whole New Testament as well as the context in which it was written, encourages respectful, mutual, and compassionate care in marriage.

are deluded if we believe that we can manufacture a sense of self-worth simply by ourselves. Writing ourselves notes of self-affirmation, giving ourselves hugs, or asserting our own value will inevitably fail to convince us of our worthiness. Rather, "we love because [God] first loved us" (1 John 4:19). Human love is radically dependent upon divine love for its very existence. Parents cannot sustain love for their children apart from a sense of being loved themselves. Ultimately all love comes from God. We cannot grow truly to value ourselves simply by willing ourselves to do so. Love is always a gift. It comes to us through the actual experience of others loving us. As we are loved and respected by others, we learn to love and respect ourselves.

Though we are to love ourselves, we are not to elevate ourselves or others in such a way that displaces God. God remains the center of our lives; God alone is to be loved with all our heart, soul, and mind. We are called not simply to meet our own needs, as if those needs were the only ones that mattered, but to glorify God by caring for all that God has created. We are to take to heart the needs of our neighbor (and indeed all of creation) with the same care as we take our own needs to heart. Here is where the biblical injunction to deny ourselves has its place. Insofar as we elevate our own needs above others or look only to our own interests and fail to take the interests of others into account, precisely then we are to honor and love others as made in the image of God, as others whose very being matters as much as our own.

Jesus always spoke specifically to each person's heart. Longing for healing, the woman with the flow of blood audaciously crept up behind Jesus and touched the hem of his robe. But Jesus did not rebuke her; on the contrary, he praised her for acting in faith (Matt 9:20–23). Similarly, blind Bartimaeus, though reprimanded by the crowd, was rewarded for his crying out for healing (Mark 10:46–51). However, those intent upon justifying themselves, such as the rich young ruler or the publican who prayed his self-satisfied prayer, are exhorted to consider the needs of others or to count others as better than themselves.

There is no uniform rule that can be applied in all contexts. Indeed, whether to focus primarily on another's need or to assert my own is a matter of daily (or even hourly) discernment. Should I assert my own need here? Or should I pay more attention to the needs of the other? What is God calling me to do in this particular situation? Compassionate communication[33] not only gives us tools for discerning our own needs and those of others, but also gives guidance toward choosing strategies that take into account all those whose needs are unmet in any given situation. The point is that everyone's needs matter, including our own.

On a practical level this means caring for ourselves as we would care for others. It is as important to know about caring for ourselves as it is to know about justification by faith alone. Indeed, justification by faith alone entails self-care at a practical level. If we believe that Jesus Christ is the one who justifies our lives, then we know we cannot earn our salvation. We see that we don't have to prove ourselves to anybody, least of all to ourselves and the tyrannical "shoulds" that drive us mercilessly toward an idealized version of ourselves.[34] We don't have to live up to the idealized self because we know that our real selves are loved and accepted by God. If God knows our worst and nevertheless forgives us and cherishes us, then we can rest secure in God's love. If God honors us by calling us to participate in the work of witness, service, and prayer, then we ought to treat ourselves with the same honor that God has already granted us.

Yet there are those in the church who seem utterly to disregard their own needs as they pour themselves out for the sake of others. In doing so, they endanger their own health and wellbeing. Some exhaust themselves to the point of burnout. Others act out, seeking to fulfill needs that they don't even know are there, clamoring for attention. Ministers of the gospel who are disconnected from their own needs and yet act them out unconsciously find themselves in tragic quagmires. All the years that they invested in preparing for their vocation—years of prayerful discernment, community encouragement, diligent study, financial resources, and hard work—come to naught. They either leave the ministry discouraged and disillusioned or are forced to leave by a community that is reeling from a sense of betrayed trust. If they had only known how to identify their needs, the tragedy could have been averted. For in and of themselves, the needs are precious and worthy of fulfillment. If the persons involved are able consciously to connect with all their needs, they can seek to meet them in ways that are in harmony with their basic values. If instead they remain disconnected from their needs, they either ignore them or act on them unconsciously, to the hurt and detriment of both neighbor and

---

33. I am using the term "compassionate communication" interchangeably with "nonviolent communication" (NVC).

34. See Horney, *Neurosis and Human Growth*, especially chapter 3, "Tyranny of the Should."

self. Lives are shattered, gifts wasted, and the splendor of God's glory lies shrouded in darkness.

Self-Pity Compared to Self-Empathy

Some people object to taking the time to pay attention to their own feelings and needs because they consider it a waste of time. In many cases, they confuse self-empathy with self-pity. It is important to differentiate between them for they lead in diametrically opposed directions. When we engage in self-pity, we see ourselves essentially as victims. We tell ourselves that we can't do whatever is asked of us and that we are powerless to initiate change on our own. We often have a story that justifies our sense of helplessness: others have power over us, and they are to blame for our disempowered state. So, we feel sorry for ourselves. Self-pity is a closed down, turned inward sort of stance. Self-empathy, by contrast, is healing and empowering, an opening up to possibility and growth. In self-empathy, we focus on our core needs. In so doing, we are able to take responsibility for ourselves. Options become apparent as we more deeply connect with what matters most to us in any particular situation. Because we are self-connected, we are able to make choices aligned with our values. In addition, the process of self-empathy itself meets our needs for self-care and compassion, as well as self-understanding. Even if our needs are not met in any particular instance, we are still able to be at peace. We trust that with time, other options will open up. Because we are not wedded to any particular strategy, we remain open to what might unfold. We may feel profound sorrow that things have not turned out as we wanted, but self-connected mourning over unmet needs is deeply healing. Instead of feeling sorry for ourselves, we feel true sorrow as we connect fully with the precious value of what we have lost. Such mourning is life-giving because it renews in us a deeper commitment to living out our values in the world.j

The Importance of Self-Empathy in Spiritual Care

It is a paradoxical fact that listening well to others is intimately tied to knowing how to listen to ourselves. In spiritual care, we need to be attentive to our own anxiety because whenever our anxiety increases, our ability to hear another decreases. As Margaret Kornfeld puts it, anxiety creates "static" in our listening.[35] When our anxiety lies outside our awareness, we are likely to fall into old habits; we might offer advice or reassurance or assume a "teaching" rather than a "listening" mode. Indeed, we are vulnerable to the "typical twelve" responses that are life-alienating when empathic understanding is needed (e.g. advising, one-upping, educating, analyzing, story-telling, minimizing, sympathizing, interrogating, reassuring, avoiding, diagnosing, or judging). Whenever we hear ourselves resorting to one of these modes of responding, it is likely a sign that our anxiety has been triggered. Our anxiety is a signal of an unmet need that wants our attention. *If we are unable to empathize with another person, it is a sign that we ourselves need empathy.* We can get the empathy we need either by reaching out to a trusted friend or colleague for help or by practicing the specific skill of self-empathy. If we start to feel angry, frustrated, helpless, or fearful, it is a sign of our own unmet needs.

In order to create a trustworthy environment for others, we need to acknowledge and address the source of our anxiety. Kornfeld notes that anxiety is often created by self-doubt. Self-doubt indeed seems to be an expression of anxiety, but knowing this is not sufficient. We need to take the next step and identify the unmet needs that fuel the self-doubt. What are the circumstances under which our self-doubt arises, and what do we need? When we are first learning the empathic skills involved in listening, for example, anxious self-doubt often arises from a need to contribute to the wellbeing of others while we ourselves are unsure about how to proceed. We might also identify needs for contribution, competence, and confidence. The spiritual challenge is to find a measure of self-acceptance as we slowly learn how to meet these important needs. It is often difficult to have compassion for ourselves as we experience the awkwardness of learning new skills.

Attitudes Toward Self and Other

It is a curious fact that our attitudes toward ourselves and our attitudes toward others are often deeply entwined. For example, some people drive themselves anxiously to accomplish task after task, while seldom letting themselves simply enjoy what they are doing in the moment. It is as if they are rushing ten feet ahead of themselves. Yet, if you were to observe them closely, you might see them driving their children in a similar way,

35. Kornfeld, *Cultivating Wholeness*, 52–58.

constantly reminding them to do this or that, hardly allowing them a minute to relax. Or to choose another example, some people have a "fix it" attitude toward others, rattling off solutions to a problem before the problem has even been fully described. If you listen closely, however, you might notice that they also become impatient with themselves whenever they are unclear about what direction to take. They don't know how to check in with themselves and accurately assess the full range of the needs they are trying to meet with any given decision. They simply want to decide and be done with it.

On the other hand, sometimes a person will speak to others with the utmost consideration and respect yet speak to himself as if he were the most despicable creature alive. If he makes a mistake, he immediately berates himself with scathing judgments or calls himself an idiot. The more he regrets a decision, the more he treats himself with scorn. He would be horrified at the thought of speaking to another in this manner, yet he speaks to himself as if he were of no value. If he were to analyze his self-talk, he might be able to recognize its origins in childhood. Perhaps a parent spoke to him in such a disparaging way, or perhaps a beloved older brother spoke of himself in this way. It may be a learned pattern, in other words, long before he became fully conscious of what he was internalizing.

Such analyses may be provisionally helpful, yet ultimately they do little to actually change the pattern. Only self-empathy can give us the skill that we need to learn how to treat ourselves with the same consideration and respect that we want to accord others. Just as we do not want to judge or blame others, so now we strive to identify the needs that are underlying any self-judgment or blame. Just as we help others to translate their negative interpretation of themselves when they compare themselves to others, so we now seek to catch ourselves in the act of comparing ourselves. When we translate the comparison into our own feelings and needs, we may experience pain, but we will also discover a hidden treasure: a bundle of unacknowledged needs that we are longing to find a way to live out fully. The others are carrying personal values of ours that we ourselves need to become more fully conscious of. In self-empathy, we learn to notice when we feel overwhelmed, sad, anxious, or distressed so that we can take the time to be with ourselves in a loving way, to listen to ourselves with the kind of compassion we would give a frightened child. When we listen to ourselves in this way, we learn to make choices that truly reflect our values, which typically gives us a sense of satisfaction and even joy.

Being "Triggered" and Asking Ourselves: What Is the Need?

Self-empathy usually begins with a "trigger." We hear, see, or remember something that brings up strong negative feelings in us. We might feel a sharp stab of hurt, the boiling up of anger, intense anxiety, or a feeling of being overwhelmed. The more powerful the emotion, the more urgent the underlying need or value. If I experience only mild anxiety about an upcoming interview, for example, it may be because I have a sense of confidence, or it may be that the interview is simply not that important to me. If I experience intense anxiety, by contrast, it may be because much is at stake. I anticipate that some vital need will be met (or not) as the outcome of the interview. The process of self-empathy would help me to assess precisely which needs of mine—and there may be many—are generating such intense feelings.

In self-empathy, we strive to stay attuned to ourselves in a bodily way. In other words, we don't think about the problem so much as feel into it. We don't analyze our anxiety with our rational capacities, but rather we pay attention to what happens in our bodies when we ask ourselves what it is about this concrete situation that matters to us. Such a process is described in vivid detail in Eugene Gendlin's groundbreaking book, *Focusing*. Developed in the 1970s at the University of Chicago, *Focusing* teaches a process of paying attention to our physiological responses in order to connect with feelings that generally lie outside of our awareness. Working with the "felt sense" in the body, Gendlin teaches us to notice when the body relaxes. When we accurately identify our feelings, there is a noticeable shift on a bodily level. For example, when we strain to remember a name that is on the tip of our tongue, there is a distinct tension that dissipates the moment the name is recalled. Calling the body a kind of "biological computer," Gendlin reminds us that "the equivalent of hundreds of thousands of cognitive operations are done in a split second by the body."[36]

When we find a word that matches the felt sense in the body, a letting go or relaxation is experienced, sometimes accompanied by a literal sigh of relief. "Ah yes, that's it! That word captures the feeling exactly," we might exclaim. At this point, Gendlin would recommend probing further to elicit even more information from the body's felt sense. Previously unconscious feelings may now begin to rise up into awareness. Gendlin

---

36. Gendlin, *Focusing*, 34.

suggests that as we pay close attention to the felt sense in our bodies, we might ask ourselves several questions: "What is it about this whole issue that makes it so . . . ? What is the worst thing about this problem? How would I feel inside if it were solved? What do I need for me not to feel so . . . 'anxious' or 'jumpy' or 'frightened,' or whatever word seems to fit the felt sense?"[37] After asking, we wait for the body to answer; we do not fill in the blanks with our conscious ideas or thoughts. Instead, we trust the inner wisdom of our body to speak.

The last question that Gendlin asks connects feelings with needs. Though the significance of connecting with one's needs remains implicit in focusing, in compassionate communication it is the master key to the whole process. Asking myself, "What do I need in this particular situation?" is the fundamental question that is able to bring about the distinct shift that Gendlin describes. What would relieve me of the anger or constriction or shame that I have identified? What need am I longing to fulfill? What need, if it were fulfilled, would bring me to a place of relaxation and peace? While focusing and compassionate communication both work with the felt sense of the body, in other words, only compassionate communication emphasizes the pivotal role that fully connecting with one's needs plays in the process. When we inquire into our needs in the same way that Gendlin suggests that we ask about our feelings—i.e., by attending to what goes on in our bodies—we are not simply connecting to words in our head. We are testing to see if the words in our minds correspond to the feelings in our bodies. Indeed, we actually pay attention to our bodies (especially to the viscera, where we find our "gut" feelings) to find our needs. The process, in other words, entails a deep integration of the cognitive, affective, and bodily components of our being.

A Simple Example of Self-Empathy

On a recent plane trip, I had fallen asleep when the flight attendant was serving drinks. Immediately upon waking, I noticed that she was collecting the cups to prepare for landing. Since I was quite thirsty, I asked for some water, explaining that I had been asleep earlier. In what sounded like an annoyed tone of voice, she replied that it was too late since the plane was about to land. She walked on by, collecting the cups. She then

---

37. These questions are paraphrases of several questions Gendlin asks in the "short form" summary in the book's appendix. See Gendlin, *Focusing*, 174.

took them to the front to dispose of them. I was upset. It was apparent that she was not going to bring me any water. I thought to myself: "How difficult would it be to get me a cup of water? I'm really thirsty. We aren't landing now anyway. Surely you have enough time." This line of thought offered no relief at all. I then switched tactics and tried to empathize with what I imagined as her feelings and needs: "Perhaps she is annoyed because she wants ease in completing all her tasks before landing." The attempt to connect empathically with her brought a slight shift but not enough to give any real relief. I was still upset.

However, when I asked myself what I needed in order to be at peace, I realized at once that my thirst was not the essential thing. I was indeed quite thirsty, but even more than water was my need for caring. I interpreted her tone of voice and her lack of action as a lack of caring. I was upset because it seemed to me that she did not care whether or not I was thirsty. When I heard myself accuse her (inwardly) of not caring, I asked myself whether caring was my deeper need. My body responded instantly with a dramatic release of inner tension. The shift was unmistakable. Caring was indeed my need. I was longing for some kind of care in her response. I thought further: "Even if she can't get me the water, if she would convey some care about my need, I could accept it. I could be at peace, if only she had said: 'I'm sorry, ma'am, but I'm unable to get you some water right now. We are about to land, and I need to return to my seat for the sake of safety.'"

To anchor myself more securely in the beauty of this need, I focused on how much I value caring. I meditated not only on how I strive to convey it in my relationships with others but also on how it feeds my soul when others convey care toward me. The longer I focused on the quality of the need itself (rather than on its absence in this particular instance), the more I felt at peace. Though still thirsty, I was no longer angry or agitated. I had connected with a value that mattered a great deal to me, one that was clamoring for attention through my feelings of distress.

Jane Connor, a certified NVC trainer, has developed a simple process for noticing what her common "triggers" are.[38] She carries a little notebook in which she jots down the exact observation (what she sees, hears, remembers, etc.) throughout the day that triggers any kind of distress or unease. At the end of the day, she meditates on each of the

---

38. I first learned of this practice in 2005 when Jane Connor and I were both participants in a yearlong training program for those wishing to teach nonviolent communication through the Bay Area Leadership Program. See www.baynvc.org.

triggers, asking herself what her feelings and needs were in each situation. In a single day, she might discover many unmet needs: for contribution, respect, understanding, meaning, acknowledgment, collaboration, choice, support, community. For example, she may observe one colleague speaking brusquely to another or refusing to answer the other's question. The moment she notices her anger flaring up, she writes down exactly what she has seen and heard. That evening when she meditates on the incident, she asks herself what she was thinking when her anger flared. By following her thoughts and attending carefully to her needs, she might discover that her unmet need is for respect. She would like her colleagues to treat each other with respect. Even when there are disagreements or different ways of viewing the world, she longs for each person to be treated respectfully.

If we make such a "trigger translation journal" a daily practice, we will become intimately acquainted with our core values. In addition, we may find places of vulnerability where we especially need healing. If our reaction is extreme, it may be that we have unresolved grief in relation to a core value. Over time, we can become acquainted with the patterns of thoughts, feelings, and needs that are repeated again and again. These patterns represent primal pathways in the brain that can be healed and transformed by empathy and self-empathy. Though the needs themselves are universal, each of us experiences them in a way peculiar to our unique make-up and history. In cases where chronic needs have remained unmet (and often unacknowledged) for years, our triggers will be correspondingly intense. Therefore, when we are intensely reactive, something of great value is at stake. Remembering this helps us to slow down and use all our skill to pay attention to the life-giving needs that are longing for acknowledgment.

Transforming Self-Judgments

In his book, *Nonviolent Communication: A Language of Life,* Marshall Rosenberg states the basic premise that lies behind the work of translating self-judgments: "Self-judgments, like all judgments, are tragic expressions of unmet needs."[39] Whenever we judge or blame ourselves, we are demonstrating that we have failed to act in harmony with our own values and needs. But it does little good to berate ourselves. That only

---

39. Rosenberg, *Nonviolent Communication*, 132.

deepens our sense of guilt, shame, powerlessness, or depression. It also perpetuates the cycle of keeping ourselves disconnected from our true needs. However, if we practice self-empathy, we can discover precisely what our needs are and look for satisfying ways to meet them.

It is an axiom in compassionate communication that all our actions are motivated by needs. If we find ourselves judging or blaming ourselves for an action we have taken, it is likely that we have failed to take into account all of our needs. For example, in ending a phone call quickly I may meet my need for efficiency, only to regret it later when I hear that my friend was hurt because she had hoped for a deeper connection with me. Now my need for caring may come to the fore. As I acknowledge the regret I feel when hearing about her disappointment in response to my action, I recognize that it emerges because I value caring in all my relationships. At the same time, however, I want to identify what need I was trying to meet with the action I took. Why did I end the conversation so abruptly? Oh yes, it was because I had a long list of tasks I was trying to accomplish before I left town for a week. I had felt a great need to be efficient in completing my checklist. Once I am fully connected to both sets of needs (in this example, both caring and efficiency), the self-judgment begins to fall away. While I may mourn the fact that I did not anticipate my friend's unexpressed need, I no longer would judge myself as inadequate or uncaring. By connecting fully with *both* sets of needs—the need I was trying to meet as well as the need I failed to meet—I am able to meet another crucial need: the need for self-acceptance.

Notice that in both examples (the example of my wanting a glass of water on the plane and the example of my ending a call abruptly) my need was the same. In both cases I identified the unmet need of caring. One of the benefits of a regular practice of self-empathy is the discovery that my need for caring entails both receiving and giving care. Self-empathy demonstrates clearly that the love of self and love of other are truly intertwined. If I value caring, its absence will trigger pain whether I am the one who fails to live it out or whether someone else fails to offer it to me. I might also be triggered when I hear a mother speaking in an exasperated tone to her children as they enter the sanctuary on Sunday morning. I may feel sad and, through self-empathy, identify caring once again as my unmet need.

Though these simple examples may seem trivial, it is helpful to practice self-empathy with relatively uncomplicated situations. Then when we are triggered by major events, in which there are whole clusters of unmet needs to be identified, we will have the basic skill mastered: the skill of connecting with all the needs at play. Once we see the self-judgments falling away in relatively simple examples, we will be motivated to keep practicing. People who are prone to shame and depression have self-judgments swirling about their minds almost constantly. In such cases the work of transforming self-judgments becomes a means of liberation. Those who have been taught to judge themselves as children (either through the explicit teaching or the modeling of a cherished other, usually a parent) often judge themselves harshly and repeatedly. They believe their self-judgments to be true and get little relief from the nearly constant inner barrage. For example, a woman once said something to me that she feared would not be acceptable. In rapid succession, the following sentences passed through her mind: "I shouldn't have said that.... I hope I haven't damaged that relationship. Eva, you're insensitive.... You should *never* have said that.... What is the *matter* with you?!"[40] An overwhelming sense of shame spiraled out of control as one sentence after another increased her sense of worthlessness. Only by slowing everything down and looking at each sentence closely could she become aware of what her needs might be. First, she regrets her words because she hopes that she hasn't damaged the relationship. She clearly values the relationship. The first step, then, would be for her to connect fully with how much she values her interpersonal relationships, acknowledging their life-giving potential in her life. The series culminates in her question: "What is the *matter* with you?" This question seems to indicate a fundamental need for self-acceptance.

The global nature of the self-judgments in this example as well as the way they were fired in such rapid succession make it difficult to trace the critical needs at stake. What is more, it is unclear what the initial observation was that set this avalanche of self-judgment in motion. What precisely was the trigger? Was there a strained silence after something that she had said? Was there a look on my face that she interpreted as disapproval? With depression, there is often a deeply ingrained habit of mind toward self-judgment, which in turn brings about a perception of others judging one as well.

---

40. Hunsinger, *Theology and Pastoral Counseling*, 164.

Deepening Needs Consciousness

In the above example, we identified a cluster of possibly unmet needs that were at work: a need for relationship, a need for acceptance, and a need for self-acceptance. There is value in identifying and connecting with each need in its own right even when they are closely interconnected. For example, the need for acceptance and self-acceptance are closely entwined. When we fear someone else's judgment, it is often the case that what we need even more than the other's acceptance is our own self-acceptance. Self-judgments are far more treacherous than the judgment of others because we so often believe them. We believe that these judgments are the truth. And because we believe they are true, we also believe that others must hold them as well. Because they go on autonomously in our minds, they are difficult to catch. One woman, for example, constantly told herself that she was lacking in basic integrity. These self-accusations would typically arise in situations in which someone would say something that she disagreed with. Rather than openly stating her disagreement, she would remain silent about her reaction and keep her opinions to herself. Even in matters of great importance, she would hesitate to speak up. Then she would berate herself for lacking the courage of her convictions. She told herself that she was simply hiding out, lacking in basic integrity. Not only was she being inauthentic by keeping her opinions to herself, she was also hiding her talents and not giving others the benefit of any possible insight that a differing perspective might impart.

Paradoxically, the action of judging herself is *itself* an attempt to meet a need. The act of self-judgment alerts her to the fact that at least one of her needs has not been met. What unmet needs did these judgments point to? Her overriding need corresponded to the loudest and most frequent judgment resounding in her mind: a need for integrity. She wanted her actions to reflect her deepest values. She wanted the freedom to express her thoughts even when they might be unpopular. She wanted to be more open, to make the contribution that might come from stating what she thought and why. She wanted to be authentically and fully herself. The cluster of unmet needs she identified as I assisted her in a process of self-empathy were: integrity, openness, freedom, contribution, authenticity, and then, surprisingly, simple connection. The need for connection took her by surprise. She had the sudden insight that by hiding her true thoughts and opinions, she had gone through life feeling lonely, not fully connecting with others because she was not revealing her authentic self.

In seeking to transform these judgments, she sought first to connect with the range of feelings that arose whenever she failed to speak up. The feelings were intense frustration, sorrow, and fear, each surfacing as she worked through the previous feeling. First, there was great frustration that no matter how much she coached herself to speak up, she remained silent and let the significant moment pass by. After exploring this frustration, she discovered a well of sadness about all the relationships in which she had failed to speak up because she didn't have the trust to say what she really thought. Once she felt the sadness fully and saw how huge her unmet need for trust really was, she became aware of the depth of her fear.

That fear needed further exploration. By asking herself about the needs connected to these feelings, she began to have compassion toward herself regarding her choice to remain silent over all these years. Though she clearly suffered from many unmet needs with this strategy, she also saw how she experienced a sense of safety by staying silent. She enjoyed relative harmony in her interpersonal and work relationships because she seldom rocked the boat. Her coworkers found her pleasant to be around, little knowing that fear of conflict kept her from speaking honestly about what she really thought and felt. At this point in the process, she took the time to consider both needs—the need to be herself and express herself fully as well as the need to have compassion for herself when she chose to stay silent. As she did this, the childhood roots of her fear filtered up into awareness, in particular, the emotional chaos and violence that had reigned in her family home. Her mother would erupt into terrifying rages out of nowhere; her sister would slap her if she said or did things that she (the sister) didn't like. Hiding her thoughts and feelings became a strategy for survival in a home where it seemed unsafe to assert herself in any way.

As she remembered these scenes concretely, even more compassion welled up within her for herself, for the frightened child who was afraid of her mother's rage and her sister's aggression. She could now appreciate the needs she was meeting through her strategy of keeping her true thoughts and feelings to herself. If she made herself as invisible as possible, she seemed able to avoid triggering irrational anger in her mother; if she kept her opinions to herself, she was able to keep her sister from slapping her. Hiding out became a way of keeping herself relatively safe in a home that seemed unsafe. Her needs for safety and harmony were so overriding that she believed it was impossible to express herself honestly in that setting.

In self-empathy, she was able to find a way to affirm, even to love, both sets of needs, the needs she was trying to meet by hiding (namely, safety and harmony) as well as the needs that she failed to meet with this strategy (integrity, authenticity, freedom, contribution, and connection). By connecting with all the needs involved, she was able gradually to find ways to take new risks, to stand by herself with compassion when she feared someone's displeasure. She discovered strategies, in other words, that met both sets of needs: the needs that were met by hiding her true thoughts as well as the needs that would be met by speaking up. Slowly but surely, as she sought and received the support she lacked as a child, she was able to find more freedom in speaking her mind fully. With that came much joy not only from the deepened connection that she had with others but also from the self-respect that came from meeting her own need for integrity.[41]

This example shows how core beliefs about herself and others kept this woman from engaging her colleagues with honesty and security. She had developed a number of stories about herself that were reinforced every time she kept silent about something that mattered to her. Concretely, these beliefs could be summarized as follows: "I will be hurt if I say what I really think. . . . The only way that I can stay safe is by hiding out, by becoming as invisible as possible." In a more extreme state, the belief was, "If I say what I really think, I will be killed." This unconscious belief was reinforced by the larger context of multiple assassinations of national figures in her childhood. In this way, the collective traumas of her historical era reinforced the neural pathways that had developed by growing up in her family of origin. The process of self-empathy enabled her to become aware of beliefs that essentially kept her stuck in old patterns. As she took more risks in which she questioned these beliefs, she found greater freedom and joy.

Self-Empathy and Prayer

Those who use self-empathy as a practical spiritual discipline sometimes find that it leads directly to prayer: to asking God for what they need. In

---

41. This example shows how nonviolent communication can be used over a period of time to promote emotional maturity in a person who is committed to a process of growth.

this way, self-empathy can deepen our connection with God. When we turn to God in prayer, having already gone through a process of self-empathy, we are unlikely simply to rattle off requests. Instead, we are likely to pray about the true nature of our need, and to offer up our requests haltingly, trusting that God, the searcher of hearts, will hear our hidden cry. "Likewise, the Spirit helps us in our weakness; for we do not know how to pray as we ought, but that very Spirit intercedes with sighs too deep for words" (Rom 8:26). Though we can sometimes be badly mistaken in assessing our true need, prayer keeps us aware of our most fundamental need: our need for God and for God's grace in its rich multiplicity of forms. Indeed, Scripture teaches us that God is the author of "every good and perfect gift" who will supply us with whatever we need for our life and wellbeing. "And my God will fully satisfy every need of yours according to his riches in glory in Christ Jesus" (Phil 4:19). "Rejoice in the Lord always; again, I will say, rejoice. . . . Do not worry about anything, but in everything by prayer and supplication with thanksgiving let your requests be made known to God" (Phil 4:4, 6). Prayer connects us to God and to all the needs fulfilled in God.

Needs, from within a Christian understanding, are all finally rooted and grounded in God. They are not ultimately understood as human qualities but rather as gifts from above. In prayer, we connect to God as the source of our needs, to Christ as the one in whom all our needs are fulfilled, and to the Spirit who searches our hearts and enables us to pray from the depths of our need. When we are discouraged, we need patience or courage. We access that patience or courage through our *koinonia* with God in prayer. If we are disappointed in ourselves, we may identify our needs as integrity or honesty. Once again, we find our center of integrity by reference to our relationship with God. At another point, we may recognize a need for trust. When we discover, again and again, that we are united to Christ and the communion of saints, we become grounded in a source of faith far greater than our own. As we confess our sins to God and each other, our needs for restoration and wholeness are met. As we lament the injustice all around us, our despair turns to hope. We are empowered to live in the "already-but-not-yet"—in this time of waiting for the fullness of God's kingdom to come.

To put it another way, self-empathy that leads to prayer supports our capacity to live compassionately. Connecting to God, the transcendent source of compassion, gives us the ability to keep our hearts open when we would otherwise be tempted to shut down. When we are overwhelmed with anxiety or despair, we have One to whom we can turn for strength. Indeed, the New Testament presents Jesus Christ as One who has taken the suffering of the entire world into his own heart. He does not leave us to suffer the anguish of loss and death, nor the consequences of our sin, alone, but actively intercedes on our behalf. Self-empathy that leads to prayer will not only become a means for preventing what is commonly called "compassion fatigue," but also can become a vital discipline for revitalizing faith.

Transforming Self-Judgments and the Forgiveness of Sin

From a Christian point of view, we are taught to seek God's forgiveness when we have not lived according to the values of our faith. Through the Holy Spirit, our conscience signals to us that we have failed to act with integrity or been fully honest. In Christian theology, when we fail to live up to God's commandments, we are counseled to confess our sin, receive God's forgiveness, make amends toward those we have hurt, and live in grateful acknowledgment of God's mercy. Transforming self-judgments, as taught by Marshall Rosenberg, is not synonymous with confession of sin, nor is it a replacement for it. While nonviolent communication lacks (and likely rejects) a concept of sin, Christian theology cannot do without it. The concept of sin, so closely tied to our understanding of our need for God and the salvation accomplished in Jesus Christ, is indispensable to our entire understanding of the life of faith. However, transforming our self-judgments gives us a deeper understanding of ourselves, which in turn transforms our practice of confession and repentance. For it enables us to encounter God with a depth of authenticity and self-awareness that are sometimes lacking in our corporate prayers of confession.

When Rosenberg acknowledges that there are times when we fail to live according to our most cherished values, he is seeking to develop a concrete tool for recognizing the dynamics at work in those situations. What he has developed is especially helpful for Christians when they get caught in cycles of self-blame and self-judgment, even when they believe that God has forgiven their sin. Though they know that they should let themselves be at peace under the mercy of God, they are unable to rest in that knowledge. Practicing self-empathy, striving to identify the unmet needs at work in their choices, gives them a practical tool for bringing their behavior into alignment with their deepest Christian beliefs. Here are the essential steps:[42]

1. Write down something you said or did which you now regret.

2. Write down all the thoughts and judgments you have about yourself regarding your behavior. Don't move into detached analysis or personal memories. Stay connected to the energy, the variety, and the intensity of all the self-judgments that come into your awareness.

3. Notice what you feel in your body. Try to identify what feelings are most alive. There might be a number of feelings connected to a single judgment or a number of judgments that bring up the same feeling.

4. Connect each feeling to an underlying need. When you notice a release or relaxation in your body, that means that you have connected with a true need.

5. Now stay connected to that need and deepen the empathy for yourself by imagining that need being fully met. Notice how your body feels when you imagine that the need is met.

6. This is the quality of life you are longing for. In other words, focus on the *presence* of the need as a personal value of yours, not on its *absence*, in this particular instance.

7. Notice how the need is an attribute of God's goodness and a gift from God's hand. Pray about this need and how much you long for it to be fulfilled. Meditate on its beauty and on the promise of God for this need to be satisfied when God's kingdom is fully lived out on earth as it is in heaven.

Self-Empathy as a Vital Practice for Christian Counselors

Among Christian counselors, caring for others is too frequently accompanied by neglecting self-care. Clergy suffer from high levels of stress, burnout, and depression. In fact, the statistics are alarming. A 2006 Episcopal

---

42. Several NVC trainers follow a format similar to this one in learning to transform self-judgments to underlying feelings, needs, and requests. For example, see Gill, Leu, and Morin, "Freeing Ourselves." This version represents my own synthesis of the steps involved in transforming self-judgments through self-empathy and connecting them to our life of faith.

Clergy Wellness Report found that stress is an emotional health risk for 73 percent of Episcopal priests and that Episcopal clergy experience significantly higher rates of depression than the overall population.[43] A 2002 study by Austin Seminary, which is affiliated with the Presbyterian Church (USA), found that nearly 20 percent of their graduates in pastoral ministry are not satisfied with their work. Forty-seven percent often feel drained in fulfilling their functions in their congregations, particularly in their attempts to manage interpersonal conflict. And 36 percent frequently experience stress from conflicting or ambiguous expectations at work.[44] Gwen W. Halaas, who has written extensively about the need for self-care among clergy within the Evangelical Lutheran Church of America (ELCA), summarizes current research on clergy wellness:

> Other studies of religious professionals found that Protestant clergy had the highest overall work-related stress and were next to the lowest in having personal resources to cope with the occupational strain. A study in 1987 found that the top three stressors for clergy were congregational conflicts and church conservatism, difficulties involved in parish commitments, and the emotional and time demands of crisis counseling. Researchers have found that one in three pastors leaving ordained ministry had family difficulties and that clergy rank third among professionals who are divorced. A study of male clergy and their wives found work-related stress on the family in two areas: the lack of available social support and the intrusion on family life. Finally, although clergy rank in the top 10 percent of the population in terms of education, their salaries rank only 325 out of 432 occupations.[45]

Self-empathy and the process of transforming self-judgments, though not a panacea for all the problems related to clergy wellness (or lack thereof), can support ministers and others in choosing a healthy life. After identifying and connecting with our own needs in self-empathy, we can make requests of ourselves or others to meet those needs. When deciding how to allocate our time and resources, we can weigh our needs, noticing which ones are most pressing at any given moment. These capacities can sustain Christian counselors in the midst of their daily activities. In the midst of conflict, when anxiety runs high, self-empathy

---

43. "Episcopal Clergy Wellness," 8.
44. Jinkins, *Survey of Recent Graduates*, 4.
45. Halaas, *Right Road*, 3.

can help us stay grounded in our most cherished values. When criticism comes our way, we can connect with our unmet needs—for understanding, support, appreciation, etc.—rather than blaming others, creating factions, or spiraling down into shame. In prayer, we can bring our needs to God, the source of all love. God's compassion then becomes the transcendent basis of our ability to have compassion on ourselves and others. God's forgiveness, mercy, and grace become the bedrock upon which our self-acceptance rests.

7

Paying Attention

The Art of Listening

Christian caregivers seek to orient persons toward God as the One who will provide for them. All ministry is Christ's ministry, in which the church is privileged to participate. In his book *Life Together*, Bonhoeffer theologically grounds our practice of listening to others in God's love for humanity. God demonstrates his love for us by listening to us when we pray. By analogy, we are to show our love for our brothers and sisters by listening to them.

In listening to others, spiritual caregivers need an empathetic imagination, and to set aside their own preoccupations. They seek to empty themselves in order to be fully present to the other. By attending to the other's story, they aim to create a bridge of understanding. What needs emerge in the narrative being told? What concerns might be brought before God in prayer? Since they aim to intercede on the other's behalf, caregivers stretch to hear the inarticulate longings beneath the needs that are expressed. They endeavor to deepen the other's connection with himself so that he might bring all of himself—his joys and sorrows, his fears and doubts, his gratitude, regret, and lament—before God.

At the same time, caregivers listen to everything that is said in the light of God's purpose and calling. There is a divine drama hidden in each person's story that cries out to be heard. Trusting that Jesus Christ is already at work in this situation, caregivers will seek guidance from God. Because the gospel addresses fundamental human needs—for forgiveness and reconciliation, for love and hope, for justice and mercy, in short, for salvation—they listen to God as well as to the other. They wait for a divine word. How might God be calling this person forth in and through this challenging situation? What word might offer comfort or hope in a day of trouble?

As caregivers listen on behalf of the other, they also monitor their own emotional reactions. How does this story touch them? Where are they moved or not moved by it? How do they enter it intelligently? Knowing how to listen to themselves gives them tools for distinguishing between the unresolved issues of the person they are seeking to serve and their own.

The key to spiritual listening lies in keeping our clear intention on being present for the other. When we pay more attention to ourselves than to the real needs of the other, we fail to hear the significance of what is being shared. Martin Buber tells of a time when he was distracted by his own inner life:

> What happened was no more than that one forenoon, after a morning of "religious" enthusiasm, I had a visit from an unknown young man, without being there in spirit. I certainly did not fail to let the meeting be friendly, I did not treat him any more remissly than all his contemporaries who were in the habit of seeking me out about this time of day. I conversed attentively and openly with him—only I omitted to guess the questions which he did not put. Later, not long after, I learned from one of his friends—he himself was no longer alive—the essential content of these questions; I learned that he had not come to me casually, but borne by destiny, not for a chat but for a decision. He had come to me; he had come in this hour. What do we expect when we are in despair and yet go to a man? Surely a presence by means of which we are told that nevertheless there is meaning.[1]

The young man died "not long after" this meeting. The unstated intimation is that he took his own life. He had come "not for a chat but for a decision"; he was in despair and yet sought something from Buber. Elsewhere Buber acknowledges that the meeting was "an event of judgment"[2] for him. Thereafter, he understood faith not as the pursuit of ecstatic experiences but as a life of attentiveness to others, the life of "I and thou" in encounter.

This incident marked a major turning point in Buber's theological understanding, a turning away from otherworldly ecstasy and a turning toward the concrete other whom God has sent. Buber suggests that the young man needed a human presence that would convey a sense of purpose. He needed a trusted other to embody faith in the meaningfulness

---

1. Buber, *Between Man and Man*, quoted in Lake, *Clinical Theology*, 6.
2. Buber, *Between Man and Man*, quoted in Lake, *Clinical Theology*, 6.

of life. A Christian appropriation of Buber's insight might suggest a person who embodies the hope of Christ in full knowledge of the shadow of the cross.

The presence that Christian caregivers are called to offer, therefore, cannot be learned simply as a technique. There is an offering of oneself in Christ that cannot be created simply by learning skills. Spiritual caregivers cannot convey "a presence by means of which [others are] told that nevertheless there is meaning" unless they understand themselves as participating in a ministry not their own, but Christ's. They cannot manufacture meaning out of their own resources. The seventeenth-century French priest St. Vincent de Paul said, "If God is the center of your life, no words are necessary. Your mere presence will touch hearts."[3] Yet no mere creatures can make God the center of their lives simply by willing it. Christ alone lived a life of obedience that truly had God at its center. Not by their own power but by virtue of their union with Christ, caregivers may witness to a compassionate presence that their own only dimly reflects.

From Empathy to Resonant Empathy

There is a spiritual dimension to every story we hear. But it is wise not to begin there lest we fall into the dead end of what has come to be called "spiritual bypassing." This term, introduced in the 1980s by the psychologist, John Welwood, speaks of it as "a tendency to use spiritual ideas and practices to sidestep or avoid facing unresolved emotional issues, psychological wounds, and unfinished developmental tasks."[4] When we begin with resonant empathy, spiritual bypassing is simply not possible because we give our attention precisely to those emotional issues, psychological wounds, and developmental tasks that need to be faced.

In the last chapter, we differentiated three related concepts: sympathy, empathy, and compassion. We argued that sympathy arises naturally in

---

3. Attard, "Saint Vincent de Paul."

4. Wikipedia, "Spiritual Bypass," https://en.wikipedia.org/wiki/Spiritual_bypass. An example would be one in which a person is urged to forgive someone who has hurt or offended them, without ever acknowledging the underlying hurt and anger that fester under the surface. Genuine forgiveness is something that comes to a person as a spiritual gift, not something accomplished through stronger and more determined "will power." See "Forgiving Abusive Parents," in Hunsinger, *Bearing the Unbearable*, chapter 4.

secure attachment relationships; empathy is a finely honed skill; and compassion is a spiritual gift, which requires the presence of the Holy Spirit.

The purpose of this chapter is to revisit some of the key features of empathy as a "finely-honed skill," and then turn our focus toward the practice of "resonant empathy," as a particular form of empathic attunement that lends itself to engaging the spiritual essence of traumatic affliction and its healing.

One of the best descriptions of empathy that I know of is that presented by A. J. van den Blink in his article, "Empathy and Diversity: Problems and Possibilities." Empathy, argues van den Blink, enables connection between people who have different cultural assumptions.

- Empathy is "inherently relational," making it the "preferred method of cross-cultural engagement."
- It involves "constant reciprocal feedback" between the persons involved. It is a *mutual* undertaking, not something that one person actively does to another who passively receives it. The presence of empathy is felt when there is a sense of rapport between persons, a mutual responsiveness.
- Empathy is a "way of knowing." It is a way of attuning oneself to another's inner and outer world in such a way that the other feels understood and valued in his uniqueness.
- Empathy enhances the sense of self of both persons, heightening each person's uniqueness even as it creates a bond between them.
- Empathy "does not imply approval or agreement." Understanding another from within the other's own frame of reference does not mean that we agree with them. Conflicts can and do arise even when empathic skill is highly developed.
- Empathy is affected by the total context in which it occurs. "There is no such thing as disembodied empathy."
- Empathy is a "respectful and caring exploration" of another's life, attempting "to discern the shape of his experience." In all empathic relating, self-disclosure and feedback are essential.[5]

In her book, *Your Resonant Self*, Sarah Peyton describes "resonance" as being different from empathy, claiming that one can have empathy

---

5. van den Blink, "Empathy Amid Diversity," 7–8.

for someone without the *mutuality* and reciprocal feedback that van den Blink identifies as central to the concept. Peyton writes: "I can have empathy for homeless people when I drive by them, and they will never know." According to my understanding, Peyton would be feeling "sympathy" for them, not empathy, because, like van den Blink, I see empathy as a *mutual* undertaking that Peyton reserves for her concept of "resonance."[6]

I believe that Peyton's conceptual development of resonance *builds on* the conceptual resources of empathy, at least those such as van den Blink sets forth, rather than *diverging* from them. In the appendix of her book, *Your Resonant Self*, Peyton describes resonance as: "the experience of sensing that another being fully understands us and sees us with emotional warmth and generosity. It is the sense that *we know* that they could try on our skin and that our feelings and longings would make sense to them."[7]

Peyton's development of the conceptual resources of resonance as well as her expansion of concrete practical skills go far beyond anything developed by van den Blink (or others) in their discussions of empathy. After many previous years devoted to honing my empathic skills, encountering Peyton's creative elaborations of resonance has enabled me to work with more precision, depth, versatility, and skill.

Peyton's singular conceptual understanding of "resonance" weaves together three different complex strands of thought, each of which contributes substantively to the skills she teaches. First, she draws on extensive research in the field of interpersonal neurobiology. This strand of her thought is then woven together with her knowledge of family constellations and her skill in facilitating them. A third strand of her expertise has evolved from her experience as a trainer of nonviolent communication. The interweaving of these three theoretical strands makes her contribution both unique and powerful. Her integrative, interdisciplinary approach in fact lays a strong foundation for grasping a sense of the complexity of the biological, interpersonal, familial, societal, and intergenerational impacts of trauma.[8]

---

6. Peyton, *Your Resonant Self*, xxiv.
7. Peyton, *Your Resonant Self*, 293.
8. Interpersonal neurobiology, begun in the late 1990s by Dr. Daniel Siegel, Peyton describes as "the study of the relational brain—not just the brain by itself but how brains affect one another—which synthesizes the fields of cognitive and social neuroscience, attachment research, complexity theory and psychology" (Peyton, *Your Resonant Self*, 291). Her work as a trained facilitator of "family constellations" arises from the creative thinking of Bert Hellinger, a German Catholic priest who later became a

The woven strands of Sarah Peyton's interdisciplinary approach also position us to unearthing the spiritual treasures that often remain hidden under a person's emotional tangles, physical symptoms, and baffling developmental obstacles. When I work as a spiritual director with other Christians, I seek to place Peyton's skills of resonance into an explicitly Christian context, in order to identify the spiritual heart of the matter. Together, we might seek to discern where and how God may be at work, or ask for God's blessing in the midst of what would otherwise seem to be hopeless. When I work with non-Christians, I use resonance to build an emotional and spiritual bridge with them, as I listen attentively to the ways that they find meaning that is in alignment with their own religious inheritance or their sense of mystery and awe.[9]

An adequate description of the depth, richness, and complexity of Peyton's achievement unfortunately lies outside the scope of this chapter.[10] I would like simply to describe three key elements that may help orient spiritual caregivers as they learn the art of paying attention. I will draw on her discussion of the importance of *attunement* and *accompaniment,* and then turn to a brief overview of the scope of her work in

---

psychotherapist. He is known for his pioneering work in investigating intergenerational trauma in the post-WWII era, as he worked with the children and grandchildren of Holocaust victims, alongside the children and grandchildren of German Nazis. "Nonviolent Communication" is a theoretical model with highly developed concrete, practical skills, created by Marshall B. Rosenberg, in which he teaches people to recognize the needs and values that lie under expressed feelings, which not only enables more clarity and ease in communication but also helps resolve (both internal and interpersonal) conflict. See Siegel, *Developing Mind*; Hellinger, *Love's Hidden Symmetry*; and Rosenberg, *Nonviolent Communication*.

9. See also chapter 8 of this volume, "Respecting Ourselves as Christian Therapists."

10. For example, beyond what is presented here, Peyton includes reflection on the impact of ACEs (Adverse Childhood Experiences) on the entire lifespan of those who have suffered from childhood trauma. She also helps people to identify and understand the impact of their own early attachment style (with parents and other early "attachment figures"). She draws on Eugene Gendlin's understanding of the "felt sense" in the body. She works creatively with Ruth Lanius' research on the sense of self that requires an integration of time, thought, body, and emotion; Stephen Porges' polyvagal theory; as well as brain research that analyzes the differentiated functions between the "instrumental" and the "relational" brain. She introduces her students to thinkers such as Daniel Siegel, Peter Levine, Allan Schore, Moshe Szyf, among others. She has found thoughtful and sensitive ways to teach about white privilege, especially in the United States, and the enormous impact of racism on the overall health of people of color. She has personally volunteered for many years to teach prisoners about resonance. As a native of Alaska, she grew up speaking both English and Russian.

resonant empathy. In conclusion, I will place the conversation back into its larger framework of Christian theology and spirituality.

Attunement

When we *attune* ourselves to another human being, we focus our attention on them and allow ourselves to be changed by their presence. We enter into relational space by making eye contact and noticing how our body responds to their presence. They are not simply an "object" in our world, something to be manipulated or made use of in some way. Each human being is completely unique, with their own singular life experience, biological and cultural inheritance, and interpersonal history.

Sarah Peyton describes it like this: "*Attunement* is the experience of someone focusing on us with warmth, respect, and curiosity. This person wonders what it is like to be us, using all available human sensitivities to tune into us."[11] Human warmth and care are conveyed, not only by our words, but also by our tone of voice, facial expression, body language, and eye contact. Peyton teaches basic skills of attunement through various exercises in which, among other things, we learn to pay attention to how our body sensations change simply by noticing how another's presence affects us. What do we notice in our torso (abdomen and chest) and in our facial expression? Are there places of tension or relaxation? What do we notice about how our breathing might have changed? How might these sensations shift as we hear the person share a brief story about "the worst moment" of something that happened during the last week? Do we make a space inside ourselves to be with whatever difficult truth the other might be experiencing without trying to "fix" or change them in any way?[12]

The Christian philosopher and theologian, Simone Weil, also speaks of attunement, as she grounds it in her desire to be of service to her neighbor.[13] The care and respect that she offers her neighbor follow

---

11. Peyton, *Your Resonant Self*, 43.

12. These questions are paraphrases from skills that Peyton gives her students opportunities to practice in break-out rooms on Zoom calls in her webinars. See sarahpeyton.com.

13. The scriptural warrant underlying her approach likely comes from the Gospel according to Matthew 22:37–39: "You shall love the Lord your God with all our heart, and with all your soul, and with all your mind. This is the great and first commandment. And a second is like it: You shall love your neighbor as yourself."

the love she bears for God and indicates the core spiritual values that her attunement seeks to embody. Her guidance in the art of paying attention captures the essential truth that while the neighbor is a person, "exactly like us," he or she is now marked "by affliction."

> The love of our neighbor in all its fullness simply means being able to say to him: "What are you going through?" It is a recognition that the sufferer exists, not only as a unit in a collection, or a specimen from the social category labeled "unfortunate," but as a person, exactly like us, who was one day stamped with a special mark by affliction. For this reason it is enough, but it is indispensable, to know how to look at him in a certain way. This way of looking is first of all attentive. The soul empties itself of all its own contents in order to receive into itself the being it is looking at, just as he is, in all his truth. Only he who is capable of attention can do this.[14]

This way of welcoming the other with warmth is also reminiscent of Karl Barth's understanding of *mitmenschlichkeit* (co-humanity) when he writes: "Human nature is the human being himself. But a person is what he is freely and from the heart. And freely and from the heart he is what he is in the secret of the encounter with his fellow-human being in which the latter is welcome, and he is with him gladly."[15]

Accompaniment

Weil's question, "What are you going through?" is an open-ended question that recognizes—and thus affirms—the otherness of the other. Though in one sense the other is "exactly like us," since we are both human beings with human longings, suffering, and joy, there is also a clear recognition of the other's pain in our desire to see them in their particularity as one who bears affliction. It shows a commitment to care for others in their uniqueness and to accompany them in their suffering.

Sarah Peyton discusses the neuroscientific basis of what enables someone to accompany another with warmth and gladness. She teaches

---

14. Weil, "Reflections on the Right Use," 115.

15. See page 84 of this volume for a discussion of Barth's theological anthropology, which captures the essential quality of welcoming the other with warmth. Barth writes that we welcome the other "gladly," which is "the secret of the whole." Barth, *Church Dogmatics* 3/2, 264. See also: Romans 15:7. "Therefore welcome one another as Christ has welcomed you, for the glory of God."

resonant healing practitioners how to widen their "window of welcome" for those who seek to heal from traumatic suffering. In order to welcome another, our own nervous system needs to be in a state of *social engagement*. When our nervous system is calm and centered in social engagement, we feel safe, creative, and responsive to others. Trust in our own belonging is not in question and we are able to be authentically ourselves ("freely and from the heart"). Our voice is alive and our breathing is relaxed.

Sympathetic activation of the nervous system happens when we experience slight to severe stress. It is the state in which our nervous system prepares us to fight or to flee. We shift out of relational space with the other whenever we do not feel safe or trust that we matter. We might feel a sense of alarm and of being all alone in the world (what Peyton calls "alarmed aloneness") with our troubles and self-preoccupation. Our thoughts might be racing, our breathing shallow, with our heart rate increasing. The body tenses up in various ways. In this state, it is impossible to give our attention to another in an open, responsive, curious, and warm way.

Immobilization is the state of the nervous system sometimes referred to as the "freeze" state. We might feel overwhelmed, hopeless, helpless, dissociated, trapped, numb, resigned, or generally "shut down." Peyton describes it in this way: "The body's response if Fight/Flight/Alarmed Aloneness is not effective: a shutdown into helplessness during stress. This state includes shock, hopelessness, frozen immobility, and dissociation."[16]

"*The window of welcome* . . . specifies the emotional expression and intensity that can actually be met with warmth and understanding."[17] We first learn to regulate our emotional expression in order to keep ourselves within the bounds of what is welcome in our family of origin, in order to belong. Studies have shown that babies at just four months of age have already learned to stay within their mother's (or mothering person's) window of welcome. Already at four months, they have learned to sense the kind and intensity of emotional expression that it is okay to have in order to belong in this particular family.[18] Peyton writes, "For humans, fitting in and belonging *are almost the same thing as survival*. . . . People are made to live with and be loved by other people in the social world. When children are securely attached, they can reach out for support from their adults in difficult moments."[19]

16. Peyton, *Your Resonant Self Workbook*, 281.
17. Peyton, *Your Resonant Self*, 216.
18. Peyton, *Your Resonant Self*, 217.
19. Peyton, *Your Resonant Self*, 216.

For example, if a mother (or father, or grandparent, i.e., primary "attachment figures") nearly always become agitated, angry, or overwhelmed by their baby's frustrated cries and cannot figure out what the baby needs, the infant will learn that such emotional expression is not welcome. Depending on the parents' own unresolved issues, children will grow up doing whatever they can to fit into their parents' window of welcome. Some parents might be unable to tolerate their child's anger and frustration, while other parents cannot bear it when their child is sad. Still others might be unable to welcome their child's exuberant energy and joy. As a result, children will wrench themselves into emotional knots in order to be loved and accepted by those upon whom their very life depends.

As spiritual caregivers who seek to accompany others in their emotional and spiritual unfolding, we need to have a wide window of welcome for the entire gamut of emotional expression. This means that it is essential for us to do our own work, which begins with widening our window of welcome for *ourselves*. When we allow *ourselves* to feel the full range of human emotion, then our welcome for *others* will also be wider and warmer. We can fully resonate with others when they are feeling numb, helpless, or hopeless while staying calm and centered ourselves. We can accurately acknowledge their anger and fury, their sadness and loneliness, their grief, fear, or disgust. We can also welcome and resonate with their feelings of pure joy, take delight in their sense of playfulness, and bask in their appreciation for beauty. As we learn the work of self-resonance, we will also learn to enjoy our own aliveness and emergence into our full personhood as we also find deep reservoirs of care for others.[20]

---

20. Neuroscientist Jaak Panksepp, in his research of the human brain (as well as other mammals) differentiated seven neuropathways (or networks) in the brain that he called our "circuits of emotion and motivation." These emotional networks are "hard wired" in our brains: seeking, panic/grief, fear, rage, lust (sexuality and emergence), care, and play. Peyton has added "disgust" to this list because of its essential role in learning to defend our own boundaries, to say "no," and in keeping ourselves safe and healthy. See Panksepp and Biven, *Archaeology of Mind*. Peyton works extensively with all the "circuits of emotion and motivation," while teaching her students how to recognize each of them in each of the nervous system states: social engagement, sympathetic activation, and immobilization.

Resonant Empathy

With help from a resonant empathy partner, we can learn to identify our own blocked emotional capacities, which will widen our window of welcome. We grow in self-trust as we learn to tolerate feelings that were somehow forbidden or scary for us to express in our original family. One mode of resonance that Sarah Peyton teaches is in learning to notice and acknowledge our body sensations. People carry habitual stress in their bodies in different places and in various levels of intensity. Some possible areas to check:

- Do you notice any constriction or contraction in your body when you feel anxious (e.g., shoulders, neck, buttocks tightening, feet curling, as well as stomach in knots, or your heart feeling like it is encased in lead?)
- Does your jaw clamp down when you start to feel something you don't want to feel?
- Does it sometimes feel like your heart is going to jump out of your chest because it is beating so hard?
- Do you find yourself literally holding your breath, so as not to cry, or digging your fingernails into your palms to stop whatever uncomfortable feeling might come up?
- Does it feel like you actually "leave" your body because what is happening feels so intolerable? (i.e., what psychologists refer to as "dissociation.")
- Can you bring warmth and compassion to *yourself* when you discover emotions that are difficult for you to bear?
- Are there certain feelings that were taboo (or dangerous) to feel or express in your family of origin? Did you banish them from your awareness or make an "unconscious vow" never to express, or perhaps never even feel that emotion?[21]

---

21. Peyton describes these unconscious contracts (or sacred vows) in this way: "When human beings have a difficult time and are too alone, it is the nature of our brains to try to prevent this from ever happening again. So, we encode a behavioral agreement, a patterned behavioral response, as a kind of program to keep the difficult moments of danger, loss, shame, or vulnerability away" (Peyton, *Your Resonant Self*, 44). See our brief discussion of unconscious contracts or sacred vows below.

Since learning to notice body sensations is one of the first steps in learning to be resonant with ourselves, it is also a necessary step in learning how to use *our own body sensations* to connect with what *others* might be feeling.

When we attune ourselves to others, when we accompany them through the various hills and valleys of their emotional landscape, we learn how to acknowledge the full scope of their life experience. They begin to feel their previously rejected emotions. They learn how to make sense of the choices they have made in their lives, and learn to trust themselves and not be bogged down with worry about the possible judgments of others. If they have regret about a past choice, they learn how not to judge or berate themselves, avoiding seemingly endless spirals of shame. Instead, they find the courage to feel the intensity of their emotions, and to acknowledge any of the circuits that might have motivated their choices, especially the four that are so greatly activated in trauma: grief (including "alarmed aloneness"), rage, fear, and disgust. This kind of acknowledgment and exploration is not possible without a trusted companion whose presence and care provide a safe container for what would otherwise be overwhelming or terrifying.

I think of resonant empathy as a form of contemplative listening, in which we walk *alongside* the people who come to us, neither ahead of them nor behind them. Our aim is to give them an experience of being understood, of knowing that they make sense because together we can make sense of their life experience. We are not trying to figure out what is wrong with them. We are not coaching them to find solutions to their problems; we are not even trying to offer them inspiration; we are simply trying to understand them as if from the inside. As they internalize our warmth and care (an outer source of resonance), they begin to build their own Resonating Self Witness (RSW), an inner resource that becomes available to them in future times of stress or emotional turmoil.

Whenever we give others the gift of warm resonance, new neural pathways will grow in their brains, enabling them to grow *through* painful experiences or old patterns they have been stuck in, to become freer, more emotionally present human beings. Their reactivity to emotional stressors will decrease as they gain a sense of safety and belonging in their interpersonal relationships. This is what Robert Stolorow calls "finding a relational home." Indeed, his very definition of trauma is the "severe emotional pain that cannot find a relational home in which it can be held."²² We provide just such a "relational home" for others as we accompany them through the emotional pain of traumatic suffering.

Sarah Peyton has developed a wide variety of online workshops in which she teaches nine forms of resonant language:

1. Identifying accurately our feelings and needs;
2. Body sensations that enable us to connect brain, heart, and viscera, to be whole;
3. Finding a fresh metaphor that captures a sense of the whole story, or a portion of it;
4. Impossible dream guesses, which open our imaginations in a playful way;
5. Poetry and the poetic imagination, which enable us to enter deeply into an experience;
6. Acknowledging what is, which acknowledges the truth of our actual lived experience;
7. Swearing, which helps capture intensity of feeling;
8. Humor, which widens our perspective or shifts it with surprising moments of delight;
9. I-you language, which opens up the relational space, enabling honest expression and unblocking the flow of energy and feeling.²³

All of these resonant skills contribute to larger complex practices of healing and resilience, in which people are accompanied as they travel imaginatively to an earlier era of their lives, as they learn to identify with precision particular moments in their history when they were severely wounded emotionally.²⁴ When accompanied with resonance, they dis-

---

22. Stolorow, *Trauma and Human Existence*, 10.

23. Peyton describes resonant language as "language that shifts us into relational space and includes wondering about and naming emotion; dreams, longings, and needs; body sensations; what is happening relationships; and fresh metaphor, visual memory, and poetry" (Peyton, *Your Resonant Self*, 293). See also Figure 1.5 in Peyton, *Your Resonant Self Workbook*, 9.

24. See especially the work of neuroscientist Ruth Lanius, on the traumatized sense of self that needs to be integrated "across time, thought, body and emotion." Peyton works with all four aspects, but her work with what she calls "time travel" to rescue the younger self who once was confronted with suffering that was too difficult or overwhelming to bear alone, is especially noteworthy. When the younger self (often a

cover possible "unconscious contracts" or "sacred vows" that they made when they were younger as a way to survive an impossible situation. While the unconscious contract once served them to get through truly unbearable circumstances, it later becomes something that constricts them. When they manage to discover the vow that had been made outside their awareness when they were young children (sometimes even before they had language to express it), they can then assess whether this is a contract that they wish to continue to keep. Usually the cost of keeping it is seen to be too high and the longing to be free of it comes fully into awareness. Alternatively, they might also see the vital emotional needs that the vow has served and may not be ready to release it. Yet, as they assess the enormity of the cost to their aliveness, they may find themselves well on their way toward claiming new blessings: to become freer and more creative, more responsive, relational, and flexible, as well as more capable of taking responsibility for their life choices.[25]

Conclusion

Every emotional issue we face has an underlying spiritual dimension to it. As I explore my emotional life I discover that at bottom, underneath all the tumultuous emotions, at heart, I need faith, hope, and love. I need to trust God's compassion and care; I need the love of others, and I need hope the way I need oxygen. I need forgiveness and repentance. I need the new life that only God can truly give, although we also need other human beings to pave the way for our ability to receive these gifts. I need worship and prayer. I need to trust God as my ultimate relational home and God as one who fully hears and understands the deep longings of my heart.[26]

---

child of a particular age) has resonant accompaniment, the person is able to integrate emotional states that previously could not be borne. This aspect of her thinking came to Sarah Peyton through studying with Susan Skye, an inspired and inventive trainer of nonviolent communication, who had also studied neuroscience. Lanius and Buczynski, "Rethinking Trauma."

25. The interested reader can read Sarah Peyton's groundbreaking book, *Your Resonant Self*. See also the companion workbook, *Your Resonant Self Workbook*. Although these two books cover much of the same material, they do so with different emphases and both repay serious study. See also her website online: http://sarahpeyton.com.

26. Each of the circuits of emotion that we have been exploring may have a corresponding spiritual gift or blessing that is revealed as we find our capacity to welcome it: *Seeking* at its spiritual depth has to do with finding our meaning and purpose in life, corresponding to a Christian understanding of *vocation* or calling. The *panic/*

Koinonia means resonant empathy at the interpersonal level and spiritual communion and prayer at the spiritual level. When we empty ourselves of our own preoccupations in order to be fully present to another, we are, in our own small way, following the example of Christ, who emptied himself of his equality with God in order to participate fully in our human plight (Phil 2). By showing tender concern for others, we point beyond ourselves to the listening God. Such conversations take place not for their own sake, but as a "sign and witness" to the God who takes our human needs and longings to heart. As members of Christ's body, we participate in Christ's tenderheartedness. When we serve others through this kind of caring listening, we strengthen faith in our God who hears every anguished cry.

---

grief circuit is in sympathetic activation when it is coping with a broken heart, evoking a longing for love and a sense of belonging. *Fear* helps us become aware of our fundamental need for trust and faith. *Rage* at its depth seeks justice and *disgust* longs for truth. *Sexuality/emergence* longs for authenticity in relationship and finding one's uniqueness and connection with others in community, or true koinonia. The spiritual gift of the *care* circuit is love, compassion, and companionship, and the gifts of the play circuit are inspiration and joy.

8

Respecting Ourselves as Christian Therapists

After recounting the labyrinthine path of his intellectual formation as a practical theologian, Ray Anderson raises the core question that he wants to address: How can a Christian psychologist function with integrity when working therapeutically with non-Christians?[1]

Professor Anderson wants to affirm the essentially spiritual nature of what it means to be human as the "common ground" on which both Christians and non-Christians can meet. By "spiritual," Anderson means that we are incapable of being (or becoming) human apart from our relationship to others. We are created for relationship with others which is the very "basis for our own spiritual identity."[2] As he says elsewhere, "The divine image is not a religious quality of the individual person, but a spiritual reality expressed through the interchange of persons in relation."[3]

All persons are thus spiritual; religious persons express that spirituality in a particular way, through various rituals, practices, and beliefs. If a Christian therapist works with someone of another (or no) religious background, Anderson wants that therapist to respect the otherness of the other and not impose theological concepts or religious definitions that the other might find alien. At the same time, he is concerned about the conceptual adequacy of so-called "secular" psychology which, he

---

1. In an issue of the journal *Edification: Journal of the Society for Christian Psychology*, entitled "Special Issue: The Work of Ray S. Anderson," Professor Anderson invited eleven practical theologians and spiritual caregivers to comment on his article, "Toward a Holistic Psychology: Putting All the Pieces in Their Proper Place." This chapter is my response to his paper in the journal.

2. Anderson, *Spiritual Caregiving*, 15.

3. Anderson, *Self Care*.

argues, cannot afford to dismiss or ignore our essentially spiritual nature if it is to be a true scientific endeavor. ("The nature of the object to be known determines the method for knowing."[4]) If the object to be known is the human being and if human beings are essentially spiritual, then psychology needs to include spirituality in its mode of inquiry.

In other words, Anderson's "holistic" psychology is an attempt to make the spirituality of persons the central key that identifies their humanity, whether or not they are "religious." Both Christian and non-Christian therapists can operate from such a "holistic" theoretical framework because all persons are spiritual. Following Bonhoeffer, Anderson dubs his holistic psychology as "nonreligious." Anderson quotes Bonhoeffer: "The individual personal spirit lives solely by virtue of sociality. Only in interaction with one another is the spirit of human beings ever revealed; this is the essence of spirit, to be oneself through being in the other."[5]

The problem with this as a definition of spirituality, as I see it, is the ambiguity in the word "sociality." If Bonhoeffer (and Anderson) mean that we live solely by virtue of our relationships with God and other human beings, then I am in agreement. I don't want the vertical dimension to be collapsed into the horizontal. For if "God is spirit, and those who worship him must worship in spirit and truth" (John 4:24), if we live by virtue of God's Spirit being breathed into our mortal frame, and if we die by virtue of its departure, then our "spirituality" is completely dependent upon the Holy Spirit of God. We are spiritual beings solely by the power of God and we grow spiritually only by virtue of our relationship to God and others. I agree with Anderson's (and Bonhoeffer's) point that Adam was not fully human apart from his partnership with Eve, but his relationship with God nevertheless remained primary. Even our (horizontal) relationships to others (*koinonia*) are mediated by the Spirit. The Holy Spirit not only binds the Father to the Son, but also Jesus Christ to the church, the church to Jesus Christ, the members of his body to one another, and the church to the world.

I must admit that I find Anderson's terminology confusing. In particular, his use of the phrase "nonreligious Christian psychology" is mystifying to me (as is his earlier term, "secular sacrament"). If a psychology is Christian, how then is it nonreligious? What would it mean for holistic psychology "to communicate, confer and affirm in a nonreligious

---

4. Anderson, *Spiritual Caregiving*, 3.
5. Anderson, *Spiritual Caregiving*, 15.

way what in theology we call grace, forgiveness, and even absolution"?[6] If someone has harmed me and I want to forgive him, by offering him the grace and forgiveness of God, how can I do all this apart from language whose web of meaning is intrinsically and irreducibly Christian? How might I communicate this in a "nonreligious" way? If I use words to communicate my intent (to offer absolution), then I cannot imagine those words apart from their specifically Christian (and therefore religious) meaning. I can communicate acceptance, unconditional positive regard, solidarity, even genuine love toward this person who has hurt me, but if I want to stand with him before God as a fellow sinner, not standing in judgment of him but assuring him of God's forgiveness as well as my own, I don't see how I can do this without using specific theological terms, made meaningful through centuries of distinctively Christian use.

One might be able to communicate something *similar* to grace, forgiveness, and absolution, in other words, but the radical loss of the multilayered richness of context-dependent theological meaning in Anderson's proposal concerns me.

None of this seems necessary. Why can't a Christian psychologist be fully and wholeheartedly Christian when meeting with people of other faiths (or no faith)? Why reduce what we have to offer to some common denominator? We can be ourselves in full integrity, respecting the beliefs of others even as we also respect our own. Naturally, therapy is no place for proselytizing, but a Christian therapist should be free to draw on his or her own distinctive theological understanding when it would illuminate or deepen the conversation. There are some things that just cannot be "translated" into another idiom. As I understand it, the uniqueness of the gospel is essentially untranslatable. It can only be approximated in other terms. As Barth writes:

> What other word speaks of the covenant between God and man? What other of its character as the work of God, and indeed of the effective and omnipotent grace of God on the basis of eternal love and election? What other of the fulfillment of this covenant in the humiliation of God for the exaltation of man? What other of comprehensive justification of man by God and sanctification for Him? What other of the fact that this reconciliation of God with man and man with God is no mere idea

---

6. Anderson, *Spiritual Caregiving*, 28.

but a once-for-all event? . . . What other is directed so concretely to each and all men?[7]

Much would be lost and little gained were we to give up the distinctiveness of the gospel.

Anderson's exegesis of Jesus' "spiritual but nonreligious" conversation with the Samaritan woman at the well seems to miss the point. The point of the conversation is neither "religious" nor "nonreligious," as I read it, but rather the self-revelation of Jesus as the Messiah to one whom the Jews would have considered a "sinner" (one of dubious character, a woman and a Samaritan). Moral rectitude is not a requirement for spiritual communion with the Lord. Anderson claims that the "transforming nature of this spiritual encounter at a purely human level led her to confess that he was the Messiah."[8] But how could this spiritual encounter have taken place "at a purely human level" since it took place with One who is uniquely human and divine? "No one can say 'Jesus is Lord' except by the Holy Spirit" (1 Cor 12:3).

Similarly, to reduce sin simply to a "distortion of human spirituality" seems to miss the very essence of the concept. As I argue in my book, *Pray Without Ceasing: Revitalizing Pastoral Care*:

> We must recognize that sin . . . pertains primarily to God and only then to human relationships. The horizontal axis, so to speak, derives meaning from the vertical axis. . . . Scripture teaches that disorder in our relationships with others is a symptom of estrangement from God. It is our connection to God that is primary and fundamental. When that is distorted, we cannot even relate to ourselves in a wholesome way.[9]

Once again, I find myself worried about losing the distinctiveness of Christian language about sin. I do, however, share Anderson's concern for understanding sin, not as an individual matter, but primarily as something that occurs between or among persons. None of us is exempt from the corporate, even universal, dimension of human sin. Yet its primary meaning is not social or moral, but theological and spiritual.

I am enriched when Buddhists are Buddhists, Hindus are Hindus, Muslims are Muslims, and Jews are Jews. I have learned about the distinctiveness of my faith by listening to those who follow other paths. Why

---

7. Barth, *Church Dogmatics* 4/1,107–8.
8. Anderson, *Spiritual Caregiving*, 27.
9. Hunsinger, *Pray Without Ceasing*, 159–60.

can't Christian therapists be fully Christian and respect others as fellow human beings made in the image of God, seeking to live out their calling as best they understand it, even as I seek to live out mine?

Perhaps I am misconstruing Anderson's argument. Certainly, there is much to ponder here. I have learned a great deal from Ray Anderson over the years and am deeply grateful for his gifts. I look forward to being further instructed by his response.

9

Vocation

An Inexpressible Gift and Joyous Task

Vocation: An Inexpressible Gift

> I sought the Lord, and afterward I knew,
> he moved my soul to seek him, seeking me;
> it was not I that found, O Savior true;
> no, I was found of thee.[1]

I have long been fascinated by a paradox that lies right at the heart of our calling to ministry. While it is true that the life of faith is riddled through and through with paradox, I find myself pondering one particular paradox as I think about what it means to help young people to discover the call of God in their lives: namely the mystery of divine and human action in the discernment of God's call.

How vividly I remember my own sense of call, coming to me in such an ordinary way out of the blue after so many years of searching, worrying, fretting, investigating, and wondering what it was that I was meant to do in this world. Then one fine October day, one of those "Mary-Queen-of-Heaven-Blue" days in Minnesota, when the air was crisp and the sun was bright, everything fell into place. I remember how distinctly etched against the sky each of the individual leaves on the trees were. I remember how it felt as if I were floating a few inches above the earth, as if my feet weren't actually touching the ground. And I remember how the cool, clear air in the world around me seemed to match a sense of inner spaciousness and feeling of freedom within.

---

1. Routley, "I Sought the Lord," 162.

After searching for so many years, it was as if I had turned a corner that day and there it was, given to me with such clarity, a complete gift. After so much effort, this was entirely effortless. It fell into my lap. Looking back now, more than fifty years later, I can see how that day changed the course of my entire life. Sometimes I wonder how my life would have evolved if I had not met that stranger that afternoon, with whom I spoke for twenty short minutes. But every time I try to imagine it, I am thrown into a place of complete wonder; it is like trying to imagine myself not being myself.

After that day, I made decisions to be sure, one after another, as I responded to what I had heard that day. But the perception has never left me: the call of God is an astonishing gift long before it becomes a human task. The task—even the many tasks which followed as I began to live out what was given me that day—hardly seems worth mentioning by comparison with the magnitude of the gift. And yet, here is what is so curious, if I hadn't been actively seeking and listening, would I have been in the position to receive the gift that God had prepared for me that day?

That's the paradox: how can something be so wondrously and completely a divine gift and yet also completely a human task and responsibility? For if I hadn't been searching for my life's work all those years, would I actually have heard God's call to me that October afternoon? Could any of it have happened as it did? It is such an imponderable mystery right there in the middle of my own life story, the event of discovering what I was meant to do with my life.

And so now I wonder about the next generation. How do we teach them about this paradox? How do we teach them both to hasten and to wait, really to trust that God will speak to them, and yet also urge them to map out their life plans as best they can by exploring and developing their gifts and interests? How do we teach them truly to ponder the question in their hearts, listening for God to guide them to their vocation, not simply a career to pursue or a way to make a living, but the discovery of their life's path, the flourishing of their uniqueness, that sense of *"yes, this is what I was put on earth to do"*?

One of the texts read at my ordination service speaks of just this kind of paradox, this mystery that lies at the heart of discerning our vocation. It is from Paul's letter to the Philippians. Since it immediately follows that wonderful hymn about Christ's self-emptying—not counting equality with God a thing to be grasped, but emptying himself, taking the form of a servant—it can easily be overlooked as something worth pondering in its own right. But it is well worth thinking about as we consider the task of helping young people find their true calling. Paul writes: "Therefore, my beloved, as you have always obeyed, so now, not only as in my presence but much more in my absence, work out your own salvation with fear and trembling; for God is at work in you, both to will and to work for his good pleasure" (Phil 2:12–13). Paul is describing here the paradox of grace that suffuses all that we do in the Christian life: the nitty-gritty working out of our salvation occurs in and through our imperfect, faltering human choices. But hidden from our eyes, God is the chief actor at work within us, sometimes despite and even against us, both willing and working out that salvation for his own good pleasure. The salvation which comes to us in the midst of our fear and trembling is at once completely God's gracious work and yet, mysteriously, also something in which we actively participate. We certainly are not the ones to bring it about, yet we need to be there, actively seeking, responding, listening all the time, participating in a profound mystery, the mystery of God at work in and through us.

The vocation we are given by God as disciples of Jesus Christ is both a divine gift and a human task. The Gospel first comes to us as a wondrous gift, freely given, something which we receive by the mercy of God. That alone is an imponderable mystery. How is it that one person is open to hearing the Gospel when another isn't? How can it be that one hears it, and it gives him life when his sisters and brothers, children of the same mother and father, neither hear, nor believe, nor receive it with joy? The calling of God is an inexpressible gift. As we hear and receive it and then weave it into our very identity and sense of purpose in life, it also becomes our joyous task. Only as we ourselves actually live by the Gospel, only as we accept it as our daily bread, can we also share it with those who are hungry. For, asks St. Paul, "What have you that you have not received?" (1 Cor 4:7).

I will first focus on vocation as the gift of God and then turn to how it becomes a human task. Of course, it is always both at the same time, both God's gift and our response. They cannot actually be separated from each other without falsifying the reality of the mystery. At the same time, however, they should not be confused with one another, for the sovereign prevenience of God's gracious call obviously forms the very presupposition and basis of our freedom, our ability to respond in a glad and wholehearted way. As for us, so also for the young people to whom we minister, they, too, are enabled to discover and live out their vocation only as they first receive it as a gift from God.

Let us first consider just how I am using the concept of vocation. In the Old Testament, vocation refers to the call of God to a whole people, to the people of Israel to be a nation set apart, to be holy to God and to worship him alone. Individuals called by God (prophets, priests, and kings) were understood as representatives of the nation, and as such they were to act on behalf of the whole people of God.

In the New Testament, Jesus called specific individuals to follow him: Simon and Andrew and James and John left their nets and followed him in response to his explicit invitation to "come, follow me" (Mark 1:20). Ordinary fishermen engaged in an ordinary day's work—yet here is the turning point of their entire lives, when they leave their nets and follow him. Like those who have come after them, they are called not by virtue of their works, but rather by virtue of God's hidden purpose (2 Tim 1:9).

Throughout the Middle Ages, "having a vocation" meant that one was committed to the monastic or priestly life. It was understood as a kind of withdrawal from the world in order to fulfill God's will for perfection. But at the time of the Reformation, Martin Luther radically redefined vocation. Since all believers were called to witness to Christ and to serve their neighbor, all evidently had a vocation that could be lived out in whatever station of life they found themselves. Since God was at work in the world and all believers were called to love and serve him, every person was in this sense a priest before God. No matter what the daily tasks set before a person, he or she was called to serve God and neighbor in and through those tasks. Thus, the milkmaid and the mother were called to serve God in humble faithfulness and diligence just as much as the magistrate or the mayor. The call to discipleship was understood to pervade every aspect of human work and form of life and not simply for those set apart by ordination or monastic vows. Rather, all persons were set apart by virtue of their baptism to love and serve God and neighbor.[2]

For Calvin, God's call was conceptually tied to his doctrine of election. As such, it was understood to be a sovereign summons, which would ensure our human response. Such effectual calling depended upon our eternal election in Christ, to be among those who were united with Christ and who would thus receive all the benefits of Christ's work of salvation.[3]

---

2. Gritsch, "Vocation," 4.245–46.
3. Packer, "Call, Called, Calling," 108–9.

Believers came to know of their election by the obvious signs of having been called to some particular service. These "posterior signs" thus reassured Christians in doubt of their being counted among the elect, that they had indeed been predestined by God to live for his glory.[4]

In contemporary usage, choosing one's vocation has generally come to mean discerning precisely in what sphere of work one is called to serve, by virtue of one's gifts and talents as well as one's very real limitations. Discerning one's vocation means to recognize "the place of responsibility" where one will live out one's Christian discipleship.[5] But this includes far more than choosing a career. It also includes discerning whether one is called to marry this or that particular person or no one at all, whether one is called to become a parent, and just how one's energies and talents are to be lived out in the fullness of one's whole life. The sign of our calling, after all, is not ordination, but rather baptism, for it is baptism that marks us for ministry. Each person called by Christ is called as a member of his body to use the gifts he or she has been given in service to others.

It is, of course, a pressing issue that faces young people today to discern precisely what they are called to do with their lives, just how they find the place of responsibility in which they can use all the gifts they have been given. And when we think about the particular young people in our care, the question of their concrete and specific calling can become urgent. How can they keep anxiety or despair at bay as the pressure rises within them to find their place in the world? For unlike Luther's day, we no longer simply reside in a particular "station of life," where, within clearly defined horizons, we can continue in the life that we have known through our parents and grandparents or through a rooted community. Certain constraints that defined the boundaries of one's sphere of life for generations, such as the place of one's birth or the occupation of one's parents, no longer set the kind of human limitations that have traditionally provided a sense of security and belonging. For middle-class Americans, even simple geography has ceased to be a defining constraint. So many young people live uprooted lives; having moved from one place to another, they have little sense of belonging anywhere or to anyone in particular. How, then, are they to face the daunting question of discerning the place and task to which they are called?

---

4. Gritsch, "Vocation," 4.245–46.
5. Barth, *Church Dogmatics* 3/4, 598, quoting Bonhoeffer.

In a situation such as this, the teaching of the church about the nature of the God who calls them according to his own purposes can provide much-needed guidance in the face of dizzying choices. For the discernment of their life path doesn't happen in a vacuum. It occurs, rather, as a response to a real call of God. In order to hear that call, young people need to have ears that are spiritually attuned. How can they even perceive the gifts God has bestowed upon them, unless they turn to him as their source of guidance? The God who created them has given particular gifts unique to each creature; the Christ who redeems them saves them from aimlessness and sin; the Holy Spirit who sustains them creates the community where they may be fully seen as who they are and where they can be called forth.

God the Creator: It is not as if young people must invent themselves out of whole cloth, or heroically just decide who they are meant to be. For they are already someone particular in God's eyes; by the time they are sixteen, eighteen, or twenty years old, they have a long history with God even if they are not yet wholly aware of it. For God knit them together in their mother's womb; he was the One who formed their inward parts in secret. Already before they were born, God beheld them and knew their unformed substance (Ps 139). The same God who created the heavens and the earth and all the creatures of the earth, also created them in all their uniqueness. Becoming conscious of their God-given uniqueness usually takes years, as young people test their strengths, encounter their limitations, and slowly begin to realize that some of the things they always took for granted about themselves might indeed be the very thing that is most needed in the world.

I have found the poetry of David Whyte, a contemporary poet originally from Wales, to reveal a pondering heart that gives voice to a profound sense of the mystery of vocation. His poems are set in a contemplative key and evoke a sense of wonder and curiosity about God's hidden purposes in my life. These lines in particular resonate with my understanding of God's having created my unique life for a purpose, a purpose that I need to discover and live out with joy: "To be human is to become visible while carrying what is hidden as a gift to others."[6] The poem evokes a kind of longing to discover my humanity as I give it away to others. It quickens my imagination to ponder what might be growing in my soul, yet unbeknownst to me, still only partially visible.

---

6. Whyte, "What to Remember When Waking," in *House of Belonging*, 27.

The poem effectively juxtaposes the ho-hum reality of daily life with its limited and limiting plans with that sense of mystery that comes when we ponder what it means to have been created as the one we are. Each human being is a whole world, an infinite mystery with a history that is unfathomable in its depth, stretching far back in time before one's birth. The Christian doctrine of election captures for many that sense of awe that we were known and loved and called by God even before we were born. Pondering Psalm 139 can be a salutary discipline for those young people whose sense of identity has been cramped into too small a space. I remember long ago studying St. Teresa of Avila's *The Interior Castle*, and being shocked into an intimation of the vast depths of my own soul. When young people are challenged to seek the "vitality hidden in [their] sleep,"[7] their sense of self can begin to expand. Augustine had a powerful sense of wonder about the mystery of the human beings created by God. In his *Confessions*, he writes, "[People] go forth to wonder at the heights of mountains, the huge waves of the sea, the broad flow of the rivers, the vast compass of the ocean, the courses of the stars; and they pass by themselves without wondering."[8]

A proper reverence for the mystery of one's own being also leads to reverence before the mystery of others. It leads to an attitude of inner expectation to find that kind of depth and beauty in others which helps to call it forth. For such an attitude assists others to become respectfully curious about the mystery of their own being. For God creates every person with particular gifts that wait to be discovered as a treasure by a world that needs them.

"To remember the other world in this world is to live in your true inheritance."[9] The young people we care for were not created simply to make their mundane plans, their "list of things to do" that gets checked off day after day, only to be replaced by a new list. No, they were created to become fully and visibly human as they carry what is hidden as a gift to others. The gift of God, the Creator, is to call them forth in splendor. Trusting that, holding on to that perception will sustain a young person through many a dark night of doubt and fear.

The true inheritance of youth is the knowledge that they are children of God, and that God calls them into a living relationship with himself. Young people are enabled to discover their vocation only as they actively

---

7. Whyte, "What to Remember When Waking," in *House of Belonging*, 26.
8. Epigraph in Nuland, *Wisdom of the Body*.
9. Whyte, "What to Remember When Waking," in *House of Belonging*, 27.

seek God's purpose for their life. For it is in their relationship with their Creator that they begin to recognize the eternal issues hidden in their daily choices; it is there that they discover what really matters in life, who they are and who they are meant to be. As they find their identity in this relationship with the One who created them, they can begin to discern what those purposes might be.

God the Redeemer

God gives himself to us wholly in the gift of his Son. "The gifts of God for the people of God."[10] These words, solemnly spoken in the liturgy of the Lord's Supper as the celebrant lifts up the elements of bread and wine and offers them to the gathered community, refer to this lavish self-giving. The sacrament of the Lord's Supper, at the very center of our life together in Christ, is that which sustains us for the tasks we are called to do. For this is the gift of Jesus Christ himself. By God's grace we are permitted and invited to partake of his body and blood and thus to incorporate him into our own substance. As we participate in Christ's own life, we are given the strength and the vision to live *sub specie aeternitatis*, under the aspect of eternity.

What does it mean to live *sub specie aeternitatis*, under the form of eternity? Concretely, for today's youth I think it means an honest recognition that the choices they make at this juncture in their lives have immense consequences. So much of gravity is decided at this time of life. Erik Erikson's focused attention on the tasks of youth highlights the crucial decisions made around questions of identity, ideology, and intimacy. "To whom do I belong? To which teachers shall I entrust myself? Which ways of understanding the world are worth learning? Where shall I put the energies of my life? And whom shall I love? To what way of life shall I commit myself?" Decisions made in these formative years about where to focus one's study or in which community to invest oneself, or whom to date or to love, these choices all carry with them profound, often unanticipated, consequences, the full extent of which is known sometimes only decades later.

In my work as a pastoral counselor and spiritual director, I have seen again and again in the lives of middle-aged adults, how the choices they made in their youth have affected the entire course of their lives. The

---

10. Holy Eucharist: Rite Two, in *Book of Common Prayer*.

reason that parents worry so much about their children getting involved with drugs or sex, of course, is that these choices are so frighteningly consequential. They can literally change the course of an entire life. Imagine yourself as a parent, bringing a child into the world by means of the blood, sweat, and tears through which every child is brought into the world and pouring your life's substance into that child. When that child finally becomes a young adult, you discover that he is addicted to alcohol or cocaine or heroin. This beloved child, this child who is bone of your bone and flesh of your flesh, is suddenly lost and cannot be reached; in fact, he seems to be in danger of losing every single God-given gift that you have nurtured for years. Such an outcome is painful almost beyond bearing.

Similarly, teenagers who buy into the culture's version of sexual fulfillment can get so far in over their heads that it can take decades, perhaps a lifetime, to come to terms with the consequences of heedless choices made in their youth. A man nearing fifty recently mused over the fact that he was with his son's mother for two short years before his son was born and for one year after. "When does it end?" he asked ruefully. Within the context of our conversation, I understood him to mean: "I don't love this woman anymore; she was just a brief episode in my life; why do I have to be involved with her after all these years?" Well, the fact is, it doesn't *ever* end. To be a father is to be a father for life. And the child's mother will remain his mother for life. Though long since divorced, this man and woman are still connected to each other through their son, and will remain so, even beyond the years of sharing the common task of raising their child to adulthood. And whatever meaning they convey to their son about the choices they made which brought him into the world will inevitably affect his whole sense of identity for good or for ill. And the worst possible outcome for him is when one or the other of his parents effectively tries to deny their common history. For no rejection screams more loudly to a child than the rejection of the half of their identity represented by the other parent. These are emotional and spiritual facts about which our culture is usually silent, but which profoundly affect the inner reality of millions of children of divorce.

Further, to engage in premarital sexual intercourse is to bear consequences that last a lifetime, even if no child is born. "Sex was never safe," writes Wendell Berry, "and it is less safe now than it ever has been. What we are actually teaching the young is an illusion of thoughtless freedom and purchasable safety, which encourages them to tamper prematurely, disrespectfully and dangerously with a great power."[11] Anyone involved in a ministry of the care of souls is given glimpses of the kind of spiritual consequences of such premature tampering. I think of the bitter tears of one woman's regret over an abortion she had chosen decades before. How could she have known in the immediate panic of discovering that she was pregnant and unmarried that the spiritual and emotional wound of deciding to terminate the pregnancy would still be open and gaping thirty years later? A middle-aged man, haunted by the memory of a former lover, has been unable to let her go even in his imagination. Despite the fact that he hasn't seen her in more than twenty years, in his mind's eye, she is still the love of his life. What could this possibly mean for his ability to live his life fully in the present? The spiritual truth is that men and women bond irrevocably when they engage in sexual intercourse, for "the two become one flesh." "You are right to say that you have no husband; for you have had five husbands and the one you have now is not your husband" (John 4:18). And yet, where in our culture today can we get a glimpse of this little-known truth about sexuality apart from the Gospel of Jesus Christ?

How can young people know this if they have never heard the Gospel? Even more crucially, how will they ever learn about God's love for them, a love so great that not even a sordid life of sexual entanglement and aimlessness and drugs can dissuade God from drawing near to them, from reaching them at the core of their being and healing, forgiving and saving them by drawing them to himself in love? Those who have carried the weight of the sins of their youth around with them for decades are mercifully renewed when they hear the Gospel faithfully preached in their middle years. But young people, too, need to hear this Gospel of forgiveness and receive it into their hearts. For they, too, are burdened with the weight of choices which they know have been disobedient to God's purposes for their lives. And as they find the grace to receive the gift of God's forgiveness, they will also find the freedom to repent, to turn away from life-denying choices toward life-giving ones. And in the newfound freedom to obey they will find the courage and hope to seek more fervently that place in the world where they can serve God.

When God calls young people to ministry, he calls them to himself. God's inexpressible gift is the gift of his Son, a gift that cannot be known or received apart from a personal relationship to Jesus Christ. Hearing

---

11. Berry, "Sex, Economy, Freedom and Community," 117–73, 142.

Christ's words of forgiveness spoken directly to you is an unforgettable moment in anyone's spiritual journey. For many, it coincides absolutely with their sense of call, with the core meaning of their life's purpose, for to experience being forgiven something which causes unbearable shame and searing regret is to be completely reoriented in one's inward being. We have only to think of St. Paul. Pain and shame and sorrow when he realized what he had been doing exploded into gratitude and joy. A new sense of purpose, indeed a complete reorientation of his whole life, rose out of the very place he had sinned most gravely. What wonder there is in this unremitting theme in the Bible, that even our most grievous sins cannot separate us from God, nor from God's finding a way to bring good out of the evil that we have perpetrated.

> Joseph wept when [his brothers] spoke to him. . . . But Joseph said to them, "Fear not, for am I in the place of God? As for you, you meant evil against me; but God meant it for good, to bring it about that many people should be kept alive, as they are today. So, do not fear; I will provide for you and your little ones." Thus, he reassured them and comforted them." (Gen 50:17–20)

The inestimable gift of our calling is Jesus Christ himself. For it is his complete self-giving in love which enables us to give ourselves to others for his sake. Jesus Christ alone has the capacity to call us forth. Through Scripture, through the Word of God, through the testimony of another human being, or through the preaching or the music or the service of the church, through the *witness*, in other words, of other human beings by word and deed, we have been given a glimpse of the living God in the life, death, and resurrection of Jesus Christ. He has actually disclosed himself to us. And then we want to know and love him ourselves. We feel summoned in such a compelling way that we cannot remain neutral.

"What have you that you have not received?" (1 Cor 4:7) asks Paul. Somewhere in your actual lived history, you have been met by the Lord Jesus Christ, himself. You have pondered the question of his significance for your own life. And if you have come to know him at all, you find yourself, like Peter, unable to imagine where else you would turn. For you recognize that Christ has the very words of life that feed you, body and soul.

God the Sustainer

Finally, when God calls us to himself, he gives us the gift of his Holy Spirit. Here I would like to emphasize three brief points. First, the Spirit grants each person a particular charism, or spiritual gift, that is distinct from, but perhaps related to, one's natural talent. Second, the Holy Spirit gathers the church, granting us the gift of true community. And third, the Holy Spirit gives the community the gift of discernment in helping each member to discover and live out his God-given gift.

What are spiritual gifts? In his letter to the church at Corinth, St. Paul labors to spell out just how each member of the body of Christ fundamentally needs every other member in order to function as a church. The spiritual gift that each person is given is absolutely essential for the thriving of the whole body. Just as every member of the body is essential to it being able to function as a living being, so also in the church. Just as the eye cannot say to the hand, "I have no need of you," nor the head to the feet, "I have no need of you" (1 Cor 12:21), so also in the church. There is not a single member of the body that is not needed for the functioning of the whole. For each member is given a spiritual gift for building up the body of Christ. Whether writing to the church at Corinth, Rome, or Ephesus, in each letter, Paul always sets his understanding of spiritual gifts in the context of this vision of how the body of Christ is to function with each member offering his or her gift for the good of all. In his first letter to the Corinthians, he writes:

> To each is given the manifestation of the Spirit for the common good. To one is given through the Spirit the utterance of wisdom, and to another the utterance of knowledge according to the same Spirit, to another faith by the same Spirit, to another gifts of healing by the one Spirit, to another the working of miracles, to another prophecy, to another the ability to distinguish between spirits, to another various kinds of tongues, to another the interpretation of tongues. All these are inspired by one and the same Spirit, who apportions to each one individually as he wills. (1 Cor 12:7–11)

Wisdom, knowledge, faith, healing, miracles, prophecy, discernment of spirits, tongues, interpretation, and finally, love, the highest of all the gifts, all these are granted by the Holy Spirit for the upbuilding of the community for both its internal mutual care and also its service to the world.

Second, the community itself is a gift of the Spirit. With all our talk about creating community, it is nevertheless something that human beings are unable to do by their own power. God is the true author of community. When each person is set free to contribute the gift he or she has been given for the sake of the community, the community as a whole comes alive and flourishes. With each member playing his part for the upbuilding of the whole, the community functions like a healthy body in which every part of the body helps every other part to function properly. When every single member is able to contribute her gift, something far greater than the sum of the parts comes into being. Radiant energy and life set this body in motion with a sense of direction and purpose and joy.

Young people are naturally drawn to such a community that is brimming over with life and radiant with health. They can see the love and respect that each member has for every other member, and they want to play a part themselves. As they are drawn into the gathered fellowship, they find that most precious of all gifts, a place where they can be seen and known for who they truly are and where they can truly belong. As they belong to Christ, they also belong to the community which is his body. And in that context, the community itself can now help them discern and call forth their gifts. For—here is the paradox again—Christ uses the community to participate in his work of calling each one. For each person in the body of Christ has been created to become "fully and visibly human as they carry what is hidden as a gift to others." This is the joyous task of vocation, to which I now turn.

Vocation: A Joyous Task

The choices before young people today are staggering in their complexity, yet what are the criteria that can help them actually make the right choices? Where is their plumb line? How do they find an orienting center to their lives? What or who calls to them? What actually has the power to call them forth to become the people they were created to be? To be without the gospel and its orienting center in Jesus Christ is a bit like being a ship on a vast sea with neither compass nor rudder.

Our culture seems to say that their choices are limitless; that anything is possible. If you have brains and a computer, the sky is the limit. The internet, after all, offers more information than any of us could pack into our brains in a lifetime. And yet there is no sorting principle. And there is seldom anyone standing by offering guidance, making considered judgments about the relative worth of one website over another. So, young people in our culture have access to all this information, yet it gives no life and imparts no purpose. Without a purpose, without an organizing center to their lives, information is just so much meaningless stuff. It is a bit like learning those "dead facts" you had to memorize in the fifth grade: China's major rivers are the Yangtze and the Hwang Ho, and their major natural resources are . . . and the list to be memorized goes all the way from aluminum to zinc. Why are fifth graders taught these facts? To what end? What does it *matter*? (Of course, if you have been to China and have understood the crucial role of these rivers and natural resources to the livelihood of the people, then such knowledge comes alive with significance. It matters a great deal, but did they tell you that in the fifth grade? Or did they just make you memorize these facts and claim that you were getting an education?)

Mere information will never sustain a hungry soul. Words that are life-giving have to reach across from one person whose heart is connected to another person, whose heart is openly seeking to know the other. Karl Barth, in his completely inimitable way, has helped me to understand something of the nature of knowledge that is really alive. He writes:

> In the language of the Bible knowledge does not mean the acquisition of neutral information, which can be expressed in statements, principles, and systems. . . . It is the process or history in which human beings . . . certainly observing and thinking, using their senses, intelligence and imagination, but also their will, action and "heart," and therefore as whole persons, become aware of another history . . . in such a compelling way that they cannot be neutral . . . but find themselves summoned to disclose and give themselves . . . in return.[12]

True knowledge is not just the dissemination of ideas nor the gathering of facts, but is the encounter with another; and here, of course, Barth is speaking of the encounter of human beings with the mystery of God. When we seek knowledge, and particularly when what we seek is a living knowledge of God's will for our lives, we open ourselves to a relationship that will change us. For spiritual communion is always at the heart of this kind of knowing. Someone once said, "All the food of this

---

12. Barth, *Church Dogmatics* 4/3, 183–84.

world is divine love made edible."[13] The same could be said of knowledge; real knowledge—of God, of the wonder of the world in which we live, and of our true calling—is a soul food feast.

Think about it. When a relationship with God is at the center of your identity, you can begin to make sense of yourself and the world in which you live. You can know many disparate things, but unless there is a center point, a point of reference that transcends all this knowing, in the end you will know only disconnected and meaningless facts, a matter of mere information rather than life-giving knowledge. Consider this contemporary parable about knowledge and knowing.

> A scholar consulted a sage as to how separate parts create a whole and what differentiates knowledge of the many from knowledge of the whole.
>
> The sage answered: What is widely dispersed becomes an entity only when it finds its center. For what is myriad achieves substance and significance only at the center, and then its abundance looks like simplicity—almost like nothing; a fruitful void, a calm force gravitating toward that which gives it meaning.
>
> To experience the whole or share in it, we do not need to know every detail; neither do we need to speak of everything nor have or do all.
>
> To enter into the heart of the city, we only have to walk through one gate. Many tones reverberate in the striking of a single bell.
>
> And when we pick a ripe apple, we need not know how it came to be as it is. We take it in our hands and eat it.
>
> The scholar, however, argued with the sage: to grasp the truth, one must first know all the facts.
>
> But the sage contradicted him: only when the truth is grown old do we know all the facts. Truth which makes us move on is risky and untried.
>
> This truth conceals its promise as the seed conceals the tree within. Therefore, if we hesitate to act because we want to know more than we need for our next step, we miss the chance to grow. We accept small change in place of riches and out of living trees make firewood.
>
> The scholar immediately remarked that this was surely only part of the answer, and begged the wise man for some more. The wise man waved aside this question, knowing that fullness resembles a barrel of fresh cider—sweet and cloudy. It

---

13. An unnamed orthodox theologian quoted in Bloom, *Beginning to Pray*, 41.

needs fermentation and sufficient time until it clears. If instead of savoring it, we try to gulp it down, we become befuddled and unsteady.[14]

"What is widely dispersed becomes an entity only when it finds a center." When our fundamental identity is grounded in the knowledge of ourselves as children of God, we are enabled to move forward out of that center. But the truth that makes us move forward in our life is always risky and untried. This is true no matter what age we are, for discerning our vocation entails an ongoing listening and living response throughout our lives. It is not as if we get a blueprint at the age of twenty-two and then follow it for the next fifty years. There is tremendous risk every day in living: the risk that we will miss an opportunity because we were preoccupied with something of lesser importance; the risk that we will attempt too much and disperse our energies fruitlessly, or that we will attempt too little because we were caught in a tangled web of fear. Discerning just where to put our efforts and energies requires a daily attunement to where God is calling us. It is a process in which we repeatedly engage, day after day, as we seek to hear God's call each new day.

"If we hesitate to act because we want to know more than we need for our next step, we miss the chance to grow." Sometimes all that we are shown is a single step forward. Enough light is shed to see whether the path veers to the right or the left, whether it is level or drops precipitously into a chasm below. We can never, especially not in today's world, know all the facts. So, we have to have a different way of orienting ourselves. How does a young person discern whether or not to marry a particular person? Whether or not to enter a particular field of study? Whether to pursue certain interests at the expense of others? What is the next step at any point in life and how are we equipped to help young people discern it in faith? None of these questions can be answered by the individual alone, nor are they meant to be. The gift of the community that we are given through the work of the Holy Spirit is the concrete context in which such discernment needs to take place.

The Vocation of the Community

Young people who have been shaped by the gospel already have an orientation in a certain direction. Certain choices as to where to invest

14. Hellinger, *Insights*, 61–63.

themselves will rise to the surface more easily than others. Churches that live out a commitment to world mission, or to feeding and clothing the poor, or to providing decent housing to members in the community, or to grappling with the devastating impact of capitalism and its so-called "free trade" on the poor of the world, or to all of these—churches, in other words, that are living out their collective vocation as disciples of Jesus Christ—will be shaping youth for years before the question ever occurs to them about where they are called to invest themselves in the world. The assumptive world that they take entirely for granted will be a world in which the hungry are fed, the homeless are given a home, and the yoke of oppression is challenged. This is no small matter, as will come home to you if you have ever had a beloved family member who has grown up without the church, without its soul-shaping gospel, without its uplifting hymns and life-giving liturgy, without its mission in the world.

When my husband and I lived in Bangor, Maine, we were involved in an organization called PICA (Peace in Central America). It was founded in 1984 during the time of the terrible civil wars in the region. In March 1985, I remember struggling to push our daughter Rachel's stroller through the snow in the march against our government's unconscionable support of the murderous Contra regime in Nicaragua. So it came as no surprise when at the age of seven, upon hearing President George Bush claim that God was on our side in the Gulf War, an incensed Rachel wrote a letter to the President of the United States. She wrote:

> Dear President Bush,
> I am a seven-year-old girl. Saddam Hussein thinks that God is on his side. You think that God is on our side. I think that God is against war.
> Love, Rachel[15]

I told her later that I would save it in a file folder for her in case our country ever tries to draft women. It would be good corroborating evidence that she had been a pacifist all her life.

Young people are profoundly shaped by their community in ways that we cannot anticipate. Even as her parents, we were surprised by the depth of passion with which she held her conviction. But it undoubtedly required a whole community to shape Rachel in these ways. It was surely the combination of what she had heard at home, what she had learned at

---

15. Her letter was subsequently published in the "Letters to the Editor," *Bangor Daily News*, January 21, 1991.

church, and what she had learned at PICA, that shaped her heart, already in pretty decisive ways by the time she was seven. When the children in our schools in Bangor had swapped drawings with the children in Carasque, El Salvador, Rachel drew a colorful bluebird bringing a big fat worm to her baby birdies in the nest. The children in Carasque drew pictures of airplanes dropping bombs and fire burning their homes. We must never consider the question of a young person's vocation in a way that is separated from the vocation of the whole church. If the church is truthfully seeking to live out its mission, young people will be affected by it in ways that cannot be predicted.

Discernment: A Community Calling

If churches have mission statements, are the youth of the church meaningfully related to them? Are they instructed and encouraged to seek the mission of their own life in the context of the church's vocation? For it is not simply a matter of discovering what you are good at and love to do, it is also a matter of deciding where you will invest those energies. If you are gifted in working with numbers, you can become an accountant for a company that sets up sweatshops around the world in order to maximize a profit for the wealthy at the expense of the workers, or you can become an accountant in an organization that reflects your most basic values and convictions. Helping young people discern their natural gifts is no small matter, but our responsibility as the body of Christ does not end there. We also need to help them discern just where they will invest their precious life energies.

As young people seek to discern what their gifts are, they are greatly blessed when they have a community around them to identify and call forth those gifts. I will never forget taking the Strong Vocational Interest Blank as a freshman in college. It was part of a regular program of vocational assessment given to all freshmen at the university where I studied and was designed to give us important clues about what kind of career path we should follow. The results that came back were disheartening, to say the least. Ranking far above any other career path were these three: artist, musician, and writer. "Great!" I thought. "I can't draw, I can't play a musical instrument, and I have no talent for writing." I was perfectly equipped for absolutely no career at all.

What a contrast that experience was to the regular communal practices of our church's high school youth group, where the young people regularly mirror back the gifts that they see in each other. Near the end of countless mission trips, they exchange notes, in which they state what they have noticed and appreciated about each other's gifts. Over the years, I have watched these young people go from strength to strength as they go out into the world. It was such a joy one Sunday to hear about Molly Christiansen's project to equip the village of Santa Maria Veleto in Oaxaca, Mexico, with eco-toilets. She had gone to this village as a health worker and seen how illness was spreading among the children because they had no proper sanitation. Trusting that her church back home would care about the plight of these people she had come to know and love, she came back to us and presented a powerful "Minute for Mission." I think she must have equipped the whole village in about a month. The exciting work of the Search Institute in Minneapolis can go a long way, I think, in helping churches to build on the strengths of our culture rather than always looking at its weaknesses. The forty developmental assets that enable young people to acquire sturdy identities should really be the birthright of every child, and churches can do a lot to build communities that will nurture their young. I was thrilled to learn of the good work of this institute and consider some of the far-reaching implications of it for building healthy communities and a new generation that is equal to the challenges of our times.[16]

It matters a great deal, therefore, to be part of a church that is a reliable community where young people know they can call upon their elders and their elders will come through for them. In his volume on theological anthropology, Karl Barth identifies what he calls the basic form of humanity. Human beings made in the image of God are created to be in relationship with God and one another. The wonderful German word, *mitmenschlichkeit*, translated into English as "co-humanity," seeks to convey the kind of active and heartfelt mutual engagement that God intends for his creatures. Only God can be *for* us; that is, only God can give us life, save us, forgive us, and create us anew. But we can be *with* one another in mutual openness and self-giving. Barth identifies four criteria or marks of true humanity.

The first mark of true humanity is the act of seeing and being seen. Only Barth is even more concrete. He says, "It is a being in which one

16. Search Institute, "Asset Approach." See their website at www.search-institute.org.

[person] looks the other in the eye."[17] The eye as the window to the soul lets the other in . . . or else it doesn't. To see the other entails allowing the other to see oneself at the same time. It is only when the seeing and the allowing oneself to be seen is mutual and reciprocal that we have a fully human relationship. Thus, isolation or hiding is a form of sin, a form of relationship not intended by God. "All seeing is inhuman in which the one who sees hides himself, refusing to be seen by the fellow human being whom he sees."[18]

The second mark of true humanity consists in mutual speaking and hearing. If we do not actively reveal ourselves to others, how can they know us as we truly are? If we are only seen, we are subject to being misperceived; we need to interpret who we are to those who want to know us by openly sharing ourselves. Just as God makes himself known to us in his self-revelation in Jesus Christ, so we also are to make ourselves known to one another.

> The human significance of speech . . . depends absolutely upon the fact that a [human being] and his fellow speak to one another and listen to one another; that the expression and address between I and thou are reciprocal. As we can look past people, we can also hear past them. . . . Most of our words, spoken or heard, are an inhuman and barbaric affair because we will not speak or listen to one another.[19]

The third mark of true humanity is offering one another mutual assistance. At the core of our humanity is the fundamental fact of our mutual need for one another. "My humanity depends on the fact that I am always aware, and my action is determined by my awareness, that I need the assistance of others as a fish needs water."[20] We can neither be left alone, nor can we leave our fellow human being without our active help and support, as each of us needs the other in order to be fully human.

Finally, true human beings engage in these three mutual and reciprocal activities—seeing and being seen, speaking and hearing, and offering mutual assistance—with gladness. The giving and the receiving that are at the core of our humanity are our common joy and therefore constitute the freedom of the encounter we have with one another. This is

---

17. Barth, *Church Dogmatics* 3/2, 250.
18. Barth, *Church Dogmatics* 3/2, 250.
19. Barth, *Church Dogmatics* 3/2, 259–60.
20. Barth, *Church Dogmatics* 3/2, 263.

the secret of the whole, that "each can affirm the other as the being with which he wants to be and cannot be without. But this leads to mutual joy, each in the existence of the other and both in the fact that they can exist together.... Human nature" says Barth, "is man himself. But man is what he is freely and from the heart."[21] We are fully human only in this free gladness to be with one another.

To do justice to Barth's rich and nuanced discussion would require an entire chapter in itself—what I have tried to summarize in two pages takes Barth twenty-five to develop—but I wanted to set forth these marks of humanity, because it is my conviction that it is only when young people are seen as they really are that their gifts can show forth and flourish. So much of contemporary life among the youth (and not only among the youth) seems to consist in covering up and hiding their true selves and letting others see only an idealized version of who they really are—avoiding being geeky at all costs. Therefore, creating an ethos where no one will be ridiculed for his or her insecurities or idiosyncrasies, where each may openly share who he or she really is, where trust and safety are sacrosanct, this may be the most important gift any youth minister can offer.

In such an atmosphere, young people can let themselves be seen. When they are seen for who they are and welcomed with gladness, it is easy to see their gifts and help them to see these gifts as well. All you have to do is ask them, "What could you talk about all night long?" Or so says a dear friend of mine who is decades younger than I am. (I knew what he meant, of course, but there is no longer anything that I could talk about all night long). Finding what you are passionate about, what makes you glad to be alive, what makes you want to sing for joy or jump out of your skin with excitement—this is undoubtedly where your vocation lies. I remember reading about the great nineteenth-century actress of the stage, Sarah Bernhardt, a few years ago. She said that she needed a life task, "big enough and toilsome enough to absorb all [her] energy." (It is interesting to note that Sarah's original ambition was to become a nun, but she was dissuaded by her family's strenuous intervention.)[22]

But some young people come to this stage of life so wounded that healing needs to take place before they dare to let anyone see them as they really are. As a church, and certainly as leaders among youth, we are also called to become communities of forgiveness and healing. A

---

21. Barth, *Church Dogmatics* 3/2, 274.
22. Cole, Chinoy, and Sheehan, *Actors on Acting*, 240.

seminary student once told me that the musicians in his field education church were instructed never to play anything in a minor key, because it was thought to be too negative. Sometimes I worry that as the church becomes more and more adapted to the culture, we are less able to speak frankly with young people about the reality of the world we live in. It may be easier to pitch our programs as "fun" activities, to offer lock-ins and cookouts, and zany games, and to avoid the life-and-death seriousness of our world situation. But the world in which today's youth are growing up is a frightening one; and if we avoid the minor key, we avoid too much of reality to enable anyone to trust us with their story.

You know the stories I mean, those who have grown up in homes whose parents speak and act violently toward each other and toward their children. Statistics here—about the twenty-five percent of American children between the ages of ten and sixteen who report being assaulted or abused within the previous year—are no mere information, no "dead facts," but rather the lived stories of young people whom you have come to know and love. All of the risk factors that have been studied over the years are known to those of you who work in the front lines: youth who are depressed, who attempt suicide, who engage in high-risk sexual activity, who binge and purge, who drink alcohol frequently and to excess.[23]

Young people need adults who will dare to reach down to a level of conviction about what they believe about God and the world we live in, what they believe about the burden of human sin, and how it is possible to keep hope alive in such a world as ours. I think often of Archbishop Anthony Bloom, whose searing words challenge us to dig deeper toward our real convictions. Bloom, a Russian émigré and priest in the Orthodox Church, who lived through the horror of two world wars, wrote:

> Whenever I speak I speak with all the conviction and belief which is in me. I stake my life on what I am saying. It's not the words themselves that are important but reaching down to the level of people's convictions. This is the basis of communication; this is where we really meet one another. If people want to ridicule me, that's fine; but if it produces a spark in them and we can talk, then it means we are really talking about something which concerns us deeply.[24]

---

23. Roan, *Our Daughter's Health*, 4.
24. Bloom, *Beginning to Pray*, 14.

How can young people entrust their hopes and fears to us if we skim along the surface of life, never letting them see how desperately we, and they, and indeed all persons need the gospel to live at all?

For even the most carefree young person, even one who has enjoyed every privilege of a comfortable home, happily married parents, acceptance among peers, economic security, a thriving church youth group, meaningful mission trips, and community service, even this young person with few emotional scars still lives in a post-September 11 world. None of us can be really alive and open to the world we live in and make it into adulthood unscathed. Wendell Berry, contemporary poet, essayist, and novelist, wrote a poem titled "Now You Know the Worst," which he dedicated "to [his] granddaughters who visited the Holocaust Museum on the day of the burial of Yitzhak Rabin."[25] This poem was given to me about six weeks after the unbearable events of September 11. As I read the opening lines, I remembered the anguish I had felt when I first had to tell our daughter, Rachel, what happened to her beloved Jesus. "Now you know the worst we humans have to know about ourselves and I am sorry."[26] She was not quite four. Christmas had come and gone, along with the many impromptu plays where Daddy was instructed to play the part of "Jophus" (sic), I was to be Mary, and she was to be the baby Jesus. Now with Holy Week approaching, I found myself stricken dumb: How could I tell her that Jesus, her precious Jesus whom she already loved with such a pure heart, was betrayed by one of his closest friends, deserted by the rest, handed over to the authorities, and killed, by hammering nails into his hands and feet and left to die on a cross? I couldn't bear to see the hurt in her eyes, or hear her uncomprehending, "Why?" Now she would know the worst we humans have to know about ourselves, and I was sorry. I wanted to protect her from this story of brutality and inhumanity. But there it was, right in the middle of the story of our faith, the cross of Jesus Christ, not to be evaded.

I remember in the early days after September 11, as I walked in a daze through the rooms of my house, I was unable to concentrate on any task whatsoever. Images of fire and collapsing towers, of human beings diving headlong to the earth to escape a living inferno of hell kept going incessantly through my mind. Fear gripped my heart at night whenever I heard planes going overhead. Over and over and over again, I would

---

25. Berry, "Now You Know the Worst," 192.
26. Berry, "Now You Know the Worst," 192.

imagine myself being on one of those airplanes that had crashed into the towers. The scene seemed to be etched permanently in my mind's eye, not unlike that other scene on November 22, 1963. Unspeakable horror. We live in a world of unspeakable horror that goes on day after day. This is the world that needs us to come alive; this is the hurting world that needs our gifts. Yet we are hurting too.

I have a number of colleagues who have been trained in critical incident stress debriefing, a method of working with communities that have undergone major trauma. In listening to their stories after the events of September 11, a certain note was sounded again and again. Never had they felt so challenged to the core. Never before in going into such communities—perhaps where there had been a devastating fire, murder, or suicide that had affected the whole community—had they themselves been so directly impacted. Always before they had been able to be a kind of stable center, around whom the community could give voice to their grief and anger, the anguish and sorrow of the trauma they had undergone. Yet now they, themselves, were reeling with grief. How were they to provide a stable anchor for the community when they, themselves, were so stricken? This is where our knowledge of God as people of faith comes alive.

What actually spoke to you, fed your soul, and gave you hope, in those days and weeks after September 11? It may sound strange, but what gave me strength in those early weeks were four words from the Apostles' Creed. Neither sermon, nor anthem, nor the great hymns of the church could reach the numbness of my heart. But then we rose to affirm our faith in words that we could all recite by rote, even in our sleep. I said the words along with the rest until I got to those four words: "He descended into hell." After that I could no longer speak because of the huge lump in my throat that could dissolve only if I consented to let the tears flow. God spoke to me through the words of the ancient creed that Sunday in September. Jesus Christ has descended into hell; he descended all the way to the bottom of that pit of godforsakenness. Jesus Christ was with those terrified passengers on the hijacked planes on September 11; Jesus Christ worked alongside those rescue workers in the midst of smoke and the smell of burning flesh; Jesus Christ loved each human being who met their end that day in such terror and despair. The unfathomable compassion of our God to be with us in suffering and death knows no limit. For he himself descended into hell.

We by ourselves cannot bring redemption to this hurting world. We, ourselves, are only weak, mortal beings, shattered by the events of our time. But the gospel, which is our lifeline, proclaims that Jesus Christ lives at the right hand of God the Father. The gospel tells us that Jesus died for us and was raised for us, that he reigns in power for us and prays for us. If this One, this One sent by God, emerged victorious over all that threatens us, not only death itself but also our own sinful hearts—our propensities toward hatred and resentment, our indifference to the suffering of those who are unlike us, our completely self-centered, rather than God-centered lives—if this One is both for us and with us, then we can emerge on the other side of such a trauma with hope.

When Nicholas Wolterstorff lost his beloved twenty-five-year-old son, Eric, in a mountaineering accident, he was plunged into a long night of grief. Questions about the goodness of God, the mystery of evil, the incomprehensibility of suffering burned within him, and he poured his anguished questions into his journal. Like his forebear in faith, Jacob, son of Isaac, who became Israel, father of the nations, Wolterstorff wrestled with God. When the new day finally dawned for him, he was led to see that "to believe in Christ's rising from the grave is to accept it as a sign of our own rising from our graves."[27] In his book, *Lament for a Son*, he writes:

> Slowly I begin to see that there is something more as well. To believe in Christ's rising and death's dying is also to live with the power and the challenge to rise up now from all our dark graves of suffering love. If sympathy for the world's wounds is not enlarged by our anguish, if love for those around us is not expanded, if gratitude for what is good does not flame up, if insight is not deepened, if commitment to what is important is not strengthened, if aching for a new day is not intensified, if hope is weakened and faith diminished, if from the experience of death comes nothing good, then death has won. Then death, be proud. So, I shall struggle to live the reality of Christ's rising and death's dying.[28]

As we dare to love this world with an open heart, we will, like the saints who have gone before us, suffer for its sake. "For to love our suffering, sinful world is to suffer."[29] But our suffering is transformed by Christ's

---

27. Wolterstorff, *Lament for a Son*, 92.
28. Wolterstorff, *Lament for a Son*, 92–93.
29. Wolterstorff, *Lament for a Son*, 90.

love as we share it in the community that he has called to himself. It is finally this suffering love that is at the heart of our vocation to ministry. "For as we share abundantly in Christ's sufferings, so through Christ we share abundantly in comfort too" (2 Cor 1:5). For the mystery at the very heart of our vocation is this mystery of participation. The New Testament calls it *koinonia*. By God's grace, we are permitted to share in Christ's own suffering and compassion for the world. As we take upon ourselves the courage to love this broken world, we are given a strange kind of comfort; not at all like the comfort that the world gives. It is not a comfort that magically makes it all better by ignoring the pain of the world around us or by trivializing the reality of evil. Rather, comfort comes in the form of a renewed passion for peace, in the form of solidarity with the meek of the earth, in the form of a "controlled fury of desire"[30] for God to fulfill his promise of redemption. It is the strange comfort that the Holy Spirit gives, groaning within us every time we cry out to God to deliver us from evil.

---

30. Katherine Paterson, quoting Frances Clarke Sayers, uses this phrase to describe art: "Art is a controlled fury of desire to share one's private revelation of life." Paterson, *Sense of Wonder*, 134.

10

A Repentance Unto Life

> "For godly grief produces a repentance that leads to salvation and brings no regret, but worldly grief produces death." (2 Cor 7:10)

Paul and the church at Corinth have a painful history together, which has caused Paul some considerable anguish. At this point in his second letter to the church, he's telling them about the emotional turmoil he has been through regarding them. After being anxious over how they might have reacted to his earlier letter, he is relieved to learn that they hadn't taken offense at his rebuke. On the contrary, they seem to have taken it completely to heart. What a relief! The risk he took in his earlier "stern" letter hadn't backfired, as he had feared it might, but seems to have brought about an earnest desire to make amends. Paul had been afraid of grieving them, but now he sees that their grief was salutary for it led to real contrition and the desire for reconciliation. For, as he goes on to say, "godly grief produces a repentance that leads to salvation and brings no regret, but worldly grief produces death."

Have you ever wondered about what had been going on in Paul's relationship with the church that makes their repentance such an occasion for joy? As is often the case in our relationships with those we love, Paul's pain over the Corinthian church was directly proportional to the depth of his love for them. We invest so much in these relationships and are sometimes willing to take huge risks to make them better. Earlier in the letter Paul had expressed his love for them openly when he exclaimed, "For I wrote you out of much affliction and anguish of heart and with many tears, not to cause you pain but to let you know the abundant love I have for you" (2 Cor 2:4). His distress was acute because so much was at stake. He saw his beloved church being led astray by false teachers who had slandered his name and tried to undermine his authority. They had accused him of many misdeeds and faults: of enriching himself at the expense of the congregation, of vacillating back and forth on important matters, of being proud and boastful, of being unskilled as a speaker, even of being weak and foolish, all with the clear implication that he was no true apostle.

Paul had suffered from their attack, but his hurt was not just personal. As one called by God to be an apostle of Jesus Christ, Paul knew that it was crucial for the Corinthians to acknowledge his authority, not for his own sake, but for the sake of the Gospel. If his apostolic authority were effectively undermined, the church would be in grave danger of receiving a "different gospel" and following "another Jesus" (11:4). So, throughout the letter, Paul is at pains to show the indivisible connection between his own life and ministry and the Gospel he preaches. As one commentator notes,

> Perhaps the central element in this letter is the close link uniting Paul's person and ministry with the kerygma he is charged to make known. Apostle and Gospel go together in indissoluble unity, just as Christ Jesus and his apostle Paul are closely associated as "Lord" and "servant." ... [They are] inextricably joined.[1]

Thus, to reject Paul was to reject the Lord he served.

While Paul was completely caught up in how the Corinthians would respond to his letter, fearing the worst but hoping for the best, his relief was also not merely personal. The fact that they took his rebuke to heart was a sign, not only of their affection toward him, but of their repentance toward God. For the deepest source of Paul's anguish had been that in remaining at odds with him, the Corinthians would cut themselves off from the Gospel. But now, after the long waiting for Titus's return, it appeared that all was well. Paul was moved by Titus's report: how grieved the Corinthians were by his letter and how much they longed for reconciliation with him! They earnestly cared for him and were indignant toward those who had offended him. So great, in fact, was their zeal for Paul that he now feared that those who had offended him would be punished overmuch and become overwhelmed by excessive sorrow. The Corinthians needed to forgive them, and Paul promised to forgive anyone whom they forgave. So, Paul was greatly relieved by the news Titus brought. Even though he had grieved them with his letter of rebuke, it was clear that the

---

1. Martin, *II Corinthians*, 63.

grief which he had inflicted had a salutary effect, for it had brought about a complete change of heart, a "*metanoia*," a radical turn in attitude and action. For Paul, it was a sure sign that God was at work within them, for Paul knew that authentic repentance is always a gift from God.

Even though things turned out well, it might be worth pausing here and consider the risk Paul had taken in rebuking the Corinthians. They might have taken offense at his words, stiffened their necks in self-defense and lashed out at him more vigorously than before. They might have refused to acknowledge the hurt they had caused him and renewed their challenges to his authority. Their grief might not have led to repentance, in other words, but only to resentment over his endeavor to call them to account. They might not have been sorrowful over their misdeeds but only sorry that they could not get away with them. Their response might have been one of denial, rationalization, and blaming. They might have renewed their accusations against Paul in an attempt to defend themselves. Such responses would surely have been a sign of the worldly grief that leads to death.

What is worldly grief? It is grief that essentially puts the self and the concerns of the self at the center of your heart, rather than God and the concerns of God. When someone calls you to account for something you have done, do you genuinely seek the truth of the matter at hand? Do you seriously consider the other's perspective, or do you seek immediately to deny responsibility and focus the guilt elsewhere? Those with some knowledge of the human heart may recognize themselves among those whose primary concern it is to defend the self. Instead of asking, "What is my part?" or, "What might be the truth in this accusation against me?" it asks, "How can I get the focus off me?" or, "How is this one rebuking me not living up to his responsibility?" Such worldly grief tends to take immediate offense at another's efforts toward correction; it is not really interested in the truth of the matter, and God's judgment is not genuinely sought. Instead, all available energy is spent on securing your position over against any accuser. It is no wonder that Paul was relieved that the Corinthians did not respond in this way.

Another sort of worldly grief, which also puts the self at the center but in a different way, would be a sorrow which refuses to be comforted. In such a scenario, the Corinthians might well have acknowledged the truth of Paul's rebuke, felt honestly convicted of their sin and experienced sincere remorse. But rather than allowing themselves to be judged and forgiven by a holy and merciful God, they might have been determined to be their own judge instead. They might have refused the consolation offered and become paralyzed by the magnitude of the wrong they had done. They might have tortured themselves with obsessive ruminations over the sin into which they had fallen. Those with some knowledge of the human heart may also be familiar with this kind of response. It occurs whenever you can readily acknowledge your sin or shortcoming but cannot bring yourself to receive God's forgiveness with simple humility. Instead, you secretly expect perfection of yourself, and in your heart of hearts, you want to be justified by your own goodness and not by the grace of God. You would rather be immobilized by self-recrimination, which is nothing but an inverted stance of pride, than allow yourself genuinely to face the consequences of your wrongdoing, confess it sincerely to God and your neighbor, and be forgiven and comforted by the One who desires to restore you. Such worldly grief leads to death because it is essentially a life without God. It is determined to be its own judge.

But neither of these things happened. The Corinthian church did not resist Paul's rebuke. They accepted its truth and grieved over the anguish they had caused him. Having accepted his chastisement, they proceeded to amend their ways and did not fall into despair over the wickedness that had brought them to that point. Rather than putting themselves at the center, they put God and God's will at the center. When God, rather than the self and its defenses or its ambitions, occupies the center of the human heart, there is no need for self-justification and defensiveness, on the one hand, nor for hopelessness and despair, on the other. There is only that "godly grief that produces a repentance that leads to salvation and brings no regret" (2 Cor 7:10 RSV).

One who genuinely repents of harming a brother or sister would be eager to find out what had caused offense, so that he could make amends. He would welcome the other, speaking as forthrightly as possible, describing those actions which caused him pain, so that he could seek to restore him. He would have no need to engage in self-justification, for he would know that attempts at self-justification always arise from self-deception. Living by faith in the Gospel, he would know that none of us stands beyond judgment; none of us can truly justify ourselves before God. He would know that all of our motives are mixed; all of our actions tainted by self-seeking.

Sorrow "according to God" is sorrow according to God's will, whose will it is to bring about true repentance. God's will works as a powerful force in the human heart, deepening our desire for reconciliation, for a renewal of trust and harmony with anyone we have hurt. When we hear about the harm that we have caused another, it is inevitable that we will feel grieved. But if we allow our sorrow to be directed by God, He will lead us to those actions which, by the power of the Holy Spirit, will move toward the other's restoration and our own redemption. The good news is that we do not have to carry the burden of our wrongdoing around with us and continue to be weighed down by it. Because God is gracious and merciful, because God desires that we confess our sins and be reconciled to our brother or sister, we are free to repent of whatever is burdening our heart.

If your brother has something against you, stop everything, don't even offer your gift at the altar of God, stop everything and go make amends to your brother. How can you worship God in spirit and in truth if your brother has something against you? How can you have harmony with God if you are at odds with those whom God loves, your brothers and sisters in Christ? It is precisely when your conscience is smitten, and you feel the full force of the pain of regret that you know that God is at work within you. For God himself is Lord of the conscience and therefore the source of all godly grief.

For it is solely by God's grace that we are led to an acknowledgment of our sins. Karl Barth goes so far as to say, "The humiliation of man is something for which he is glad and thankful."[2] When we are brought to a true recognition of our sin, there is a tremendous release. Finally, we don't have to pretend anymore, nor do we have to hide. When we are brought low, we at last understand the proper ordering of our relationship to God; we see our complete dependence upon him and his saving work in our life. No longer do we have to spend such immense energy trying to justify ourselves or our actions. No longer do we have to assert, maintain, or advertise ourselves. We can simply look to God as the giver of all good gifts, as the sustainer of our lives, as the source of truth, as the One who forgives our sins and redeems our life from the Pit. What a relief it is no longer to focus on ourselves and try to justify what we have done or failed to do. At last, we can simply focus on God and trust in his judgment and forgiveness.

There is no question that repentance is painful. But it is pain which, curiously, has joy at its center. For whenever we repent of our sins, we do so in the context of the knowledge of faith. It is because we know

---

2. Barth, *Church Dogmatics* 4/1, 363.

something about God's gracious judgment; it is because we know that God wants us to live as free people in glad communion with him and with our neighbor that we are able to repent. It is because we know God's desire for us to live according to the truth, that we are able to let go of the lies we tell ourselves whenever we seek to justify ourselves.

As we come together for worship and hear the Gospel preached week after week, we are given the opportunity to know ourselves as the sinner whom God wants to restore to life:

- I am the prodigal son who shamefully squanders all that my Father has given me—not just the material wealth which I spend on things which corrupt my soul—but the immense love which he has poured into me, hoping that I will make something of the life he has given me.
- I am the Samaritan woman, looking for a love which can satisfy the deep thirst of my soul, but never finding it despite having given myself to one man after another.
- I am Peter who is so sure of myself that I brag about my faithfulness, certain that I would never deny my Lord, but in finding myself afraid for my life, swear that I have never known him.
- I am the disciple who looks at Jesus' hands and side and sees what my disobedience and betrayal and denial have cost him. Hiding in the upper room, filled with guilt and shame and fear, I am astonished to be offered Jesus' peace and forgiveness.
- We are the beloved church at Corinth, who boast in our superior knowledge, who sit in judgment over others in the church, who wrongfully slander those in authority over us, and who cling to our cherished factions rather than recognize the unity of the body of Christ.

In each case, and in countless others, we are faced with a truth about God that is intimately joined to a truth about ourselves. The truth about God is that He loves us with a fierce tenderness, with a depth impossible to fathom, with overflowing generosity. His rebuke may be gentle when gentleness is needed, but there is also a kind of no-nonsense insistence on facing the truth. There is judgment in God's lovingkindness. How could it be otherwise, given that we are sinners who rebel against God? But the judgment itself is merciful; that is to say, God's judgment puts a limit to the bottomless pit of our bent toward self-destruction. It is God's loving judgment that brings the prodigal son to himself. He is finally released from the imprisonment of his obstinate heart and is set free to go to his father and confess his unworthiness. It is Jesus' loving judgment that does not skirt the truth of the Samaritan woman's sordid sexual history; in fact, he "tells her everything she has ever done," yet he does it in such a way that she is filled with awe and joy and is set free to begin her life anew. For Peter, the moment of judgment comes when the cock crows the third time and Jesus looks at him (With reproach? With sorrowful love?), and he goes out and weeps bitterly. The disciples' immersion in fear and grief and shame comes to an unexpected end when the Crucified One appears in their midst and gives them the gift of his inexpressible peace. Paul's love reaches the Corinthians, smiting their conscience and bringing about a godly grief that produces a repentance unto life.

"It is a fearful thing," said Max Scheler, "that we can win life only on the dark via dolorosa of repentance. But it is glorious that we have any way to life."[3] Jesus, the Crucified One, appears in the midst of his disciples with a heart overflowing with love. The One we betrayed and denied and deserted appears among us with his gift of peace. How is this possible? We cannot comprehend nor can we fathom the depth of a love like this. We only know that it makes us ashamed of all our bickering and pride and our pathetic little attempts at making ourselves important. Faced with such a love, we can let all that go. We no longer have to focus on ourselves at all. Now we can focus on the One who gives us life and hope and his inexpressible peace. "Love so amazing, so divine, demands my soul, my life, my all." Amen.

---

3. Scheler, *On the Eternal in Man*, 61–62.

11

Our Life Together

Called to Compassion

The healing of Bartimaeus is just one of the many stories recorded in the New Testament that enables us to see the depth of Jesus' compassion for human suffering. Over the years, I have returned to this story again and again for inspiration and instruction. I imagine the blind man sitting by the roadside for weeks with his ears wide open, waiting to hear if Jesus will pass by. When he hears the jostling crowds this day, he strains to identify who is making such a commotion. Upon hearing that it is indeed Jesus, he knows that his moment has come! He immediately cries out, "Jesus, Son of David, have mercy on me!" When those around him try to hush him up, it only increases his determination to be heard all the more. He cries out again, "Son of David, have mercy on me!" (Mark 10:47–48). And Jesus stops and calls him.

Have you ever noticed how often Jesus stops whatever he is doing and pays attention to the one who cries to him for help? So many stories flood the mind: Jairus, pleading on behalf of his dying daughter; the leper who comes to him, begging to be made clean; the disciples terrified by the storm on the Sea of Galilee; the demoniac who cries out in anguish night and day; even the hemorrhaging woman who sneaks up behind him, desperate for the healing that has eluded her despite years of searching. Though each person's situation is unique, Jesus sees what is truly in their hearts and addresses each one in their particular distress.

These stories sound like concrete illustrations of Psalm 107 with its litany-like refrain, "Then in their trouble they cried to the Lord, and you delivered them from their distress" (Ps 107:6, 13, 19, 28). In the psalm, we are given an imagination for the myriad circumstances in which God hears our cries for help: whether we are wandering in desert wastes, hungry and thirsty, or are prisoners in misery and gloom; whether we are afflicted with illness or with guilt, or are simply overwhelmed by the storms of life, crashing in on us.

Although Bartimaeus cries out for mercy, not compassion, mercy and compassion are so closely interconnected in Scripture that they are used almost interchangeably. The rhetorical device of parallelism used in Romans 9, for example, underscores the importance of what is being said by saying it twice, each with its own nuance:

- "I will have mercy on whom I have mercy, and I will have compassion on whom I have compassion." (Rom 9:15)
- The Gospel of Luke combines the two attributes by speaking of God's "merciful compassion." (Luke 1:78)
- While both are features of God's grace and lovingkindness, mercy especially emphasizes God's sovereign power to save and compassion his willingness to enter fully into our human plight.
- The Lord's decision to be God-with-us is evident in how profoundly he takes our suffering to heart.

The mercy of God, as described by Karl Barth, reveals the "free inclination of an unconditionally superior one toward one who is unconditionally subordinate" and is characterized by God's "readiness to share in sympathy the distress of another, a readiness which stamps all his doing and being."[1]

By calling on Jesus as the Son of David, Bartimaeus acknowledges Jesus' royal power, as one in the lineage of David, the King of all Israel. He thus recognizes Jesus as God's designated agent, as one who has the power of a King to grant mercy to a supplicant. The gap between the powerlessness of the beggar and the power of the King is especially pronounced.

Jesus Christ as one who is *both* fully God and fully human combines these attributes: the mercy of God Almighty with the compassion of one like us, a fellow sufferer. According to Mark, Jesus is moved with compassion when he looks out at the gathering crowds, "because they [are] like sheep without a shepherd" (Mark 6:34).

- This is not simply a passing feeling, but rather something that affects him at the core of his being.
- Profound caring for another's distress was thought to reside in the very bowels of a person.

1. Barth, *Church Dogmatics* 2/1, 369.

- Saying that his response is gut-wrenching would capture something of the flavor of the Greek word: *splanchnizomai*.
- Jesus is moved to his very entrails when he sees the masses so hungry and desolate, so in need of sustenance, healing, and hope.
- And though surrounded by multitudes day after day, he still hears each individual's cry.

It is also striking to notice how the one called blind in this story is in fact the only one who has the eyes (i.e., the spiritual perception) to see who Jesus truly is. Though he suffers from the affliction of physical blindness, he sees more clearly than many in the crowd around him. For Bartimaeus not only acknowledges Jesus' royal power, but also trusts in his loving compassion from the start, when he cries out to him.

- From the very beginning of the dramatic scene, we are clued in to the fact that Bartimaeus sees with eyes of faith.
- He is at the ready and seizes the moment when it comes.
- If he could only make his voice heard over the din of the crowd, then Jesus would hear him and be gracious to him.
- Amid all the noise and clamor, Jesus does hear his voice and says, "Call him."
- The crowd, which had been so eager to silence him, is now instructed to assist him.
- He who has sat invisibly at the margins of the community is now thrust into its center.
- For when Bartimaeus hears that Jesus is calling him, he throws off his mantle and springs up.
- He leaps into decisive action and is at Jesus' side in an instant.

A helpless blind beggar throws off his cloak and springs up? Don't you feel wonder-struck when you hear that? Here is our clue that a miracle is already underway, even before Bartimaeus asks for what he needs. Faith in the loving heart and inexpressible power of God is mysteriously already his. Upon seeing his faith, Jesus asks him directly, "What do you want me to do for you?" Bartimaeus doesn't miss a beat. He knows his heart's desire. "Master, let me receive my sight." I imagine that this has been his prayer for a long, long time.

I suspect that those who have committed themselves to a life of prayer will know their need when Jesus stands before them. Those who are aware of their complete dependence upon God for the gift of life itself—

- for their daily bread,
- for the forgiveness of their sins,
- for deliverance from temptation and evil,
- for the healing of their bodies and spirits,
- for the willingness to forgive those who have hurt them,
- indeed, for the wisdom, courage, and hope that come from God's Spirit alone—
- when Jesus stands before them, asking about what they need, they will be ready with their answer. They won't hesitate.
- Like Bartimaeus, they will entrust themselves to him entirely. They will spring up in joy!

Here I am reminded of those strange sayings that we know as the Beatitudes. Jesus speaks of blessings that belong to the meek, the broken-hearted, the poor and humble, to those who ache for justice and peace, or who are persecuted for seeking it. All those who suffer because of their yearning for God's Kingdom to come, these are the ones who are blessed. But how can such affliction be a blessing? The blessing is not in the affliction itself, but rather in the durable faith that grows as they learn to depend upon God. The blessing is the rock-solid trust that God will see them through.

By contrast, when we are accustomed to relying exclusively on our own strength, on our natural gifts, or intelligence or education, then we might not see the depths of God's compassion until we are brought low. Nicholas Wolterstorff, professor of philosophical theology *emeritus* at Yale Divinity School, writes of how his understanding of God shifted after his first-born son fell from a mountain slope at the age of twenty-five and died. In his book, *Lament for a Son*, Wolterstorff writes:

> For a long time, I knew that God is not the impassive, unresponsive, unchanging being portrayed by the classical theologians. I knew of the pathos of God. . . . But strangely, his suffering I never saw before. God is not only the God of the sufferers but the God who suffers. The pain and fallenness of humanity have entered into his heart. Through the prism of my tears, I have

seen a suffering God.... And great mystery: to redeem our brokenness and lovelessness, the God who suffers with us did not strike some mighty blow of power but sent his beloved son to suffer like us, through his suffering to redeem us from suffering and evil. Instead of explaining our suffering, God shares it. But I never saw it. Though I confessed that the man of sorrows was God himself, I never saw the God of sorrows.[2]

Those who have really seen Jesus' compassionate heart, and who have come to trust that Jesus is the living presence of God, will find themselves shouting out with the psalmist: "You have shown me the path of life. In your presence, there is fullness of joy" (Ps 16).

Such fullness of joy becomes a wellspring of life inside us, to which we can return for refreshment, even in the midst of struggle and sorrow. Compassion, in the sense that I am speaking of it, is not an abstract theological principle, but rather an attribute of our living Lord. It is not a human virtue that we must struggle to develop, but rather a divine gift, given to us as we participate in *God's* work among us. No longer blinded to God's power at work among us, we become witnesses to Jesus Christ by offering others the compassion that we ourselves have, by grace, received.

The blessing of a life together, centered on worship and the communal study of God's life-giving Word, as we are privileged to enjoy, is an incomparable gift. Dietrich Bonhoeffer reminds us on the first page of his book, *Life Together*, that "it is not to be taken for granted that the Christian has the privilege of living among other Christians." Bonhoeffer wrote these words just as his own community was threatened at its core, as the Nazi party in Germany was sending some off to war, some off to prison, and others, including Bonhoeffer himself a few years later, off to concentration camps.

We are faced today with enormous challenges in our nation, in our world, and also here at Princeton Seminary. Recent events in our common life prompt me to ask: If you were to imagine Jesus standing before our community, asking, "What do you want me to do for you?" what would your answer be?

- I am asking this question, not simply about your individual distress, but more so about the distress you experience as a member of this community.

---

2. Wolterstorff, *Lament for a Son*, 81–82.

- Of course, the two are inseparable, but the focus of my question is on how you perceive the needs of *our shared life* together and not simply your personal need.
- Would you be ready with your answer when Jesus sees your mustard seed of faith?
- Would you have the courage of Bartimaeus to cry out your lament?

In light of an email I read this summer about our community, I found myself crying out to God once again for the healing of racial tensions and divisions among us.

- The email spoke of an act of "hate speech that seemed to be directed as a racial slur against one of our families."
- I felt heartsick as I read it. My stomach tensed up, tears burned at the back of my eyes, and I felt dread in my belly, a confusing knot of alarm and anger, bewilderment, fear, and sorrow.
- I imagined the shock, the hurt, the fear, and the anger that the targeted families or other racial minorities might be feeling.
- I also thought about the many efforts that have been made in recent years to work toward racial reconciliation and lamented that such an act of violence might undermine the good work and good will of so many.
- A single incident like this affects our entire community. A comment by Harry Emerson Fosdick seems apt: "We have even secret sins which poison the wells from which other people drink."[3] Though done in secret, this racial slur poisons us all.

Kaethe Weingarten, a psychologist and professor emerita at Harvard Medical School, has named experiences like this as "common shock."[4] Common shock is widespread because it includes not only the direct victims of violence and violation, but also all those who are witnesses. Common shock affects all of us, but each of us in an idiosyncratic way, as we each attempt to make meaning out of what has occurred. When we "experience events and exchanges that disturb us," Weingarten comments: "every one of us must metabolize daily jolts. Since few people are aware of the chronically debilitating effects of common shock, few people know how to deal

---

3. Fosdick, *Riverside Sermons*, 297.
4. Weingarten, "Witnessing the Effects of Political Violence," 51.

with it themselves, or crucially, help children do so."[5] Her comment is very much to the point in our situation, for I imagine that those with children would feel the impact of this incident all the more viscerally.

African Americans, immigrants, people of color, or anyone perceiving themselves to be the targets of a racial slur may be especially concerned over how to talk about it with their children. Weingarten illuminates the dilemma when she writes: "A parental imperative is to keep one's children from harm. Warning children about danger is a primary means of safeguarding them. However, when the warnings themselves terrify and have the potential to harm, parents are in a terrible bind."[6]

From my study of the neuroscience of trauma in recent years, I have come to appreciate how impossible it is for children (or any of us) to learn and grow if they are surrounded by threat and violence. Without a sense of safety, none of us can take in new information, let alone interact with it creatively, connecting it to what is already known, so that it becomes meaningful knowledge. Such a realization is obviously important to an academic institution, which cannot function at all apart from an optimal learning environment for all its members. So, I was encouraged as I read in the email that we will be provided with opportunities to "grow as a learning community in identifying and rooting out racism, discrimination, and other impediments to inclusion of all members of our community and beyond."

What might this entail? How might we go about the huge task before us with some degree of confidence or hope that we can succeed? Since we are a learning community, a reading community, we will no doubt read what others have written, to consider and discuss their ideas. As we do so, however, we cannot afford to distance ourselves emotionally from the impact of what we read. We need to find a way to reach one another's hearts as we read together. Here I am reminded of something James Baldwin said more than fifty years ago:

> You think your pain and your heartbreak are unprecedented in the history of the world, but then you read. It was Dostoevsky and Dickens who taught me that the things that tormented me most were the very things that connected me with all the people who were alive, or who ever had been alive. Only if we face these open wounds in ourselves can we understand them in other people.[7]

5. Weingarten, "Witnessing the Effects of Political Violence," 51.
6. Weingarten, "Witnessing the Effects of Political Violence," 51.
7. As quoted by Howard, "Doom and Glory," 89.

Can we use this opportunity to discover that the things that torment us most are the very things that connect us with each other? Can we find a way for this open wound to draw us together as a community called to compassion? "If one member suffers, we all suffer together." Baldwin wisely notes, "Not everything that is faced can be changed. But nothing can be changed until it is faced."[8]

This is the question I want to address: Can we find a way together, as one body bound together in our love for Jesus Christ, to bear the unbearable burden of racism in our beloved community so that it does not separate and estrange us from one another?

It is important to note that though we all suffer this burden, the suffering of the witness is not to be confused with the suffering of those whose group has been harmed directly by violence.

In his book, *Suffering Witness: The Quandary of Responsibility after the Irreparable*, James Hatley writes:

> By witness is meant a mode of responding to the other's plight that ... becomes an ethical involvement. One must not only utter a truth about the victim but also remain true to her or him. In this latter mode of response, one is summoned to attentiveness, which is to say, a heartfelt concern for and acknowledgment of the gravity of violence directed toward particular others. In this attentiveness, the wounding of the other is registered in the first place not as an objective fact but as a subjective blow, a persecution, a trauma.... We find that our witness of the other who suffers is itself suffered.... We suffer, so to speak, the impossibility of suffering the other's suffering.[9]

Those of us who are witnesses, and not directly targeted, are "summoned to attentiveness" and directed toward the ones who are hurting. In order to hear the wounding "not as an objective fact but as a subjective blow," we need to take the time to listen to how it affects our neighbors personally. To listen, to pay attention. To find out what matters to each one. It is the subjective blow, the experience of persecution, the trauma that has been suffered that needs to be heard with tenderness. Our solidarity and caring are conveyed as we listen and respond to the hurt, or the anger, or to the fear of each one.

His last point, "that we suffer, so to speak, the impossibility of suffering the other's suffering," is also important to grasp. No matter how much

8. Baldwin, "As Much Truth as One Can Bear."
9. Hatley, *Suffering Witness*, 3, 5.

we care for those who have been hurt or been made afraid, we might never fully understand what they are going through. Unlike Jesus, we cannot see truly what is in another's heart. Our understanding is limited. Weingarten reminds us that it is important to "ensure that at no point do we ever confuse whatever suffering might come from witnessing with the suffering that we are witnessing." They "are not akin to each other," and we "have an ethical responsibility to ensure that we are not confused by this."[10]

Weingarten differentiates the task of the sufferer from the task of the witness. While the task for the sufferer is to *resist isolation*, the task for the witness is to *refuse indifference*. I want to address each of these in turn.

First, for those who understand themselves to be directly impacted by this racial slur or by other violating acts and attitudes within our community: *Resist isolation*. Do not take the hateful act into your heart and let it fester there. It has nothing to do with you and everything to do with the one perpetrating the violence. Talk to your neighbors to get support. Ask your friends to hold you in prayer. If the incident triggers traumatic symptoms, such that you are unable to focus your mind on your studies, let your feet lead you to our Student Counseling Center, where there is a cadre of therapists and counselors who are trained specifically to work with trauma, anxiety, and depression. Don't suffer alone in silence. Let your crying out to Jesus be heard by the members of his body, right here at our seminary.

Second, for those who are witnesses to this or other acts of violence in our community: refuse indifference. It is true that those in a position of privilege can more easily distance themselves from the impact, or even resort to minimizing it, thinking, perhaps, that I am "making a mountain out of a molehill." Whenever we insist on interpreting any kind of violence as a minor issue, we blind ourselves to someone's pain. Another way to distance ourselves is to spend our energy looking for a scapegoat. It is tempting to think that the racial slur might have come from someone outside our community and so excuse ourselves. And while I hope the perpetrator of this violent speech will be held accountable for his or her actions, we ought not to waver from our essential task, which is to care for those who have been harmed, to provide a sanctuary for grief to be shared, and to build whatever bridges of trust that we can by listening attentively and compassionately to our neighbors' pain. And to pray without ceasing for Jesus Christ to break down the dividing walls of hostility.

---

10. Denborough, "Trauma, Meaning, Witnessing, and Action."

The psychiatrist Vamik Volkan writes: "When members of the victim group are unable to mourn such losses or reverse their humiliation, they pass on to their offspring the images of their injured selves and even the object images of those who hurt them. . . . The next generation is given, unconsciously as well as consciously, tasks to carry out for their ancestors, such as completing the mourning process or reversing the humiliation."[11]

Traumatic loss, heartbreak, the humiliation of entire peoples: Can we begin small, right here, in our own place of belonging to mourn together our country's history of apartheid—the radical separation among ethnic and racial groups—and our repeated failures to love one another? Can we listen to one another with respect and love, especially to those who have been harmed in such devastating ways? Can we together call upon our compassionate God to have mercy upon us, to help us find a way to hear one another into speech?

In his book *Life Together*, Bonhoeffer reminds us that Jesus Christ stands between each of us and every other member of the community. He writes, "We can meet others only through the mediation of Christ," and that "we will find full fellowship with [our brother or sister] only in the Christ who alone binds us together."[12] He goes on to say that "the most direct way to others is always through prayer to Christ and that love of others is wholly dependent upon the truth in Christ."[13] As we commit ourselves to pray for the afflicted in our community, we will also be drawn to them in a spirit of open-hearted listening. Our compassion will become palpable when it depends upon, but not apart from, Christ's own compassion.

The humiliation and trauma suffered by generations of African Americans, by generations of Native Americans, by generations of immigrants from around the world, is a burden too heavy for us to carry. It is too heavy for any individual to bear, or even, I believe, for a whole community to bear alone. We cannot atone for the sins of our ancestors, nor can we heal the suffering that people of color endured and continue to endure to this very day. It is only as we call upon Christ to intercede for us that we can enter into this space at all. We are mortal, fallen human beings who cannot right the balance. We cannot simply declare ourselves forgiven. We can only entrust ourselves to Jesus and cry out for his mercy.

---

11. Weingarten, quoting Volkan, "Tree Model," 143.
12. Bonhoeffer, *Life Together*, 36.
13. Bonhoeffer, *Life Together*, 36–37.

By God's grace, we are able to take what we have heard—all that we understand and all that we have failed to understand—and lay it at the feet of Jesus. Together, we can pray for deliverance. In his book, *Raging with Compassion: Pastoral Responses to the Problem of Evil*, John Swinton writes: "If we are to resist and transform evil, then it is vital to find ways to reclaim the practice of lament."[14] I believe that the Black Church has given the world church a priceless treasure in the cries of lament that have come to us as African American spirituals. Centuries of affliction and oppression have been metabolized and transformed into inexpressible beauty, resilient hope, and durable trust in the God who hears our cry.

Each of us needs to claim our particular gifts and give of them gladly for the good of the whole. "If the ear should say, 'Because I am not an eye, I do not belong to the body,' that would not make it any less a part of the body. If the whole body were an eye, where would be the hearing? If the whole body were an ear, where would be the sense of smell?" (1 Cor 12:16–17 RSV). Each person brings unique gifts to the community that no one else has. Each of you belongs to Christ's body as the unique and irreplaceable individual that you are; and you are essential to the working of the whole. The community needs to hear your voice even if, like Bartimaeus, you stand at the margins, even if you have experienced others trying to silence you. Do not allow yourself to be silenced. "Take heart, rise, he is calling you" (Mark 10:49).

---

14. Swinton, *Raging with Compassion*, 121.

12

Spiritual Trauma Care

Lifelines for a Healing Journey

In one way or another, many of us all over the world are coping with traumatic stress at this point in our collective life history—either through recent overwhelming losses, or through past trauma that threatens to be reactivated, through vicarious trauma as we witness the suffering of others, or perhaps through the sheer magnitude of the current collective trauma—the hugeness and profound uncertainty of it all. I believe that it is only as we learn to face our situation together in community that we can build the collective resilience and strength we need "to turn with [our] will intact to go wherever [we] need to go."[1]

As I meditate on the experience of trauma affecting people throughout the world, as country after country reports growing numbers of those afflicted with the coronavirus, I find myself in danger of being swept out to sea—a kind of panicky feeling of a powerful undertow taking over. A second image—that of being in a very small boat surrounded by the vast ocean, afraid of being tossed into the raging sea and shouting for a lifeline—also lives in me. Sometimes, I see myself with the disciples in the storm on the Sea of Galilee, crying out for Jesus to wake up, for heaven's sake, and save us from the mounting chaos. These images all point to something unimaginably huge that has come our way which requires us to find a trustworthy lifeline that will bring us securely to a place of safety and rest.

Hence, the word "lifelines" in the chapter title "Spiritual Trauma Care: Lifelines for a Healing Journey." The primary definition for the word "lifeline" appears in my dictionary as follows: "a line (such as a

---

1. Kunitz, "Layers," 217–18.

rope) used for saving or preserving life: such as a line along the outer edge of the deck of a boat or ship."[2]

Though I write this in the early days of what is considered to be a worldwide pandemic, it is not affecting everyone in the same way. The complexity of it staggers the mind. In every community, there are some who have been immersed in firsthand experiences of death for months (as in exhausted medical personnel), while others complain that their gym has closed, or that their eyes hurt from all the Zoom meetings they have to attend. Vast numbers of people are isolated from those they love. Just when people need one another the most, they are instructed to stay at home, and to distance themselves from neighbors, friends, and loved ones. The enormous disparities between the rich and the poor are set in stark relief. Some people do not know a single person who has died from COVID-19, while others are coping with the devastation of losing multiple family members in a single week. When illness strikes, the grief and fear are immense, as people are forbidden to be with their loved ones in the hospital during their time of need.

While the focus of my remarks will be from my own historical context, for that is the only one I know from the inside, I trust that there will be similarities to be found in other contexts. While it is crucial to be fully responsive to our own particular time and place, all of us the world over have been affected by *collective* trauma. It was here long before we were born. The particular historical, social, and cultural context *in which each of us lives also lives in each of us*. Trauma lives *in our bodies* even if the traumatic events we have experienced involve no bodily injury. It is for this reason that personal experiences of traumatic stress can easily be reactivated when collective trauma strikes.

In the early days of the pandemic, the storm seemed still to be outside me. But then the chaos threatened to come closer. Fears and anxieties began to pop up, sometimes related to my personal health and wellbeing, sometimes related to those I love and care for. But then, they spiked exponentially when George Floyd was murdered by a police officer in Minneapolis on May 25, 2020. It wasn't the first brutal murder of an African American man by police in my country. And appallingly, it wasn't the last. But it seemed to be a decisive moment in our collective history. It struck such a deep chord in the collective body of which I am a part, a sense of living through a watershed moment. Alicia Garza,

---

2. *Merriam-Webster*, "lifeline," https://www.merriam-webster.com/dictionary/lifeline.

co-founder of the Black Lives Matter movement, wrote in early August, 2020: "Everyone right now is longing for something different, something better. In the midst of all the grief and rage and pain, there's a hopefulness. There is a longing for who we can be."[3]

With these words, she gave voice to deep longings of our collective body, longings that can be painful to acknowledge because they emerge in the wake of grief and rage and pain. I do not believe that we can get to the hopefulness apart from *acknowledging* the depth of our collective grief, rage, and pain, and finding a collective *willingness* to face it together.

With the murder of George Floyd, COVID-19 suddenly became the backdrop for this other issue, seemingly more urgent, much more painful, with layers upon layers going deep in the collective psyche of my nation—the centuries-old wound that has never healed, the legacy of the enslavement of African peoples and their ongoing brutalization which we try to sum up with words like racism or white privilege, but which so poorly convey the centuries of collective terror, grief, and rage always present, even if festering just below the surface.

Trauma is triggered by "an inescapably stressful event that overwhelms people's existing coping mechanisms."[4] It is no wonder that so many people around the world felt overwhelmed by this murder. Hopelessness set in for unimaginable numbers of people who have spent their lives trying to heal this deeply ingrained collective trauma. The compounded effect of this brutal public murder coming when everyone's nervous systems were already taxed makes it understandable that this would be the "proverbial straw" that pushed people into such a state of frenzied intensity: the urgent need to take action. Either fight or flee! Or else just freeze, so overwhelmed that you have to dissociate and make yourself numb. This urgent need to act was felt by vast numbers, exacerbated by the weeks of feeling trapped or constrained by the "lockdown" orders of various governments around the world.

The urgent need to take action comes about as the autonomic nervous system goes on high alert; stress hormones are released, and the body prepares itself to fight the danger or to flee from it. We experience an elevated heart rate, difficulty in breathing, rising blood pressure, and an inability to stay warm. Our brains and nervous systems are finely tuned to perceive threat whenever it draws near. The vagus nerve that

---

3. Hartigan, "She Co-Founded Black Lives Matter," para. 18.
4. van der Kolk, McFarlane, and Weisaeth, *Traumatic Stress*, 279.

runs from the brainstem to the gut sends messages primarily from the gut to the brain, whenever the body senses danger. This happens in less than a split second. Every single experience from your past is stored in your body with an exquisite inner alarm system in place, priming you to flee, to fight, or, if neither of those are possible, to freeze. The freeze reaction, now called immobilization, shifts your consciousness dramatically. A kind of quiet detachment sets in.

Such a dissociative state is a numbing reaction to the intensity of what would otherwise be overwhelming pain. It doesn't always occur, but when it does, it indicates a greater likelihood of suffering post-traumatic stress disorder (PTSD). Psychiatrist Judith Herman writes that, "Studies of survivors of disasters, terrorist attacks, and combat have demonstrated that people who enter a dissociative state are among those most likely to develop long-lasting PTSD."[5] Fight, flight, or freeze all happen automatically, which means that they are outside a person's conscious control.

Trauma is unbelievably complex. It is not a single thing, nor even a *single set* of things, that you can identify from the outside, saying: yes, this is clearly a traumatic experience; or *no*, that one is not. Trauma arises from a *subjective* feeling of threat that cannot be adequately processed. The felt sense in the body is I AM NOT SAFE, or I DO NOT MATTER. The feeling of being overwhelmed cannot be predicted by the nature, magnitude, or intensity of the triggering event. "A traumatic reaction needs to be treated as valid, regardless of how the event that induced it appears to anyone else."[6]

With an unresolved traumatic experience, you go through life expecting the worst to happen. Instead of a sense of adventure over new opportunities, you feel scared and uncertain, afraid that something terrible might happen. Neuroscientists remind us that "neurons that fire together, wire together."[7] Our brains develop a vast web of interconnected associations such that visual, aural, olfactory, or other sensory cues in the world are wired together with the circumstances in which they first occurred, especially those circumstances that have a high emotional valence. When something reminds your neuro-circuitry of the trauma, symptoms can be unleashed, because of what has been wired together in your neural pathways. A. J. van den Blink writes: "Painful life experiences get encoded in our brains and bodies and can be reactivated with great intensity by the

---

5. Herman, *Trauma and Recovery*, 239.
6. Yoder, *Little Book of Trauma Healing*, 11.
7. Siegel, *Developing Mind*, 26.

right kind of trigger decades later, even if we believe we have dealt with them or have completely forgotten about them."[8]

The hyperarousal of the nervous system is like being on permanent alert, always poised for danger. It is as if there is an inner tornado constantly swirling inside your body, wreaking havoc with stress reactions.[9] Disturbing intrusive thoughts and emotions can be activated by events associated with the trauma, but which are not consciously remembered. For example, you might become intensely afraid of dogs, but have no conscious memory that a dog was barking loudly when you were assaulted. It is as if the event is in the body's tissues, but not in your narrative memory.

Victims of trauma might struggle to make sense of their symptoms because they don't have access to the larger context in which those symptoms initially arose. Frightened by the irrationality of their thoughts and emotions, they may develop intense feelings of anxiety or shame. They become fearful not only of the traumatic event itself (which often remains outside their awareness) but also of their reactions to it. Unable to make sense of their reactions, they may fear that they are "going crazy" and do whatever they can to suppress the pain or avoid anything that might remind them of the traumatic situation. This numbing response entails a kind of constriction of awareness which can sometimes be severe. For some people, it is like losing a piece of themselves, splitting off the painful experience so completely from consciousness, and remaining unaware that they have done so, but becoming numb or dead inside.

The felt sense of being overwhelmed can arise after a single terrifying event or it can grow over a period of years when chronic stress exists, such as under conditions of poverty or oppression, or in childhood developmental trauma. Children who grow up with terrified or terrifying parents experience high levels of chronic stress. When they suffer neglect or abuse at the hands of those upon whom they depend utterly, they may hold a number of ACEs (or Adverse Childhood Experiences). The more Adverse Childhood Experiences children suffer, the more prone they are not only to later trauma, but also to major chronic illness throughout their lives.[10]

Daniel Siegel, a psychiatrist who has studied the neuroscience of trauma, teaches people to approach the painful sensations, emotions, or memories with what he calls mindful presence.

8. van den Blink, "Trauma and Spirituality," 38.
9. Levine, *Waking the Tiger*, 20.
10. "Adverse Childhood Experiences (ACEs)."

The idea of mindfulness, developed originally in the context of Buddhist thought, has been shown to help people gain emotional resilience, even while living under trying circumstances. Here are the four elements he identifies: C-O-A-L: Curiosity, Openness, Acceptance, and Love. Though I am using his acronym, I develop it in my own way.[11]

If memories of trauma begin to emerge, instead of clenching in fear and shutting down your emotional receptivity, *get curious* about what is happening in your mind and body. Ask yourself gently: When did I notice my anxiety starting to rise? Was it a thought or an image that sparked it, or perhaps a sensation in my body? Was it something that someone said? What are the actual sensations that I am experiencing in my body: a quickened breath; a tight jaw or shoulders; a knot in my stomach; shaking in my legs or hands? What is the overall "shape" of it? Does a metaphor come to mind? A word or phrase that captures it?

Are there certain thoughts that I hear myself repeating such as "I cannot bear this"; or "I'll never get any relief"; or "This will never change because it has already happened, and I cannot change the past." Thoughts such as these, repeated over and over again, only serve to reinforce the traumatic cycle of suffering. Instead of *reinforcing the trauma* by thinking about your helplessness, ask yourself questions about what you are actually experiencing in the here and now. *Stay curious.*

Second, *stay open* to what is happening. There are good reasons (that you may not yet fully understand) for you to feel as you do. Trauma symptoms are not a sign that you are sick or crazy; they are your body's way of speaking about its distress so that you can pay attention to it and heal it. Be open to what is happening without judging it. Judgments about what should be only reinforce pain without creating the emotional space needed for true mourning. Even a slight shift in thinking from, "My husband *should* be here to walk our daughter down the aisle on her wedding day," to, "I *feel so sad* that my husband has died and will not be with us that day. It opens an aching hole of longing in my chest and *it hurts* to see my daughter's pain on top of my own." Shifting from judging what is happening to feeling what is happening could seem like a small shift, but experientially, it is huge. The "shoulds" keep us stuck whereas expressing our pain enables us to heal.

Siegel's third characteristic is developing an attitude of *acceptance*. For whatever reason, you are feeling anxious. Accepting this fact instead

---

11. Siegel, *Mindful Brain*, 15–20.

of fighting against it paradoxically makes it easier to tolerate. Acceptance doesn't mean it will always be this way. Nor does it mean that you are giving up or giving in. Instead, it is an attitude that says something like: "OK, this is where I am at. Right now, this is my experience." A certain level of acceptance frees you to become aware of your actual surroundings in the present. You are here in this room in the here and now. You are not there and then in the place of terror. It shifts your brain into relaxation mode and restores a sense of agency and choice. It also helps you to acknowledge the crucial fact that you actually have survived the traumatic experience.

Finally, *love*. This is an attitude of kind compassion toward yourself that you would extend to anyone going through something frightening, a dear friend or spouse, or a child whom you love. This is the key element, learning to offer yourself loving attention. If you cannot manage this on your own, you will need to turn to someone who can be with you, offering you their loving attention, helping you to regulate your own nervous system with their presence and love.

When people are unable to find a way to settle their bodies or calm their nervous systems when feeling overwhelmed, they will need to turn to someone they trust and ask them for help as they try to metabolize all the chaotic, overwhelming feelings. Those who learned early in life to keep themselves safe by not trusting others when feeling frightened and vulnerable, face a kind of catch-22: they actually need the strength and calm presence of another person to self-regulate their own nervous system, but to ask for help requires that they acknowledge how frightened and alone they feel. This can actually increase the overwhelmed feeling because they believe that they are safe only when they do not admit how fearful they feel. They learned as small children to protect themselves by pretending or hiding their true feelings, by not showing up as their truly authentic selves.

One of the single most painful aspects of traumatic suffering is the experience of what one author has called "alarmed aloneness."[12] It is a feeling that no one sees you, perhaps a belief that no one can be trusted, or that it wouldn't matter to anyone whether you lived or died. You feel all alone in the world, overwhelmed, and helpless. Allowing another into your inner world of fears, acknowledging your sense of helplessness, is

---

12. Peyton, author of *Your Resonant Self*, teaches about "alarmed aloneness" as a key constituent of traumatic suffering. See Concept #8 at Peyton, "10 Key Concepts." https://sarahpeyton.com/10-key-concepts-of-resonant-healing/.

the key factor in healing this sense of utter aloneness. This is what Robert Stolorow calls "finding a relational home" for traumatic suffering.[13] "Severe emotional pain cannot be endured, if it does not have a relational home, someone to hold what cannot otherwise be borne."[14]

Besides primary trauma, which happens to an individual, two other forms of trauma need to be mentioned—secondary trauma and intergenerational trauma—before we turn to the multiple collective traumas of our current world situation.

Secondary trauma is what you experience when you witness the primary trauma of another, often someone you care about, but not always; sometimes just hearing about what has happened to a stranger while listening to a news program can trigger secondary trauma. It is surely what happened to millions of people in the USA and also around the world as they watched the video clip of a white police officer kneeling on George Floyd's neck for more than eight interminably long minutes. Witnesses to murder frequently experience traumatic shock or vicarious trauma. People poured into the streets in outrage around the world and the grief, fear, and rage only increased as they were met by military force and brutal tactics of violence.

Secondary trauma especially afflicts those caregivers whose own unresolved and unhealed trauma is triggered as they listen to the suffering of those they care for. Whenever there is no acknowledgment of a caregiver's own unresolved pain, she might find herself struggling with a compulsion to "fix" the other as a way of alleviating her own distress. Those whose work exposes them daily to the pain and brokenheartedness of others are especially vulnerable to secondary or vicarious trauma. Weingarten names five career paths whose workers experience what she calls double jeopardy, whose personal traumas are constantly being re-triggered as they listen to the sad and frightening things that happen in the lives of those they serve: clergy, health workers, teachers, police, and journalists.[15]

All trauma involves witnesses. When those witnesses (such as those identified above) are awake and present—and able to stay present and truly hear the victims, the ones directly affected are able to process the event emotionally and move on. In fact, it is more important to notice what happens after a terrifying incident than it is to focus on the traumatic

---

13. Stolorow, *Trauma and Human Existence*, 10.
14. Hunsinger, *Bearing the Unbearable*, 18.
15. Weingarten, *Common Shock*, chapter 5.

trigger itself. People who have a compassionate witness are able to process, literally to metabolize emotionally, their sense of overwhelm. The witness is the one who throws the lifeline. The volatile energy of the traumatic event doesn't get frozen in the victims' bodies but is able to move through them. The afflicted ones are held in the warmth of their caring witnesses, their relational home, where they can be restored to a sense of safety. As they find themselves being fully received by another, they begin to recognize and acknowledge that they actually survived the trauma.[16]

Intergenerational trauma occurs when your parents or grandparents (or even your more distant ancestors) experienced trauma of such great a magnitude that they could not adequately metabolize their terror, rage, and grief. Immigration, poverty, suicide, physical or sexual abuse, alcohol or drug addiction, or the tragic loss of children (or a parent) at an early age; indeed, any unbearable family trauma will live on in the bodies of the children and grandchildren of those directly affected. Understanding something of the intergenerational transmission of trauma originally grew out of studies done of the children and grandchildren of Holocaust victims.[17] "Symptoms described by offspring as related to hearing about the Holocaust corresponded to symptoms described by people who had lived through the Holocaust, both of which were associated with lower than normal cortisol levels."[18] Anyone who has pondered their own family's history in any depth will intuitively grasp how this might be true. Bert Hellinger, originally a Catholic priest from Germany, then a missionary for twenty-five years in South Africa, and finally a trained psychologist, worked for decades in safe, carefully structured rituals, with the grandchildren of Holocaust survivors and the grandchildren of Nazis to help them acknowledge and bear witness to the unprocessed grief that has lived in their bodies all their lives, enabling them to engage in a process of conscious collective witnessing and mourning. His work addresses intergenerational family trauma as it intersects with the major collective traumas of the twentieth century.[19]

We have only to name some of these to imagine the vast scope of the collective trauma that lives in us whether or not we acknowledge

16. Babette Rothschild names this—recognizing and acknowledging that they have in fact *survived* the trauma—as the *first essential key* to trauma recovery. See her book: *Eight Keys to Safe Trauma Recovery*, 10.

17. Weingarten, *Common Shock*, 120.

18. Weingarten, *Common Shock*, 120.

19. Hellinger, *Love's Hidden Symmetry*.

it: the catastrophic immensity of the Holocaust; the bombing of cities throughout Europe and the nuclear bombing of Japan; unceasing wars since the end of World War II; famine; rape and sexual slavery; the sexual abuse of children (especially by trusted members of the clergy); the mass incarceration, public murder, and systemic oppression of people of color; 9/11 and the reactive wars perpetrated on the peoples of Iraq, Afghanistan, and Syria, leading to a refugee crisis of unfathomable proportions; apartheid in South Africa, Israel/Palestine, and the United States; assassinations of political leaders around the world; assassinations by drones; torture as a matter of policy; war crimes; widespread electromagnetic field pollution; the nuclear disasters of Fukushima and Chernobyl; climate change of catastrophic proportions; ocean pollution; the melting of the icecaps; massive extinctions of species and losses of biodiversity; fires that cannot be contained; hurricanes; earthquakes; volcanoes; tornadoes. Today, worldwide economic instability and threats of future wars encircle the globe.

It is impossible to acknowledge even a few of these accumulated collective traumas that live in our bodies and minds unless we can gird ourselves with a whole network of supportive friendships and daily practices. We need to gain an understanding of our collective history, particularly the catastrophic events of the twentieth century, in which genocide and ecocide became "normalized"; to receive a daily influx of poetry, song, and beauty, by which the human spirit can be uplifted; to gain the courage and resilience that comes from a "conspiracy of hope"[20] generated by the kind of nonviolent political action that is grounded in love for this world; to uncover a profound sense of belonging with our very own ancestors, with our actual neighbors, our religious and spiritual communities, and our extended and nuclear families. The greater the sense of belonging and vital participation in the communities that we actually belong to, the safer we will feel as we dare to acknowledge the level of pain, grief, and fear that we are coping with.

The more we are able to give voice both to our longings and our hopes, the more we will be able to consent to enter into a depth of collective mourning. Profound mourning in collective gatherings paradoxically gives rise to hope. Mourning together reduces shame, opens our hearts to the sheer magnitude of our love for the world, and deepens our

---

20. Hammer, "Lived Experience," 5: "Given the challenging odds of the wager of our generation, we require a conspiracy of hope to galvanize a transformation of global consciousness and action."

desire to act together in a responsive and responsible way, rather than in an outraged and reactive way. We need to have access to our ability to think clearly by staying connected to our prefrontal cortex. This is impossible to do if we remain in an alarmed state of fight, flight, or freeze reactivity. It is only as whole-brained and whole-hearted persons that we can think creatively and coherently about our situation.

The lifeline for collective trauma is collective awareness, collective mourning, and collective action. We need to find ways to create collective healing modalities that will enable us to integrate the legacies of our past and to mourn together. Many of us watched in awe as the collective creativity of various cultures found ways to promote courage and resilience. I'm remembering with gratitude the early weeks of the coronavirus outbreaks, where the people of Rome went out onto their balconies and began singing arias to their neighbors. It was so quintessentially Italian! They tapped into the collective wealth of the history of Italian opera, with all its tragedy and inexpressible beauty, and sang to each other.

Then I noticed that many people began giving away their gifts for free on the internet. Webinars on every imaginable self-care topic, daily meditations and prayer, yoga classes, rich poetry exchanges; somehow the internet became our village green, our commonwealth, where we could go to be with others and not feel so alone. There we could gaze into the faces of others, seeing them eye to eye, without their faces half-covered with masks. Funerals and weddings, hymn sings and coffee hours sprouted up in those communities whose resources enabled them to meet on the internet.[21]

Martha Cabrera, a psychologist who worked in post-war Nicaragua (just after the devastation wrought by Hurricane Mitch), described her country as a "multiply wounded, multiply traumatized, multiply mourning country."[22] Perplexed by the apathy, numbness, and sense of isolation among the people, she found ways to open up conversation about the losses that had been sustained but never talked about. She writes, "Unprocessed traumas and other wounds and grief explain much of the current lack of mobilization."[23] A kind of collective numbness had set in because of all the accumulated, unprocessed pain. She set about to create intentional structured spaces that could hold the collective suffering

---

21. Once again, it is important to acknowledge the shameful disparities that exist between the rich and the poor all over the world.

22. Cabrera, "Living and Surviving," 1.

23. Cabrera, "Living and Surviving," 3.

of each community. She notes how personal and social change are inextricably bound together. Not only is the personal political, but the political is also personal. After months of holding restorative circles, where people began to speak openly about how the calamities of the war and the hurricane had affected them, she concludes, "Our field work has led us to believe that we have to talk about that past, in fact our whole past history, if we want to heal ourselves."[24]

Our relational capacities can unleash tremendous power for healing and resilience, when we entrust ourselves to a process of mutual listening, speaking, and caring, when we come into one another's presence committed to speaking honestly and courageously about what we have found to be true. When we join our community with open hearts and open ears, we join as humble participants, knowing that the whole is far greater than the sum of its parts. We are just one small part of the whole, but every voice matters. The eye cannot say to the hand, "I have no need of you," nor again the head to the feet, "I have no need of you."[25]

A living faith functions as an indispensable lifeline. Anyone who loves Scripture will be uplifted by the stories that have sustained people of faith throughout the ages: stories of a trustworthy God who has delivered generations from every kind of devastation: from the ruin of the land (Jeremiah), from the intolerable oppression of enforced slavery (Exodus), and from countless personal afflictions (the Gospel narratives). The witness of Scripture is that our merciful God hears the cries of his people.

Our relationship with God is alive at every level of trauma, both individually and collectively calling upon our faith (or lack of it) with each kind of traumatic trigger. If the scope of trauma's impact is envisioned as an ever-widening circle of harm, "the gospel's restorative power is understood to emanate outward as the presence and work of Jesus Christ mercifully address every kind of human misery and need."[26] The lifeline of God's grace is the one that undergirds and upholds us during every kind of trouble. When we entrust ourselves, body and soul into God's and one another's care, we can stay afloat in turbulent waters.

Those of us in the church can also turn to the lifeline of prayer. When a practice of daily prayer has been strengthened by a living faith over time, trust will deepen and new risks will be ventured. Those who turn to God in prayer in both prosperity and adversity know in their

---

24. Cabrera, "Living and Surviving," 8.
25. 1 Cor 12:21 RSV.
26. Hunsinger, *Bearing the Unbearable*, 12.

bodies (not just their minds)—in their whole nervous system, from their gut to their brainstem, to their limbic system, to their whole embodied self, that they have a "relational home" in God. They know they can take their sorrow, outrage, and anguish to the One who has promised to take them to heart.[27]

While collective trauma has the capacity to intensify or reignite individual unhealed trauma, so also collective restorative practices can have a profound healing impact on personal trauma. That which is most deeply personal becomes part of the communal lament of the people of God through the ages. Years ago, Walter Brueggemann reminded us that:

> [The] public dimension of grief is deep underneath personal loss, and for the most part, not easily articulated among us. But grief will not be worked well or adequately until attention goes underneath the personal to the public and communal. My expectation is that pastors, liturgically and pastorally, most need to provide opportunity and script for lament and complaint and grief for a long time. No second maneuver after grief shall be permitted to crowd in upon this raw, elemental requirement.[28]

Whenever we consent to descend into our collective grief with a community we love, within the secure boundaries of ritual space, hope and trust are paradoxically restored.

Those of us who have witnessed the power of the gospel in our lives and in the lives of countless people we love, its power to bring joy, freedom, justice, peace, wholeness, in a word, God's own shalom, need to embody the hope that the gospel has given us. We who have witnessed its power to bring deep refreshment in times of drought, creativity, and new life when we least expect it, and the sheer grit to get through hard times, are called upon to speak. We are called upon to testify to the foundational lifeline of trust in a God whose faithfulness has carried generations of our forebears through trauma and tragedy. In the community of the church, we can share with one another the paradoxical comfort of participating in the sufferings and sorrows of our God as we have come to know him in Jesus Christ. We are given the spiritual solace of a relational home in God's love and in the mutual care of a whole community. We are also

---

27. Hunsinger, *Pray Without Ceasing*.

28. Brueggemann, as cited by John Swinton in *Raging with Compassion*, 121. See also "Unspeakable Things Spoken," by Cedric Johnson in Greider, Hunsinger, and Kelcourse, *Healing Wisdom*, for a description and analysis of a whole community engaged in a transformative healing process as it confronts horrific historic and ongoing trauma.

given countless opportunities for joining our voices in prayers of lament, in which our grief and rage and pain can all be expressed. By God's grace, our collective mourning will melt the frozen numbness of our hearts and paradoxically restore a sense of agency and hope.

Robert Jenson writes: "In historical fact and by manifest anthropological necessity, nothing but final hope ever sustains genuine suffering or enables creative historic action."[29]

Nothing but final hope. If we are to be sustained through the suffering of traumatic experience, it is only because we have been able to ground our lives in hope. We are given access to this final hope when we entrust our lives to the God who created us, to the One who has redeemed us, and the One who sustains us every day of our lives. Healing, whether physical, emotional, or spiritual, is always set within the unimaginable reaches of God's salvation. It is through the promises of the Gospel that we have access to the One in whom we can place our trust.

> The LORD is my light and my salvation;
> whom shall I fear?
> The LORD is the stronghold of my life;
> of whom shall I be afraid?
> I believe that I shall see the goodness of the LORD
> In the land of the living!
> Wait for the LORD;
> be strong, and let your heart take courage;
> yea, wait for the LORD![30]

---

29. Jenson, "Story and Promise in Pastoral Care," 113-23.
30. Ps 27:1-2, 13-14, RSV.

Bibliography

"Adverse Childhood Experiences (ACEs)." Centers for Disease Control and Prevention, April 2, 2021. https://www.cdc.gov/violenceprevention/aces/index.html.
Allen, Jon G. *Coping with Trauma: Hope Through Understanding.* Washington, DC: American Psychiatric Association, 2005.
Anderson, Ray S. *Self Care: A Theology of Personal Empowerment and Spiritual Healing.* Wheaton, IL: Victor, 1995.
———. *Spiritual Caregiving as Secular Sacrament: A Practical Theology for Professional Caregivers.* London: Jessica Kingsley, 2003.
———. "Toward a Holistic Psychology: Putting All the Pieces in Their Proper Place." *Edification: Journal of the Society of Christian Psychology* 1.2 (2007) 5–16.
Attard, Mario, Father. "Saint Vincent de Paul: The Apostle of Love." *Catholic Insight*, September 27, 2021. https://catholicinsight.com/saint-vincent-de-paul-the-apostle-of-love/.
Augsburger, David. *Hate-Work: Working Through the Pain and Pleasures of Hate.* Louisville: Westminster John Knox, 2004.
Baillie, John. *A Diary of Private Prayer.* New York: Oxford, 1936.
"Letters to the Editor." *Bangor Daily News*, January 21, 1991.
Baldwin, James. "As Much Truth as One Can Bear." *New York Times Book Review*, January 14, 1962. https://www.nytimes.com/1962/01/14/archives/as-much-truth-as-one-can-bear-to-speak-out-about-the-world-as-it-is.html.
Barth, Karl. *Church Dogmatics.* 4 vols. Edinburgh: T. & T. Clark, 1956–75.
Bass, Ellen, and Laura Davis. *The Courage to Heal.* New York: Harper, 2008.
Berry, Wendell. "Now You Know the Worst." In *A Timbered Choir: The Sabbath Poems 1979–1997*, by Wendell Berry, 192. Washington, DC: Counterpoint, 1998.
———. "Pray Without Ceasing." In *Fidelity: Five Stories*, 3–60. New York: Pantheon, 1992.
———. "Sex, Economy, Freedom and Community." In *Sex, Economy, Freedom and Community*, 117–73. New York: Pantheon, 1993.
Bloom, Anthony. *Beginning to Pray.* London: Darton, Longman & Todd, 1970.
———. *School for Prayer.* London: Darton, Longman & Todd, 1970.
Bonhoeffer, Dietrich. *The Cost of Discipleship.* New York: Touchstone, 1995.
———. *Life Together: Prayerbook of the Bible.* Dietrich Bonhoeffer Works 5. Minneapolis: Fortress, 1996.

The Book of Common Prayer. New York: Seabury, 1979.

Browning, Don. "Pastoral Care and the Study of the Congregation." In *Beyond Clericalism: The Congregation as a Focus for Theological Education*, edited by J. Hough and B. Wheeler, 103–18. Atlanta: Scholars, 1988.

Buber, Martin. *Between Man and Man*. New York: Macmillan, 1948.

Cabrera, Martha. "Living and Surviving in a Multiply Wounded Country." Revista Envío. https://www.medico.de/download/report26/ps_cabrera_en.pdf.

Calvin, John. *Institutes of the Christian Religion*. Translated by John Allen. Philadelphia: Presbyterian Board of Publication, 1902.

———. *Institutes of the Christian Religion*. 2 vols. Edited by John T. McNeill and Ford Lewis Battles. Louisville: Westminster John Knox, 1960.

Cane, Patricia Mathes. *Trauma Healing and Transformation*. Watsonville, CA: Capacitar, 2000.

Cole, Toby, Helen Kirch Chinoy, and Patrick Sheehan. *Actors on Acting*. New York: Three Rivers, 1970.

Del, Martin. *Battered Wives*. New York: Pocket, 1976.

Denborough, David. "Trauma, Meaning, Witnessing and Action: An Interview with Kaethe Weingarten." *The International Journal of Narrative and Community Work* 3/4 (2005) 72–76.

Diagnostic and Statistical Manual of Mental Disorders: DSM-III-R. United Kingdom: American Psychiatric Association, 1987.

"Domestic Violence Timeline." The Pennsylvania Child Welfare Resource Center, Handout 3. https://www.pacwrc.pitt.edu/Curriculum/310DomesticViolence IssuesAnIntroductionforChildWelfareProfessionals/Handouts/HO3Domestic ViolenceTimeline.pdf.

Duckro, P. N., and P. R. Magaletta. "The Effect of Prayer on Physical Health: Experimental Evidence." *Journal of Religion and Health* 33.3 (1994) 211–19.

Eddy, K. W. *Celtic Prayers*. Edited by Avery Brooke. New York: Seabury, 1981.

Eddy, Robert, and Kathy Wonson Eddy. *Cry of the Wild Goose: Celtic Prayers and Songs of Resurrection*. Compact Disc. Randolph, VT: Quaker Hill, 1984.

"Episcopal Clergy Wellness: A Report to the Church on the State of Clergy Wellness, June 2006." Credo Institute, 2006. https://www.cpg.org/globalassets/documents/ publications/credo-clergy-wellness-report.pdf.

Felitti, V. J., et al. "Relationship of Childhood Abuse and Household Dysfunction to Many of the Leading Causes of Death in Adults: The Adverse Childhood Experiences (ACE) Study." *American Journal of Preventative Medicine* 14.4 (1998) 245–58.

Fenhagen, James C. *Mutual Ministry*. New York: Seabury, 1977.

Frei, Hans W. "An Afterword to Eberhard Busch's Biography of Barth." In *Karl Barth in Re-View*, 95–116. Pittsburgh Theological Monograph Series 30. Eugene, OR: Pickwick, 1981.

Fortune, Marie. *Keeping the Faith: Guidance for Christian Women Facing Abuse*. San Francisco: HarperOne, 1995.

Fosdick, Harry Emerson. *Riverside Sermons*. New York: Harper & Brothers, 1958.

Gendlin, Eugene. *Focusing*. New York: Bantam, 1981.

Gill, Raj, Lucy Leu, and Judi Morin. "Freeing Ourselves of Self-Violence." In *NVC Toolkit for Facilitators*, 227–33. Charleston, SC: BookSurge, 2009.

Gilligan, James. *Violence: Reflections on a National Epidemic*. New York: Random House, 1996.

Greider, Kathleen, Deborah van Deusen Hunsinger, and Felicity Brock Kelcourse. *Healing Wisdom: Depth Psychology and the Pastoral Ministry*. Grand Rapids: Eerdmans, 2010.

Gritsch, Eric W. "Vocation." In vol. 4 of *The Oxford Encyclopedia of the Reformation*, edited by Hans Hillerbrand, 245–46. New York: Oxford, 1996.

Halaas, Gwen W. *The Right Road: Life Choice for Clergy*. Minneapolis: Augsburg, 2004.

Hammer, Dean. "The Lived Experience of a Psychologist Activist." *Psychotherapy and Politics International* 18 (June 2020) 1–5. https://onlinelibrary.wiley.com/doi/abs/10.1002/ppi.1536.

Harrison, Everett. "Compassion." In *Baker's Dictionary of Theology*, by Everett Harrison et al., 132. Grand Rapids: Baker, 1960.

Hartigan, Rachel. "She Co-Founded Black Lives Matter. Here's Why She's So Hopeful for the Future." *National Geographic*, May 3, 2021. https://www.nationalgeographic.com/history/article/alicia-garza-co-founded-black-lives-matter-why-future-hopeful?cmpid=org&rid=67192388F48109F9D1726384F5AEC7BA.

Hatley, James. *Suffering Witness: The Quandary of Responsibility after the Irreparable*. Albany: SUNY, 2000.

Hellinger, Bert. *Insights*. Heidelberg: Carl-Auer-Systeme Verlag, 2002.

———. *Love's Hidden Symmetry*. Phoenix: Zeig Tucker and Co., 1998.

Herman, Judith. *Trauma and Recovery: The Aftermath of Violence—From Domestic Abuse to Political Terror*. New York: Basic Books, 1992.

Horney, Karen. *Neurosis and Human Growth*. New York: Norton, 1950.

Howard, Jane. "Doom and Glory of Knowing Who You Are." *LIFE* 54.21 (1963) 89.

Hunsinger, Deborah van Deusen. *Bearing the Unbearable: Trauma, Gospel and Pastoral Care*. Grand Rapids: Eerdmans, 2015.

———. "Bearing the Unbearable: Trauma, Gospel and Pastoral Care." *Theology Today* 68 (2011) 8–25.

———. "The Chalcedonian Pattern." In *Between Two Languages: Spiritual Guidance and Communication of Christian Faith*, edited by Tjeu van Knippenberg, 27–28. Netherlands: Tilburg University Press, 1998.

———. "Forgiving Abusive Parents." In *Forgiveness and Truth*, edited by Alistair McFadyen and Marcel Sarot, 71–98. New York: T. & T. Clark, 2001.

———. "Keeping an Open Heart in Troubled Times: Self-empathy as a Christian Spiritual Practice." In *A Spiritual Life: Perspectives from Poets, Prophets, and Preachers*, edited by Allan Hugh Cole Jr., 67–69. Louisville: Westminster John Knox, 2011.

———. "The Master Key: Unlocking the Relationship of Theology and Psychology." *Inspire* 5.2 (2001) 22.

———. "Prayers of Lament." In *Pray Without Ceasing: Revitalizing Pastoral Care*, by Deborah van Deusen Hunsinger, 138–56. Grand Rapids: Eerdmans, 2006.

———. *Pray Without Ceasing: Revitalizing Pastoral Care*. Grand Rapids: Eerdmans, 2006.

———. *Theology and Pastoral Counseling: A New Interdisciplinary Approach*. Grand Rapids: Eerdmans, 1995.

Hunsinger, George. *Evangelical, Catholic and Reformed: Doctrinal Essays on Barth and Related Themes*. Grand Rapids: Eerdmans, 2015.

———. *How to Read Karl Barth: The Shape of His Theology*. New York: Oxford University Press, 1991.

Jaeger, Marietta. *The Lost Child*. Grand Rapids: Zondervan, 1983.
Jenson, Robert W. "Story and Promise in Pastoral Care." *Pastoral Psychology* 26.7 (1977) 113–23.
Jinkins, Michael. *Survey of Recent Graduates Working in Pastoral Ministry*. Austin: Austin Presbyterian Theological Seminary, 2002.
Jones, Serene. *Trauma and Grace: Theology in a Ruptured World*. Louisville: Westminster/John Knox, 2009.
Jordan, Judith. "The Meaning of Mutuality." In *Women's Growth in Connection: Writings From the Stone Center*, edited by J. V. Jordan et al., 87–88. New York: Guilford, 1991.
Journey of Hope. "Our History." Journey of Hope. https://www.journeyofhope.org/mission/.
Kaplan, Alexandra G. "Empathic Communication in the Psychotherapy Relationship." In *Women's Growth in Connection: Writings from the Stone Center*, edited by Judith V. Jordan et al., 44–50. New York: Guilford, 1991.
Kaufman, Gershen. *Shame: The Power of Caring*. Cambridge: Schenkman, 1980.
Kohut, Heinz. *The Restoration of the Self*. New York: International Universities, 1977.
Kornfeld, Margaret. *Cultivating Wholeness: A Guide to Care and Counseling in Faith Communities*. New York: Continuum, 2000.
Küng, Hans. *The Church*. New York: Sheed and Ward, 1967.
Kunitz, Stanley. "The Layers." In *The Collected Poems of Stanley Kunitz*, 217–18. New York: W. W. Norton, 2002.
Lake, Frank. *Clinical Theology*. London: Darton, Longman and Todd, 1966.
Lanius, Ruth, and Ruth Buczynski. "Rethinking Trauma: How Neuroscience Can Give Us a Clearer Picture of Trauma Treatment." National Institute for the Clinical Application of Behavioral Medicine. https://s3.amazonaws.com/nicabm-stealthseminar/Rethinking-trauma-new/Ruth/NICABM-RuthLanius-Transcript.pdf.
Levine, Peter A. *Waking the Tiger: Healing Trauma: The Innate Capacity to Transform Overwhelming Experiences*. Berkeley: North Atlantic, 1997.
Lin, Bonnie E., "All This Is from God: Augsburger, Lederach, Barth, and Coutts on Forgiveness." *Pro Ecclesia* 28 (2019) 39–59.
Lindbeck, George. "Scripture, Consensus and Community." In *Biblical Interpretation in Crisis*, edited by Richard John Neuhaus, 74–101. Grand Rapids: Eerdmans, 1989.
Loder, James E., and W. Jim Neidhardt. *The Knight's Move*. Colorado Springs: Helmers & Howard, 1992.
MacNair, Robert. *Perpetration-Induced Traumatic Stress: The Psychological Consequences of Killing*. Westport, CT: Praeger, 2002.
Maloney, Newton. "Review of *Psychology, Theology and Spirituality in Christian Counseling*, by Mark McMinn." *Journal of Pastoral Care* 51.1 (1997) 119–20.
Martin, Del. *Battered Wives*. New York: Pocket, 1976.
Martin, Ralph. *II Corinthians*. Word Biblical Commentary. Grand Rapids: Zondervan, 1992.
Martyn, Dorothy W. "A Child and Adam: A Parable of the Two Ages." *Journal of Religion and Health* 16.4 (1977) 275–87.
Milbrandt, Jay. *The Daring Heart of David Livingstone: Exile, American Slavery, and the Publicity Stunt that Saved Millions*. Nashville: Thomas Nelson, 2014.

Miller, Jean Baker, and Irene Pierce Stiver. *The Healing Connection: How Women Form Relationships in Therapy and in Life*. Boston: Beacon, 1997.

Miller-McLemore, Bonnie. "Cognitive Neuroscience and the Question of Theological Method." *Journal of Pastoral Theology* 20 (Winter 2011) 64–92.

Nuland, Sherwin. *The Wisdom of the Body*. United Kingdom: Chatto & Windus, 1997.

Packer, James I. "Call, Called, Calling." In *Baker's Dictionary of Theology*, edited by Everett F. Harrison, 108–9. Grand Rapids: Baker, 1987.

Panksepp, Jaak, and Lucy Biven. *The Archaeology of Mind: Neuro-evolutionary Origins of Human Emotions*. New York: Norton, 2012.

Paterson, Katherine. *A Sense of Wonder: On Reading and Writing Books for Children*. New York: Penguin, 1995.

Patton, John. *Pastoral Care in Context*. Louisville: Westminster/John Knox, 1993.

Peyton, Sarah. "10 Key Concepts of Resonant Healing." Sarah Peyton (blog), November 11, 2020. https://sarahpeyton.com/10-key-concepts-of-resonant-healing/.

———. *Your Resonant Self: Guided Meditations and Exercises to Engage Your Brain's Capacity for Healing*. New York: Norton, 2017.

———. *Your Resonant Self Workbook: From Self-Sabotage to Self-Care*. New York: Norton, 2021.

Polanyi, Michael. *The Tacit Dimension*. Gloucester, MA: Peter Smith, 1983.

Purves, Andrew. *Reconstructing Pastoral Theology: A Christological Foundation*. Louisville: Westminster/John Knox, 2004.

———. *The Search for Compassion: Spirituality and Ministry*. Louisville: Presbyterian Publishing, 1989.

Reumann, John. "Koinonia." In vol. 1 of *The Encyclopedia of Christianity*, edited by Erwin Fahlbusch et al., 134–36. Grand Rapids: Eerdmans, 2003.

Rienstra, Marchienne Vroon. *Swallow's Nest: A Feminine Reading of the Psalms*. Grand Rapids: Eerdmans, 1992.

Roan, Sharon L. *Our Daughter's Health*. New York: Hyperion, 2001.

Rodenburg, Patsy. *The Need for Words*. New York: Routledge, 1993.

Rogers, C. R. "The Necessary and Sufficient Conditions of Theraputic Personality Change." *Journal of Consulting Psychology* 21(2) 95–103. https://doi.org/10.1037/h0045357.

Rosenberg, Marshall. *Nonviolent Communication: A Language of Life*. Encinitas, CA: Puddle Dancer, 2003.

Rothschild, Babette. "Applying the Brakes: In Trauma Treatment, Creating Safety Is Essential." *Psythotherapy Networker, Inc.* (January/February 2004) 1–4. https://yogafordepression.com/wp-content/uploads/applying-the-brakes-rothschild.pdf.

———. *The Body Remembers*. New York: W. W. Norton, 2000.

———. *Eight Keys to Safe Trauma Recovery: Take-Charge Strategies to Empower Your Healing*. New York: Norton, 2010.

Routley, Erik. "I Sought the Lord." In *Rejoice in the Lord*, by Erik Routley, 162. Grand Rapids: Eerdmans, 1985.

SAMHSA. "Trauma-Informed Care in Behavioral Health Services." Substance Abuse and Mental Health Services Administration, US Department of Health and Human Services, 2014. https://www.ncbi.nlm.nih.gov/books/NBK207191/box/part1_ch3.box16/.

Schaff, Philip. *The Creeds of Christendom: With a History and Critical Notes*. Vol. 2. New York: Harper, 1931.

Scheler, Max. *On the Eternal in Man*. New York: Routledge: 2009.
Search Institute. "The Asset Approach: 40 Elements of Healthy Development." Search Institute, 2017. https://www.search-institute.org/product/the-asset-approach-40-elements-of-healthy-development-2017-update/.
Siegel, Daniel. *The Developing Mind: How Relationships and the Brain Interact to Shape Who We Are*. New York: Guilford,1999.
———. *The Mindful Brain*. New York: Norton, 2007.
"STAR: Strategies for Trauma Awareness and Resilience." The Center for Justice and Peacebuilding. https://emu.edu/cjp/star/.
Stolorow, Robert D. *Trauma and Human Existence: Autobiographical, Psychoanalytic, and Philosophical Reflections*. New York: Routledge, 2007.
Sutton, Jeanette. "Convergence of the Faithful: Spiritual Care Response to Disaster and Mass Casualty Events."*Journal of Pastoral Theology* 16.1 (Fall 2006) 18–29.
Swinton, John. *Raging with Compassion: Pastoral Responses to the Problem of Evil*. Grand Rapids: Eerdmans, 2007.
Tedeschi, R. G. "Violence Transformed: Posttraumatic Growth in Survivors and Their Societies." *Aggression and Violent Behavior* 4 (1999) 319–41.
Tietje, Adam. "*Contra* Rambo's 'Theology of Remaining': A Chalcedonian and Pastoral Conception of Trauma." *Pro Ecclesia* 28.1 (2019) 22–38.
Torrance, James B. *Worship, Community and the Triune God of Grace*. Carlisle, UK: Paternoster, 1996.
Torrance, T. F. *The Christian Doctrine of God: One Being, Three Persons*. Edinburgh: T. & T. Clark, 1996.
Trible, Phyllis. *Texts of Terror: Literary-Feminist Readings of Biblical Narratives*. Philadelphia: Fortress, 1984.
Tutu, Desmond. *No Future without Forgiveness*. New York: Doubleday, 1999.
Ulanov, Ann Belford. *The Functioning Transcendent: A Study in Analytical Psychology*. Wilmette, IL: Chiron, 1996.
———. *The Unshuttered Heart*. Nashville: Abingdon, 2007.
van den Blink, A. J. "Empathy Amid Diversity: Problems and Possibilities." *Journal of Pastoral Theology* 3 (1993) 1–14.
———. "Trauma and Spirituality." *Reflective Practice: Formation and Supervision in Ministry* 28 (2008) 30–47. https://journals.sfu.ca/rpfs/index.php/rpfs/article/view/153/152.
van der Kolk, Bessel. *The Body Keeps the Score*. New York: Penguin, 2015.
van der Kolk, Bessel, Alexander C. McFarlane, and Lars Weisaeth, eds. *Traumatic Stress: The Effects of Overwhelming Experience on Mind, Body and Society*. New York: Guilford, 2012.
Volkan, Vamik. *Blind Trust: Large Groups and Their Leaders in Times of Crisis and Terror*. Charlottesville, VA: Pitchstone, 2004.
———. "The Tree Model: A Comprehensive Psycho-Political Approach to Unofficial Diplomacy and the Reduction of Ethnic Tension." *Mind and Human Interaction* 10 (1999) 142–206.
Webster, Richard. "The Bewildered Visionary." *The Times Literary Supplement*, 1997.
Weil, Simone. "Reflections on the Right Use of School Studies with a View to the Love of God." In *Waiting for God*, 105–16. https://www.themathesontrust.org/papers/christianity/Weil-Reflections.pdf.

Weingarten, Kaethe. *Common Shock: Witnessing Violence Everyday.* New York: New American Library, 2003.
———. "Witnessing the Effects of Political Violence in Families: Mechanisms of Intergenerational Transmission and Clinical Interventions." *Journal of Marital and Family Therapy* 30 (2004) 45–59.
Whyte, David. *The House of Belonging.* Langley, WA: Many River, 1997.
Wimberly, Edward P. *Prayer in Pastoral Counseling.* Louisville: Westminster John Knox, 1990.
Wilmer, Harry, "The Healing Nightmare: A Study of the War Dreams of Vietnam Combat Veterans." *Quadrant* 19 (1986) 47–61.
Wolterstorff, Nicholas. *Lament for a Son.* Grand Rapids: Eerdmans, 1987.
Yoder, Carolyn. *The Little Book of Trauma Healing.* Intercourse, PA: Good Books, 2005.
Zehr, Howard. "Doing Justice, Healing Trauma: The Role of Restorative Justice in Peacebuilding." *South Asian Journal of Peacebuilding* 1 (2008) 1–16.
———. *The Little Book of Restorative Justice.* Intercourse, PA: Good Books, 2002.

Index

acceptance, 204–5
accompaniment, 142–44
addictive behaviors, 17
Adverse Childhood Experiences (ACE), 71, 140n10, 203
alarmed aloneness, 143, 205–6
Allen, Jon G., 24
American Psychiatric Association, 12
Anderson, Ray, 5, 115, 150–54
anxiety, among spiritual caregivers, 119
Apostles' Creed, 63
apprenticeships, 54–55
associative empathy, 111
asymmetrical relationship
    basic theses for, 55–56
    conceptual integration, 39–41
    logical precedence of theology, 43–46
    translation, of logical levels concept, 41–45
    two natures of Jesus, 37–38
atonement, work of, 95
attachment, 108, 140n10
attentiveness, 195
attitudes, toward self and other, 119–20
attunement, 141–42
Augsburger, David, 17, 24
Augustine, of Hippo, Saint, 161
Austin Seminary study (2002), 133

Baillie, John, 88
Baldwin James, 194–95
baptism, 96

Barth, Karl
    approach to pastoral theology, 77–78
    background of, 57–58
    Chalcedonian imagination, 64–70
    Chalcedonian Pattern, 65, 68–69, 74
    Church Dogmatics, 57, 58, 59
    on God's identity, 47
    on God's mercy, 189
    on human dignity, 97
    on humanity, 173–75
    indestructible order, 34, 66–67
    on Jesus Christ as sinner, 36
    on Jesus' two natures, 37
    mitmenschlichkeit (co-humanity), 83, 142, 173
    on nature of knowledge, 168–70
    normative criteria for theological anthropology, 58–60
    on prayer, 87, 92
    pre-eminent practical test, 73–75
    recognition of our sin, 185
    as Reformed theologian, 4
    on relationships, 83–84, 86n4
    secular parables of truth, 62–64
    speculative theories *vs.* exact science, 60–62
    on theological understanding, 152–53
    trauma, a case study, 70–71
    trauma studies, dialogue, 72–76
Barth, Markus, 68
Bernhardt, Sarah, 175

Berry, Wendell, 163, 177
Black Lives Matter movement, 200–201
Bloom, Anthony, 176
body, felt sense in, 121
body sensations, 145, 145n21
Bonhoeffer, Dietrich
    God's listening to us, 105
    Life Together, 135, 192, 197
    loving one another through Christ, 86, 90
    on spirituality, 151
Browning, Don, 101–2
Brueggemann, Walter, 28, 211
Brunner, Emil, 57
Buber, Martin, 136–37

Cabrera, Martha, 209–10
Calvin, John, 61, 79, 113–14, 158
capital punishment, 24
care circuit, term usage, 149n26
Chalcedonian Definition, 33–34, 63, 64–65
Chalcedonian imagination, 6, 57, 64–72
Chalcedonian Pattern
    Barth and, 65, 68–69, 74
    conceptual integration, 39–41
    healing, context for, 50–53
    indestructible order, 37–38, 66–67
    indissoluble differentiation, 34–35, 65–66
    inseparable unity, 35–37, 66
    interdisciplinary map, 30–32
    logical precedence of theology, 43–46
    process, attention to, 53–55
    sorting "puzzle pieces," 7
    theological compass, 32–34, 45–46
    theological imagination and, 8
    theory of the unconscious, 46–50
    translation, of logical levels concept, 41–43
children
    attitudes towards, 119–20
    chronic stress in, 202
    trauma among, 21n47, 71, 75–76, 128–29, 140n8
    window of welcome, 143–44
    See also infants

Christian counselors
    interdisciplinary map, 30–32
    respecting self, 150–54
    self-empathy and, 132–34
Christian spirituality, description of, 3–4
Christians, direct access to God, 93
Christiansen, Molly, 173
The Church (Küng), 92
Church Dogmatics (Barth), 57, 58, 59
clericalism, in church community, 92
C-O-A-L: Curiosity, Openness, Acceptance, and Love, 8–9, 203–4
collective trauma, 1, 8, 129, 199–212
common shock, 193–94
community
    discernment, 172–80
    gifts of the Spirit, 167
    healing of, 192–98
    importance of, 4, 8–9
    learning prayers in church, 91–92
    pastoral care as work of, 92–98
    response to trauma, 28–29
    secular parable for, 75–76
    vocation from, 170–72
    See also koinonia
compassion
    attitudes, toward self and other, 119–20
    of God, 104–6
    nature of, 106–7
    needs, meeting of, 127–29
    related concepts, 106–13
    self-empathy, 113–19, 129–31
    self-judgments, 124–29
    self-pity, 118
    term usage, 112
    we are called to, 188–98
    See also self-empathy
compassionate communication, term usage, 116–17, 117n33
complex trauma, 1
conceptual integration, 39–41
Confessions (Augustine), 161
confessions of the church, 63
Connor, Jane, 123
constriction, term usage, 14
contemplative listening, 146

INDEX

core human needs, 8
core values, 124, 129
Council of Chalcedon (451), 32–33, 64
COVID-19, impact of, 199–212
curiosity, 204

de Paul, St. Vincent, 137
death, 108n13
demonic possession example, 49
depression, 126, 133
despair, 136
Diagnostic and Statistical Manual (1980), 12
A Diary of Private Prayer (Baillie), 88
discernment, 159–60, 172–80
disgust circuit, term usage, 149n26
doctrine of election
    Barth on, 60, 152
    Calvin on, 158–59
    knowing love of God and, 161
dogmatic affirmations about humanity, 73
dreams, 47

emotion circuit, term usage, 148–49n26
emotional connectedness, 112
empathetic imagination, 135
empathy
    description of, 109–10, 138
    to resonant empathy, 137–41
"Empathy and Diversity" (van den Blink), 138
Episcopal Clergy Wellness Report (2006), 132–33
Erikson, Erik, 162
Evangelical Lutheran Church of America (ELCA), 133
exact science *vs.* speculative theories, 60–62, 66

fear circuit, term usage, 149n26
felt sense, in the body, 121–22
Fenhagen, James C., 100
fight or flight, 14–15, 143, 201–2
flashbacks, 16
Floyd, George, 200–201, 206
Focusing (Gendlin), 121
forgiveness, 23–24, 96, 131–32, 137n4, 165

Fosdick, Harry Emerson, 193
freedom, to obey God, 59
freeze response, 15, 201–2
Freud, Sigmund, 18, 47, 52–53, 111
fruits of the Holy Spirit, 9, 64–72

Garza, Alicia, 200–201
Gendlin, Eugene, 121–22
Gilligan, James, 18
God
    of all comfort, 28
    Barth's normative criteria on, 58–60
    Christians, direct access to, 93
    compassion of, 104–6, 115
    the Creator, 160
    crying out to, 25
    dependence on, 191
    imago Dei, 83–84, 114
    loving judgment, 186–87
    mercy, 188–89
    the Redeemer, 162–65
    the Sustainer, 166–67
    as Trinity, 81–82
    See also Holy Spirit; Jesus Christ
godly grief, 7, 181–83
Gospel/Scripture
    Bartimaeus' healing, 116, 188–91, 193, 198
    Bible reading, 96
    healing to the suffering, 21–26, 44–45, 188–89
    Jesus Christ's trauma, 10
    Job, story of, 44
    love of God and neighbor/self, 113–16, 142
    need for agreement with, 72–73
    Samaritan woman, 153
    sinners in, 186–87
    story of Job, 67
grief, 181–87

Halaas, Gwen W., 133
Hatley, James, 195
healing
    context, 50–53
    prayers as resource for, 43–44, 54
    to the suffering (scripture), 21–26, 44–45, 188–89
Hellinger, Bert, 94–95, 139–40n8, 207

Herman, Judith, 12–13, 14, 73, 202
holistic psychology, 150–51
Holy Spirit
   fruits of, 9, 64–72
   gifts of, 98–101, 166
   'Jesus is Lord,' 153
   Trinity and, 82
   See also God; Jesus Christ
hope, 23–24, 208, 212
Horney, Karen, 17n33
human needs, 135
humanity, basic form of, 173–75
Hunsinger, George, 64, 65
hyperarousal of the nervous system
   defensive patterns, 17
   response, 15–17
   term usage, 14
   triggers, 15–16, 16n31
hypostatic union, 36

imago Dei, 83–84, 114
immobilization, 143
indestructible order, 34, 37–38, 66–67
indissoluble differentiation, 34–35, 65–66
inexpressible gift, vocation, 155–62
infants
   abuse of, 47
   attachment, 144
   mother-infant bond, 51
   sympathy among, 107–8
   See also children
inseparable unity, 35–37, 66
Institutes of the Christian Religion (Calvin), 114
interdisciplinary dialogue, 72–76
interdisciplinary map, 30–32
intergenerational trauma, 5, 207
The Interior Castle (Teresa of Avila), 161
interpersonal neurobiology, 139n8
intrusion, term usage, 14

Jaeger-Lane, Marietta, 24, 107
Janet, Pierre, 16
Jean Baker Miller Training Institute, Wellesley College, 110, 112
Jenson, Robert, 212

Jesus Christ
   Council of Chalcedon (451) on, 32–33
   healing, to the suffering, 188–89
   incarnation of, 37
   as mediator, 85–86
   message of salvation, 95
   modes of relationship with humans, 86
   as the One mediator, 85–89
   redemption, purpose of, 22–23
   relationship with God, 58–60
   trauma suffered, 10
   two natures of, 34–35, 37–38
   See also God; Holy Spirit
Jones, Serene, 10n1, 17n33
Jordan, Judith, 107–8
judgment, 186–87, 204
Jung, Carl, 47

Kaplan, Alexandra, 111
Kierkegaard, Søren, 34
King, Martin Luther, Jr., 107
knowledge
   empathy and, 112
   nature of, 168–70
Kohut, Heinz, 109
koinonia
   description of, 79–81
   as end in itself, 89–91
   Jesus as the One mediator, 85–89
   ministry, equipping for, 98–102
   pastoral care as work of, 92–98
   relationships, 81–84
   resonant empathy and, 149
   in scripture, 80
Kornfeld, Margaret, 118–19
Küng, Hans
   direct relationship to God, 93–94
   exercise priestly rights and functions, 92–93
   on gifts of the Holy Spirit, 98–99

Lake, Frank, 79–80
Lament for a Son (Wolterstorff), 179, 191–92
Lanius, Ruth, 147n24
Levine, Peter, 13

Life Together (Bonhoeffer), 135, 192, 197
lifelines of a spiritual trauma, 199–212
Lindbeck, George, 31n2, 96
listening
    accompaniment, 142–44
    art of, 135–37
    attunement, 141–42
    empathy to resonant empathy, 137–41
    first service to community, 105–6
    Kornfeld on, 119
    Lake on, 79
    resonant empathy, 145–48
Livingstone, David, 15
logical precedence of theology, 43–46
loneliness, 102, 205–6
Lord's Supper, 96–97, 162
love
    attitude of, 205
    of God, 86, 113–16, 142, 161
    of neighbor, 113–16, 142
    self-love, 113–17
Luther, Martin, 92, 158

Maloney, Newton, 44, 70
Mandela, Nelson, 19n40, 107
McFarlane, Alexander C., 12n12
Mechthild of Magdeburg, 26
meditation example, 123–24
mercy of God, 188–89
Mhlauli, Babalwa, 24
Middle Ages, vocation in, 158
Miller, Jean Baker, 111
mindful presence, 203–4
ministry, equipping for, 98–102
mourning, healing process, 19, 208–9
Murder Victims' Families for Reconciliation (MVFR), 24, 107

National Child Traumatic Stress Network, 21n47
need
    connecting feelings with, 122, 124–29
    types of, 135
neighbor, love of, 113–16, 142
nervous system, states of, 143, 144n20
New Testament, vocation in, 158

Nicene-Constantinopolitan Creed, 63
No Future Without Forgiveness (Tutu), 107
nonreligious psychology, 151–52
nonverbal signals, 110
nonviolent communication, 117n33, 129n41, 139, 148n24
Nonviolent Communication (Rosenberg), 124
"Now You Know the Worst" (Berry), 177

openness, 204
order, indestructible, 37–38

painful life experiences, 16n31
panic/grief circuit, term usage, 148–49n26
Panksepp, Jaak, 144n20
parents, for a lifetime, 163
pastoral care
    case example, 90–91
    community outreach, 26–28, 27n61
    dual role of, 27n64
    opening channels of communication, 27
    practice of, 89–90
    prayers, need for, 11
    as work of community, 92–98
Patton, John, 90–91
Peace in Central America (PICA), 171–72
penultimate values, 45
perpetrators of violence, 22–23
Peyton, Sarah
    on accompaniment, 142–43
    on attunement, 141–42
    on body sensations, 145, 145n21
    on nonviolent communication, 139
    on resonance, 139–40
    resonant language, forms of, 147, 147–48n24, 147n23
    Your Resonant Self, 138–39
PICA (Peace in Central America), 171–72
Polanyi, Michael, 39–41
post-traumatic stress disorder (PTSD), 1, 12–13, 13n16, 25n56, 202
Pray Without Ceasing (Hunsinger), 153

prayers/praying
    in community, 91–92
    essential in Spiritual care, 79, 84
    "The Eye of God (St. Patrick), 87–88
    Jesus' to all disciples, 85
    John Baillie's, 88
    of lament, 25
    Lord's Prayer, 87
    need for, 4, 11
    for others, 97
    resource for healing, 43–44, 54
    self-empathy and, 129–31
pre-eminent practical test, 73–75
Presbyterian Church (USA), 133
Presbyterian Disaster Assistance (PDA), 27n64
Princeton Theological Seminary, 8
process, attention, 53–55
professionalism, in church community, 92
Purves, Andrew, 104

rage circuit, term usage, 149n26
Raging with Compassion (Swinton), 198
Redeemer, God, 162–65
Reformation, impact of, 92, 96, 158
relational home
    finding, 146–47
    for traumatic experience, 26
relationships. *See* koinonia
repentance, 181–87
repetition compulsion, 18
resonance, 110, 139
resonant empathy, 137–41, 145–48
resonant language, forms of, 147, 147n23
Resonating Self Witness (RSW), 146
responses, types of, 14–15, 17–18, 119
revenge response, 17–18
Rodenburg, Patsy, 102n30
Rogers, Carl, 109
Rosenberg, Marshall, 109, 124, 131, 140n8
Rothschild, Babette, 20n44, 207n16

sacraments, 96–97, 162
sacred vows, 148
sacrifices, spiritual, 94

safe environment for processing, 20–21, 20n44
Scheler, Max, 187
secondary trauma, 206
"secular" psychology, 150–51
seeking circuit, term usage, 148n26
self, respecting as Christian counselors, 150–54
self-doubt, 118–19
self-empathy
    art of, 113–18
    importance of, 113–19
    meeting needs, 129
    prayer and, 129–31
    self-pity and, 118–19
    simple example of, 122–24
    steps to alignment with Christian beliefs, 132
    stress among clergy, 132–34
    triggers, 121–22
self-judgments, 124–29, 131–32
self-love, 113–17
self-pity, 118–19
self-talk, 120
self-worth, 112
September 11, terrorist attack, 177–78
sexual abuse by clergy, 75
sexuality/emergence circuit, term usage, 149n26
shame
    concept of, 41–43
    self-judgments, 126
shock, responses to, 14–15
Siegel, Daniel, 8–9, 108, 110–11, 139n8, 203–5
sin
    estrangement from God, 153
    forgiveness of, 23–24, 131–32
    grace and, 66
    recognition of, 185–86
    shame and, 42–43
    trauma and, 22–23, 50, 74
Skye, Susan, 148n24
small faith communities, 102–3
social engagement, 143
sorrow, 184–85
South African Truth and Reconciliation Commission, 24

speculative theories *vs.* exact science, 60–62
spiritual but nonreligious, 153
spiritual bypassing, 137, 137n4
spiritual discernment, 101
spiritual gifts (charisms), 166–67
spiritual practice, 4, 94
spiritual trauma, 199–212
Stolorow, Robert, 26, 146, 206
Stone Center, Wellesley College, 110
stress, 21n47, 133, 145
　　See also post-traumatic stress disorder (PTSD)
suffering, 179–80
Suffering Witness (Hatley), 195
support groups, 12
Sutton, Jeannette, 27n61
Swinton, John, 28–29, 198
sympathetic activation, 143
sympathy, 107–8, 108n13

The Tacit Dimension (Polanyi), 39
teens, trauma among, 21n47
television viewing of, 102n30
Teresa of Avila, Saint, 161
"The Eye of God (St. Patrick), 87–88
theological anthropology, normative criteria for, 58–60
theological compass, 32–34, 45–46
theology, gifts of
　　pastoral relationship for healing, 50–53
　　process, paying attention to, 53–55
　　theory of the unconscious, 46–50
theology, logical precedence of, 43–46
Theology and Pastoral Counseling (Hunsinger), 5, 30–31
theology and psychology, how related, 30–32
theory of the unconscious, 46–50
Torrance, T. F., 37
"Toward a Holistic Psychology" (Anderson), 5
transference, concept of, 51–53
translation, of logical levels concept, 41–43

trauma
　　breaking free from, 19–21
　　case study, 70–71
　　definition of, 13, 146–47, 202
　　fields of study for understanding, 5
　　hearers of, effect on, 10–18
　　intergenerational trauma, 5, 207
　　as a lived experience, 5–6
　　perpetrators of, 22–23, 23n49
　　support groups, 12
　　"Trauma and Spirituality" (van den Blink), 3–4
trauma studies, dialogue, 72–76
traumatized sense of self, 147–48n24
trigger translation journal, 123–24
triggers, self-empathy and, 121–22
Trinity
　　God' love and, 86
　　understanding of, 81–82
truth
　　from a sage, 169–70
　　through God, 60–62
truth, secular parables of, 62–64
Tutu, Desmond (Bishop), 24, 107
"typical twelve" responses, 119

Ulanov, Ann, 18, 19, 47
unconscious, theory of the, 46–50, 112
unconscious contracts, 148
unity, inseparable, 35–37

van den Blink, A. J., 3, 138, 202–3
van der Kolk, Bessel, 12n12, 16, 19n40
Vietnam Veterans Against the War, 12, 70
violence
　　perpetrators of, 22–23, 23n49
　　suffering of others and, 195–96
　　systems of, 1
　　toward women and children, 75–76
vocation
　　Calvin on election, 158–59
　　of the community, 170–72
　　in different eras, 158–59
　　discernment, 172–80
　　God the Redeemer, 162–65
　　God the Sustainer, 166–67
　　an inexpressible gift, 155–62
　　a joyous task, 167–70

vocation circuit, term usage, 148n26
Volkan, Vamik, 197

war, traumatic impact of, 12, 76
Weil, Simone, 141
Weingarten, Kaethe, 193–94, 195, 206
Weisaeth, Lars, 12n12
Welwood, John, 137
Whyte, David, 160
window of welcome, 143–44
Winnicott, D. W., 51

witness
  giving of, 95–96
  responding to other's plight, 195–96, 206–7
Wolterstorff, Nicholas and Eric, 179, 191–92
women, 21–26, 75–76, 116
worldly grief, 7, 183–84

Yoder, Carolyn, 14
Your Resonant Self (Peyton), 138–39

zest, feeling of, 112